Contents

****

Contents

****

Chapter 4 Pronouns

Chapter 5 Adjectives

Chapter 6 Adverbs

Chapter 7 Prepositions

Chapter 8 Determiners and Interjections

Contents

****

Chapter 9 Conjunctions

Part 2 Analysis, Transformation & Synthesis

Chapter 10 Phrases

Chapter 11 Clauses

Chapter 12 Sentences

****

Part 3 Punctuation

Chapter 13 Punctuation

Part 4 Written Communication

Chapter 14 Social Letter Writing

Contents

****

Some examples of social letters

Chapter 15 Business Communication

Examples of some business letters

V111   Contents

****

Introduction

. Introduction

Like other languages, the English language can be spoken and written. For both purposes we require vocabulary and grammar. Vocabulary consists of words. Grammar has rules for combining words for meaningful communication in spoken and written English. By vocabulary, we mean all the words in English or any other language. No one knows precisely how many words there are in the English language. One of the main reasons is that it is a dynamic language, which is continuously changing. The other reason is that experts have different views on what constitutes a distinct word, and whether we should include scientific words in the English vocabulary. However, it is generally understood that the English language, excluding scientific words, as about one million words. Some words do become obsolete, and some new words are being continuously included.

It is interesting to imagine for a moment what is required to build a strong and safe brick wall. You will need some bricks. If you just pile these up on top of each other, the wall will not be a strong and safe structure. Therefore, you would require some lime or cement and sand in order to mix these with water to make some mortar. The mortar is used to hold the bricks together. By using the right amount of mortar between bricks, you can create a strong and safe brick wall structure.

Like bricks, **vocabulary (words)** by itself is insufficient for both writing and speaking purposes. To create a language **structure**, such as a phrase or a sentence, what is needed is **_a set of rules of grammar_** (mortar). Like mortar, the correct application of the rules of English grammar can convert a meaningless combination of words into a meaningful structure.

Here, the word **structure** means the way some words are arranged, in accordance with the rules of grammar, into phrases, clauses, etc. There are numerous types of structures such as a human body structure, building structure and so on. We are interested in the **grammatical structure** of the English language.

A particular **style** is a distinct way in which something is organised, arranged or done for whatever purpose. For instance, a manager can be kind, friendly and assertive when dealing with staff in order to get the job done. We can label this manager's style as a 'friendly style of management'.

2   **Introduction**

****

On the other hand, another manager can be nasty, unfriendly and authoritarian. This is an 'autocratic style of management'. These are two distinct styles of management. Similarly, there are many styles of using the language. For example:

- *simple style* – some people prefer a simple style – they use common words, short phrases and sentences mainly in private conversation and personal letters
- *complex style* – some people find simple writing and speaking dull – they use complicated words and *jargon* (words and phrases that are used by some group of people and are difficult for others to understand)
- *colourful style* – some people such as toastmasters, writers and speakers who make money by writing and speech making, use very colourful language(metaphor, alliteration, simile, hyperbole and wordplay)
- *colloquial style* – some people use very simple words and phrases. This style is not for formal speech and writing. It is used in private conversation

One can think of many other styles such as a *humorous style*, *prose style*, *archaic style*, etc.

The English language is widely used in the world and therefore it has many different forms. I am concerned with the contemporary English in use in Britain. Despite the fact that there are many regional variations, there is **standard English**. Standard English is the form of the language that is nationally used in Britain. It is the medium of communication at the national level. It is used by institutions including educational bodies, text books, newspapers, broadcasting services, government agencies, etc. Standard English is socially accepted as the most correct form of the English language. Speakers of other languages also learn standard English.

A number of words can be put together without applying any rules of grammar. Let's consider the phrase *'any grammar book'*, in which three words are side by side. We do understand the meaning of the combination of these three words. If you exchange places of two words in this combination, or pattern of words, it will not make any sense. The reason is that we do not say 'book grammar any'. This new combination of words becomes no more than a meaningless jumble of words.

If you ask a number of native speakers of English, they will immediately recognise both the correct and incorrect pattern of these words. They use mental pictures which help them to recognise these groups of words as meaningful or meaningless. It is not only the combination of words that native speakers recognise, but also the meaning associated with that combination of words.

They apply their knowledge of the order in patterns of words, and their associated meanings, by using their familiar vocabulary.

Native speakers use the language in its complexity from early childhood. They have been using the language up to the present time in their lives, and their knowledge of grammar is stored somewhere in their memories, just like the memory of a computer. Often, they are able to recall it and use it intuitively. They might have forgotten the technical terms needed to explain why the structure, such as a complicated sentence, is unrecognisable, or difficult to understand. Whether you are a native speaker or a student of the English language, you must learn *English grammar* in order:

- . to be able to put words into recognised structures, namely phrases, clauses, sentences and paragraphs
- . to identify grammatical structures, e.g. sentences, etc.
- . to understand the meaning associated with these structures
- . to analyse these structures in order to explain them to others, if there is a need for it

What is grammar? *Grammar* is an umbrella term. In essence, it is concerned with the words of a language and the mechanism, or rules of combining, or joining them together in meaningful phrases, clauses and sentences. It can also mean a person's knowledge and use of a language. For our purpose, the word *rule* means a recognised standard way of constructing structures. Therefore, the rules of grammar are principles for both spoken and written language.

In this age of the World Wide Web, the use of English is expanding exponentially through the Internet, and the correct use of English and its grammar is increasingly becoming highly desirable. Boldly speaking, it can be said that you are only as good as your grammar.

The prime aim of this book is to describe, and explain with the aid of numerous helpful examples, those aspects of English which are essential for both written and spoken standard English. The general objective of this book is to enable readers to improve their knowledge and skills in using the language with confidence. If you are an intermediate or advanced learner of English, or a teacher of English, you will find this book invaluable. The *prescriptive method* of grammar explanation is applied in this book. This approach is concerned with prescribing what is correct. It means discussing how the language should be used.

Diagram 1 shows that the relationship between words and rules is inseparable as indicated by a double arrow between them. The rules of grammar govern words and words are needed to make rules about them. All illustrations are numbered simply as 1,2, etc. within chapters.

The *linguistic* aspects of the English grammar are beyond the scope of this book. In passing, *linguistics* is the scientific study of language. Linguistic is connected with linguistics. A *linguist* studies languages and works in the linguistic field, mainly in the academic world. In this book, uncommon words, such as *discourse* (for combining sentences) and *lexis* (the words of a language) i.e. linguistic terminology used by linguists, are not included.

. How to use this book

This book consists of four parts. These are:

Part 1 starts with word classes which are also known as parts of speech. As words are the building blocks of language, it is, therefore, vitally important to understand how they are classified and governed by the rules of the English grammar.

Part 2 is devoted to analysis, transformation and synthesis of different types of phrases, clauses and sentences. This part follows Part 1 so that the reader can fully grasp the importance of each class of words and the role that can be played by different words in phrases, clauses and sentences.

Part 3 deals with punctuation. Punctuation makes written communication clear.

Part 4 examines writing skills for letter writers. It demonstrates good letter writing basic requirements in the English-speaking world.

It is suggested that Parts 1 and 2 are to be read consecutively. Parts 3-4 may be read in any order.

Test Your Knowledge section has some exercises. It is recommended that self-learners and students work the exercises out for themselves first and then compare them with the solutions provided.

The glossary contains an alphabetical list of definitions of terms used in this book.

Addendum contains some information on word formation, such as phrasal verbs.

The book finishes with **an index**. This can be used for reference at any time. Illustrations, diagrams and tables are numbered simply as 1,2,3…etc. within chapters.

Part 1
Word Classes

. Getting started

Word Classes at first glance

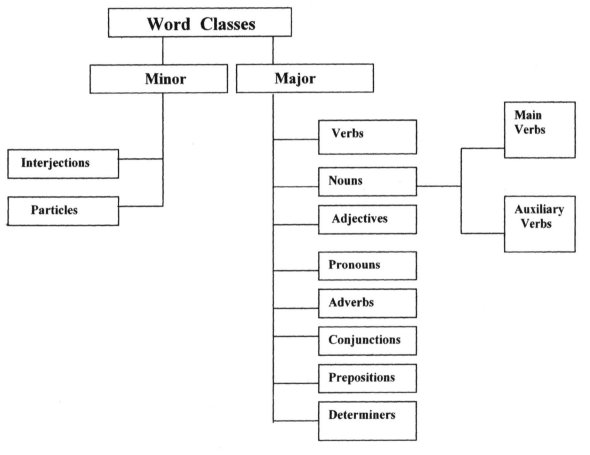

Diagram 1

There are different word classes as depicted in Diagram 1 above. These are also known as parts of speech. You may find that different books have different numbers of word classes. If you see differences in this respect, you have to decide for yourself which classification is the most appropriate and meets your specific needs. Minor word classes have very few words in them, but it is important to recognise them as classes, at least for the sake of clarity.

Diagram 1 is self-explanatory. However, many words can be placed in more than one word class. Even so, the idea of word classes helps us to group words with similar features together, and know exactly how they are used.

A word is a single and independent unit of vocabulary. It can be recognised in both speech and writing (or print). Many words have several meanings. A recognised word has the following features:

- it has a distinct sound, which can be a combination of sounds
- it has a meaning, i.e. definition
- a written word is recognisable by its structure, i.e. the number of letters in it and their combination pattern.

Yes, you can have words consisting of not only alphabetic letters but also other elements such as recognised symbols, e.g. £ sign.

For instance, the word *table* consists of five alphabetic letters. To speakers of English, it is recognisable as a combination of five letters when arranged in this given order. Therefore, when this word is used in *speech*, a speaker of the English language knows it by its distinct sound. This sound is produced by the sounds of four letters in it because the last letter 'e' is silent. When the same word is *written* (printed), a reader of the English language identifies it by the pattern of letters put together side by side to structure it.

We know that a table is a piece of furniture, which has a flat top on legs, trestles or pillars. It can hold things *(meaning/definition)*. When it is a part of a sentence, we are interested in understanding what role *(function)* it plays in the sentence. You know many such words, and most likely you consider them as the building blocks of the English language. Now consider the following sentence:

She listened carefully to my story.

This text has spaces between the words which make it easy to identify and count the words used there. It has six words. Normally, in English writing, there are spaces between words, but there are occasions when word identification as a single independent unit is not so easy. For example, when two or more words make a single unit. *A compound word* is composed of two or more words.

- It can be written with *a hyphen* (hyphenated word) between words, as exemplified below:

    (1) . mother-in-law

    (2) . man-made fibres such as polyester

    (3) . dark-haired

    (4) . passer-by

- It can be written <u>without</u> any spaces between words. This is illustrated below:

    (5) . teapot ⇐ two words joined together

    (6) . housewife ⇐ two words joined together

- It can be written <u>with or without spaces between</u> words constituting a compound word. For example:

    (7) . troublemaker or trouble-maker ⇐ hyphenated word

    (8) . teamwork or team-work ⇐ hyphenated word

    (9) . plant pot ⇐ a space between them - in speech it is considered as a single word ⇒ plantpot

    (10) . world war ⇐ a space between them – some people spell it as a single word ⇒ worldwar

<u>All these words and many more in terms of meaning are singular words.</u> These and many similar words can cause some confusion to learners of English, as they do not appear to be single words. However, they are considered as single words, meaning something is singular.

Furthermore, *in an idiomatic expression* a word does not usually give its own meaning. This can be a really serious problem to learners of English. For example, **a hard nut to crack** is a group of five individual words forming an **idiomatic expression**. In this expression, each word does not have its own dictionary meaning. Such an expression is fixed, and its meaning is deduced from the context in which it is used. For instance:

    (11) . Financing a stand at this international IT exhibition will be *<u>a hard nut to crack</u>* for us.

an idiomatic expression↵

In this context, it means that we will find it difficult to finance a stand at this international exhibition. Here, each underlined individual word does not render its dictionary meaning. The idiomatic expression "a hard nut to crack" means a difficult problem, but its real sense is deduced from the context in which it is used. An idiomatic phrase by itself often does not make sense* to those whose mother tongue is not English. The same is true about idioms in other languages.

---

* **make sense** is also an idiom – it means something has a meaning that one can easily understand. Or something is easy to do, understand or explain. For instance: It is now midnight. We must stop this party. It makes sense.

All major word classes shown in Diagram 1 are discussed next in Part 1 in considerable depth with the aid of scores of helpful and practical examples. Each major word class has its own chapter. The other two minor word classes are so small that they are often not discussed separately. Particles class is out-lined below. The other minor class is discussed in Chapter 8.

. **Particles class** is a very small word class. Particles are used
   with verbs to make phrasal verbs (multi-word verbs). For instance:

> (12) . She tore up his letter. *tore up* ⟹ *phrasal verb*

> (13) . He fell off the stairs. *fell off* ⟹ *phrasal verb*

> (14) . Our car broke down. *broke down* ⟹ *phrasal verb*

In these sentences, *up, off* and *down* are particles. These three words are ac-tually adverbs as well as prepositions. When you use them with verbs to make phrasal verbs such as *tear up, fall off* and *break down*, these are then known as particles. Many writers do not discuss particles class as a word class in its own right, because there are only a few words in it.

. Some writers classify numerals as a separate class. In this book,
   numerals are discussed as determiners.

. Determiners, pronouns and conjunctions are much smaller classes than
   verbs, nouns, adjectives and adverbs.

. Sentence, subject, predicate and object

A group of words that makes complete sense is called a **sentence**. For example:

> (1) . <u>John</u> is my friend.
> subject⏎

> (2) . <u>Alex and Sofia</u> are brother and sister.
> subject⏎

> (3) . <u>The postage</u> was £2.75.
> subject⏎

Each of the above examples is a sentence, as they all make complete sense.

Each sentence has two parts, namely:

1. **subject** – the part of the sentence, which refers or names someone or thing. In other words, the person or thing we are speaking about.
   In the above examples, the subject is indicated by an arrow. One can imagine the subject as the **doer** of the action.

2. **predicate** – it is that part of the sentence, which says something about the subject of the sentence. The predicates of the above sentences are **highlighted** in the above examples. It is everything in the sentence apart from the subject.

. Sometimes the verb in the predicate takes either one object or two objects. When a verb takes two objects, one is **direct object** and the other is **indirect object,** e.g.

(4) . She wrote **a letter** yesterday morning.

object↵

Action passes from the subject ⟹ *she* (doer) to the object ⟹ *a letter*

(5) . I was reading a **book**.

object↵

Action passes from the subject ⟹ *I* (doer) to the object ⟹ *a book*

(6) . I bought **some flowers** for **my wife**.

direct object↵   indirect object↵

. In example (6), the action of the verb 'bought' **directly affects** some flowers (*primary effect of the verb*) as I bought them. For this reason, *some flowers* are considered as **direct object**.

. At the same time, my wife is indirectly affected by the action(*secondary effect*) of the verb, 'bought'. Thus, it is called the **indirect object**.

. In the following examples **indirect objects** are shown in **bold-type** words.

(7) . She promised (to) **me** a ticket.

(8) . My brother gave (to) **Jane** his car.

(9) . The architect has already sent **us** your property survey report.

In each case, the **indirect object** is dependent on the underlined direct object.

. Phrases and clauses

A phrase is a small group of words. For instance:

. My car   . A beautiful garden   . Some books on that shelf
        . get out!   . Shut up!
. Home sweet home miles away from here.

All these above phrases make some sense, but not complete sense in a way that informs us about the situation to which they refer. A group of words larger than a phrase, which has a subject and a predicate is called a **clause.** For instance:

> . **She** is my best student in this class.
> . **I** was running very fast on the track.
> . **Rachel** likes her two children very much.

These examples contain a subject which is **highlighted** and a predicate. You may be saying to yourself, 'there is hardly any difference between a sentence and a clause.' It seems so, but there is a difference between these two grammatical units. A clause is usually smaller than a sentence, as a sentence can have more than one clause as illustrated below:

> . **He has two new friends**, but *they are from Russia.*
> . **I could have done it on time this afternoon,** if *you were not interfering with my work.*

Note: 'but' and 'if' are conjunctions used to join clauses together. See conjunctions. Each of these sentences contains two clauses —one clause is **highlighted** and the other clause is *printed in italics.* Thus, a sentence can have more than one verb, because each clause in a sentence has its own verb. A clause is smaller than a sentence, but like the sentence, it has only one subject and a predicate.

. The above illustration shows similarities and differences between
   clauses and sentences.

. You will see that it is the function - in other words the **use** of the word
   that determines to which word class a word belongs in a sentence,
   clause or phrase. In fact, often the same word in accordance with its
   use may be placed in more than one word class. Here are some
   examples:

Word	**Word class**	**Use of the word**
. **Above**	Adverb	He was obeying orders from above.
	Adjective	The above address is correct.
	Preposition	We were flying above the clouds.
. **Before**	Adverb	I have never met him before.
	Preposition	In fact he left the party **before** me.
	Conjunction	Before you resign, you must think carefully about your career.

In summary, this preliminary detail lays the foundation for exploring more extensively these in the next and subsequent chapters.

Chapter 1
Verbs

. Introduction

The word verb is derived from the Latin word *verbum*. In Latin, it means 'the word'. A verb is a central part of speech and writing. A verb can be a word or a group of words. The reason for its pivotal importance is that as a word or a group of words, it is required to construct a sentence. Generally speaking, people think of a verb as a *doing* or *action* word. Indeed, most readers would have learnt this idea of a verb at school. In fact, verbs are also used to describe the *state* or *condition* of something. Now, consider the following two sentences:

> (1) . Andrea *received* a large bouquet of fresh roses.
>
>   verb ↵

Here the verb clearly shows the physical action of Andrea , **'doing'**. Many verbs are used for this type of **action** of doing something.

> (2) . John *believes* in her good character.
>
>   verb ↵

In this example, the verb indicates *'John's state of mind'*, which is not his physical action of doing something. There are many such verbs in English that indicate a state or a condition. If a word can be marked by inflection for *tenses*, then the word is a verb. This is the major difference between verbs and any other classes of words. Tenses are discussed under tenses in the next chapter. Like nouns, many verbs have more than one form. The verb is at the heart of sentences and clauses, and thus it is the most important part of speech.

. Verbs undergo changes

Verbs do change their spellings or forms when we use them to express all kind of situations in the present, past and future tenses or times. Most verbs, which change their forms are known as **weak** or **regular or ordinary** verbs. The reason for calling them weak is that they follow rules to express tense, time or mood. There are many thousands of regular verbs. On the other hand, there are only about three hundred verbs, which are so stubborn that they do not follow any set of rules, and thus change some of their forms unexpectedly. These are **strong or irregular verbs**.

See ⇒ regular and irregular verbs   See also ⇒ inflection

. <u>Verb forms</u>

Verbs have the following forms:
. Base form   . s-form   . Participle   . Past Participle

. <u>Base Form</u>

Verbs in a dictionary are listed in their base forms. The base form is also known as *bare infinitive*, *root form* or *stem*. It is without the particle *to*. The following verbs are in their base forms:

be, sing, dance, laugh, work, run, wonder.

Sometimes, the bare infinitive is preceded by *to*, e.g. *to wash, to wish, to go*, etc. For instance:

(1) . I <u>wanted</u> ***to wash*** my hands.

verb⏎   ⇑ = to +verb

it is ***to-infinitive*** *form* of the verb **wash**

Here is another example:

(2) . I <u>promised</u> ***to send*** some flowers to Anne.

verb⏎   ⇑ = to + verb

to- infinitive *form* of the verb **send**

When a verb is preceded by the word *to*, it is known as ***to-infinitive***. The word ***to*** is used as ***to-infinitive marker.*** It also functions as an adverb and a preposition. See ⇒adverbs and also see ⇒Prepositions.

. <u>s-form</u>

The bare infinitive form is inflected in relation to the third person singular of the subject by adding –*s* to the verb. This is discussed under concord or agreement. Here are some examples of such verbs : **look(+s)**, **run(+s)**, **see(+s)**, **play(+s)**, **smile(+s)** and **jump(+s)**. The following examples demonstrate the use of the s-form of the verb:

(1) . She <u>looks</u> happy.

s- form of the bare infinitive **look** ⏎

(2) . Frank <u>loves</u> Elena.

s- form of the bare infinitive **love** ⏎

. <u>Participle –ing form</u>

It is that part of the verb which ends in -*ing*, e.g. going, coming, seeing, missing, jumping, etc. Its use is illustrated below:

(1) . I am **writing** a letter.

-*ing* participle form of the verb **write** ⏎

(2) . Alexander is **playing** with his toys.

-ing form of the verb **play** ↵

. Past Participle form

It is that part of the verb which ends in *-ed* in regular verbs, e.g.
happened, disappeared, etc. For instance:

(1) . I **joined** him at London Victoria Station.

-**ed** of the verb **join** ↵

It is used to form the simple past tense. See ⟹ tenses

(2) . They have **worked** for us.

-**ed** of the verb work ↵

It is used to form the present perfect tense. See ⟹ tenses

. In irregular verbs the past participle ends with *-en'* or some other
endings, e.g. *fallen, struck, undergone, laid*, etc. For instance:

(3) . She **became** his wife.

past participle form of the verb **become** ↵ - simple past tense

. Inflection

Inflection means a change in the form of a word or its spelling in accordance
with its grammatical function. In English, many words have inflected forms.
Verbs are also inflected. For instance:

(1) . She **laughs** a lot.
(2) . Why **are** you **panicking**?
(3) . They **ran** fast.
(4) . They **interviewed** me for nearly one hour.

In these examples, 'laughs', 'are', 'panicking' 'ran' and 'interviewed' are inflected forms of the verbs 'laugh', 'be', 'panic', 'run' and 'interview' respectively. At this juncture, it is desirable to discuss the meaning and use of
moods. At the end of moods, inflection is further explored because verbs undergo changes. See also above ⟹ verbs undergo changes

. Regular and Irregular Verbs

Verbs are divided into regular and irregular verbs. The forms of **regular/
weak/ordinary verbs** are determined in accordance with the changes they
undergo in order to express tense (time) or mood. The four different forms of
regular verbs and how they are formed are shown in Table 1. A vast majority
of verbs are regular. In fact, there are thousands of regular verbs.

14   **Word Classes**   **Verbs**

****

Some Regular Verbs

Base Form or Infinitive (bare) or Root or Stem	Present Form -s (/es) added to infinitive form	Participle Form - ing added to infinitive form	Past Participle Form -ed added to infinitive form
abuse	abuses	Abusing	abused
accuse	accuses	Accusing	accused
advise	advises	Advising	advised
blame	blames	Blaming	blamed
blush	blushes	Blushing	blushed
bore	bores	Boring	bored
cease	ceases	ceasing	ceased
disturb	disturbs	Disturbing	disturbed
enter	enters	Entering	entered
guide	guides	Guiding	guided
help	helps	Helping	helped
interview	interviews	interviewing	interviewed
join	joins	Joining	joined
knock	knocks	Knocking	knocked
laugh	laughs	Laughing	laughed
look	looks	Looking	looked
love	loves	Loving	loved
miss	misses	Missing	missed
manage	manages	Managing	managed
note	notes	Noting	noted
owe	owes	Owing	owed
push	pushes	Pushing	pushed
rate	rates	Rating	rated
scatter	scatters	Scattering	scattered
turn	turns	Turning	turned
unfold	unfolds	Unfolding	unfolded
vanish	vanishes	Vanishing	vanished
wash	washes	Washing	washed
wish	wishes	Wishing	wished
work	works	Working	worked
yearn	yearns	Yearning	yearned
zoom	zooms	Zooming	zoomed

Table 1

Like regular verbs, **irregular verbs** also change their shapes, but unexpectedly. There are three forms of irregular verbs. These are listed below.

Base form	**Past tense form**	**Past participle form**
arise	arose	arisen
be	was, were	been
bid	bade or bid	bidden or bid

Due to their stubbornness, they are also known as **strong verbs.** A good thing is that most verbs are regular. The total of irregular verbs comes nowhere near to the total of regular verbs. In fact, there are about 300 irregular verbs. You have to know these forms in order to be able to construct **tenses** correctly. You may find all these listed towards the end of your quality English Dictionary.

. Moods

In grammar, the word mood is used to mean a manner in which a statement is made. In both speech and writing, the verb enables us to express three types of moods, namely:

. **Indicative mood** – it is used to make a statement, state a fact or ask a question. In the following examples verbs are in the indicative mood:

(1) . Mr. Smith **was** here about five minutes ago.

(2) . What **is** the matter with you ?

(3) . I am very **busy** today.

These examples illustrate that we use the indicative mood when we require information or to indicate information. In these examples **highlighted verbs** are used in the indicative mood.

. **Imperative mood** – it is used to give a command or an order. The command or order can also be of a polite nature, e.g. **forgive me**. The following examples illustrate this type of mood:

(4) . **Go** away from here!

(5) . **Sit** or **leave** the classroom.

(6) . Please **telephone** your mother.

(7) . Let's **walk**.

In each of these examples the verb is said to be in the **imperative mood**. In example 7, **let's** or **let us** is the first person plural. In this example, the verb **walk** is in the indicative mood. It is implying here both command and suggestion. We often omit the subject (**you**) in the indicative mood, as its presence is understood.

. **Subjunctive mood** – it is used to express a possibility, uncertainty, condition or supposition. It is not as commonly used in English as in other European languages such as German and French. For instance:

(8). They wished they were at the meeting.

(9). I wish I knew her name.

(10). He talks as though he was drunk.

In English, the most common subjunctive expressions start as
'**If I were...**', e.g.

(11). If I were a millionaire, I would have built homes for homeless people.

(12). If you were to climb Mount Everest, you would be world famous overnight.

Both statements imply impossibility and supposition rather than the likelihood of occurrence. It should be mentioned that there are situations which involve supposition, when a positive outcome is also possible, e.g.

(13). If you can pass that car, I'd be able to turn left.

On the other hand, the following example implies a negative outcome, i.e. most unlikely to happen, because you are sure that 'he' will not be able to do so.

(14). If he were to give up gambling, he'd be able to payback his debts.

The same statement is written as:

(15). If he gives up gambling, he'd be able to payback his debts.

This statement also implies supposition, but it is more positive, i.e. you think that he will be able to give up gambling. Thus, one should use the subjunctive mood only when something is highly unlikely to happen.

. Person and number

The use of verbs is often described in terms of **three persons** and **two numbers**. These are shown in the panel below:

	1st person	2nd person	3rd person
Singular	I eat	You eat	he/she/ one/it eats
Plural	we eat	you eat	they eat

The correct use of both person and number is essential. For instance:

(1). I **am** young.

(2). You **are** not so young.

(3). **She is young** as well.

(4). They **are** also young.

These sentences have the same verb '**be**' and the same present tense, but

****

the verb form is different in all four sentences. <u>A verb in a sentence must agree with the person and the number</u> (see tenses). In each of these sentences, the basic verb form has changed, i.e. inflected. The inflection is discussed

below. See also⇒ inflection

.Tenses and Verb Agreement

The following examples illustrate that verbs help us to express the time when the action or the state or condition of a verb takes place. The present tense means *now* (time). It enables us to indicate the action, the state or condition of something at the present time. Similarly, the past tense means *then* (past time). It assists us to put into words the action or the state of something which took place in the past.

In English, the verb tense is marked by inflection for only the *present tense* and *the past tense*. However, the form of the verb is controlled by the person or thing and number of the subject. **The future tense** can be expressed by the present time. The construction of the future tense is discussed under tenses. Now examine the following sentences:

(1) . <u>Janet</u> **hates** no one.

subject - singular third person ↵

present tense –*s* form of the regular verb ⇒ **hate**

state of mind/behaviour/attitude shown by this verb↵

(2) . <u>I</u> *held* my hand in her soft hand.

subject - singular 1st person ↵

past tense - irregular verb ⇒ **hold**

action denoted by the verb↵

<u>See verb concord or agreement in the next chapter for further discussion.</u>

. Voice

In a speech as well as in writing you have two choices in relation to the subject:

(1) . <u>When the subject has to act or experience a state or a condition, your construction of the clause or the sentence is said to have an active verb or an active voice.</u> In other words, <u>the subject is the doer.</u> For instance:

(i) . She **loved** her husband.

Here, the verb is in the active voice because '**she**'- the subject is the doer, i.e. felt affection. The object – her husband is the receiver of her affection. Here are some more examples of the active voice:

(ii) . We played cricket last Sunday.

(iii) . Who did this to you?

(iv) . He will visit us next week.

(2) . <u>The above examples are re-structured by altering the form of the verb in each example. The object of each above example is now in the subject position in examples (v) to (viii) below:</u>
   (v) . Her husband was loved by her.
   (vi) . The cricket was played by us last Saturday.
   (vii) . By whom was this done to you?
   (viii) . We will be visited by him next week.

These examples show that the subject is **acted upon by the object**. In other words, **the subject is the receiver** of something, i.e. the subject is passive. When the subject is at the receiving end(receiver of something), the verb of the clause or the sentence is in the **passive voice**.

If you compare examples (i) to (iv) with examples (v) to (viii), you can find:
   (a) . verbs in examples (i) to (iv) are transitive verbs as they are followed by an object;
   (b) . the object in examples (i) to (iv) became the subject of the passive voice/verb in examples (v) to (viii);
   (c) . in examples (v) to (viii) the verb is in the passive voice, i.e. converted from the active voice in examples (i) to (iv); and thus it is the transitive verb which can be used in the passive voice*.

---

* Some verbs function only intransitively and thus take no object. Such verbs cannot be used in the passive voice. Intransitive verbs are used alone, i.e. without the object, i.e.
. She disappeared <u>from view</u>.
. Our founder members toiled <u>for a long time at making our party</u> strong.

In both examples, the verb is followed by <u>a prepositional phrase not an</u> **object.** Prepositional phrases are underlined above. See ⇒ phrases

---

. <u>**When should you use the active voice or the passive voice?**</u>

Certainly, the active voice is more direct and simpler. Therefore, it is used more frequently than the passive voice. However, one should apply the active voice when the subject is prominent, i.e. the doer performing the relevant action, experiencing a state or condition. On the other hand, the passive voice may be preferred when you definitely do not know the subject, i.e. 'we', 'they', 'someone's name', etc. In such cases, the use of the passive voice is preferred for emphasis. Let's consider the following question and two answers:

. Who drove the car at the time of the accident?

(1) . My wife drove the car at the time of the accident.

(2) . The car was driven by my wife at the time of the accident.

Here, in example (1), we know the subject,' my wife'. It is the active voice. The same example is re-written in the passive voice, in order to place emphasis on the driver 'my wife'. Thus, in this case, the passive voice is preferred. It may be so that someone prefers (1), because they may find it more direct.

The comprehension of both mood and voice ideas can enhance your practical skills of both spoken and written English.

. Verb Classes

In diagram 1 on page 31, you can see at a glance the division of verbs into main/ordinary/lexical and auxiliary verbs. Speaking grammatically, most verbs are known as lexical or main verbs. In the English language, there are thousands of such verbs, but a small number of verbs are called auxiliary verbs. The word 'auxiliary' is derived from the Latin word **auxilium**, which means help. Indeed, these verbs are helpers, i.e. help other verbs form their tenses, voices or moods. There are only sixteen auxiliary verbs, which are classified as:

. Primary/basic auxiliary verb

These are only **be, do,** and **have**.

. Modal auxiliary verbs

These are:

can	could	dare	may
might	must	need	ought
shall	should	used (to)	will
would			

Note: In some publications, you may find less than thirteen modal verbs. In some other books, fourteen modal verbs, as they include **have to**.

. Modal verbs have only one form as shown above. Thus they are not inflected and therefore they do not have **-ing** , **-ed** or **–s** forms.
. Modal verbs are followed by the infinitive form of another verb, without 'to', with the exceptions of **ought (to)** and **used (to)**
. Negative sentences with modal verbs are constructed with either **not** or **-n't** (short form of not).
. **do, does** or **did** are not used with modal verbs.

. How do primary auxiliary verbs help main verbs?

The following examples demonstrate how the primary auxiliary verbs are used as helpers:

> (1) . He **is** reading a book.
>
> (2) . Where **do** you come from?
>
> (3). We **have** bought a new car.
>
> (4) . Anne **has** made this beautiful dress for me.

In these examples:

> (1) . 'is' derived from the primary auxiliary verb **be**. Here, it is helping the participle 'ing' form of the lexical verb **read** to form a compound verb - **is reading**.
>
> (2) . 'do' is one of the basic auxiliary verbs. It is helping the base form of the lexical verb **come** to form a compound verb - **do come**.
>
> (3) . 'have' is one of the primary auxiliary verbs. It is helping the past participle form of the main verb **buy** to form the compound verb - **have bought**.
>
> (4) . 'has' is the present tense form of the primary auxiliary verb **have**. Here, it is used with the third person singular **she** to help the past participle form of the primary verb **make** to form the compound verb - **has made**.

The following examples also illustrate the application of the primary auxiliary verbs as giving a helping hand to the main verbs to express different situations:

> (5) . They **are** working very hard to finish the job on time.

'be' in the form of are ↵ -The **participle 'ing'** form of the verb - **work** is supported be the primary auxiliary verb.

> (6). We **have** not discussed the contents of this report yet.

primary auxiliary verb↵ - The past participle form of the main verb **discuss** is supported be the primary auxiliary with 'not' for negation.

> (7). She **does** show a sign of worry.

do in the form of **does** ↵ - The base form of the lexical verb show is being helped by the primary auxiliary form a compound verb in order to emphasise a point.

- **Modal auxiliaries** - like the primary auxiliaries, they also help the main verb to express a variety of meanings. The following examples illustrate the range of meanings rendered by modal auxiliaries:

  . *Can*

  (1) . She can knit a pullover for you. ⇐ ability indicated

  (2) . She cannot/can't knit a pullover for you. ⇐ inability pointed out

  (3) . Sarah can't dance like me. ⇐ inability/negative form

****

. *Could*

(1) . When Sarah was three, she could read. ⇐ ability shown

(2) . Last night, she could not sing well. ⇐ meaning unable

(3) . My manager said, 'You <u>could</u> leave the office at 4.30 pm.'

　　　　　permission granted ↵

(4) . I am so tired of mountaineering that I <u>could fall sleep</u>.

　　　　　　　　prediction/outcome↵

(5) . <u>Could</u> you at least direct us to the nearest post office?

　　⇑

　　strong request or demand

(6) . Could you help me to finish this job? ⇐ demand/instruction/

　　　　　　　　　　　　　　　　　request

(7) . You could write to us from Japan. ⇐ making a suggestion

(8) . I have already worked for 17 hours today non-stop that I could

　　　breakdown. ⇐ predicting the future

(9) . Could you please tell me the time? ⇐ asking/requesting

(10) . <u>Could you speak up</u> , as we can't hear?

ordering/instructing↵

. *dare*

This verb requires special care when using it. It can be used as a modal verb
as well as an ordinary verb. As a modal verb, it is usually used in the present
tense negative forms, e.g.

(1) . She didn't dare **(to)** interrupt the honourable guest speaker.

(2) . John didn't dare **(to)** tell his father about damaging his car.

. When it is used as a modal verb, it is followed by the base form of the
  verb without '**to**'. For this reason 'to' is enclosed within ( ) in
  examples (1) and (2) - not required.

. **In what ways does the use of 'dare' differ when it is used as an
  ordinary verb?**

  a) When in spoken English the verb **dare** is used as an ordinary verb, it is
      usually followed by the base form of the verb, i.e. without the
      to- infinitive maker 'to', e.g.

      (3) . Don't you dare walk out of home without my permission.

      (4) . He didn't dare open his mouth against me.

  b) As an ordinary verb, dare is followed in both questions and in negative
      forms by the **to-infinitive** form of the verb, e.g.

      (5) . He won't dare to speak against me.

      (6) . Have you asked Mr. Bull about your salary rise?

22   **Word Classes**   **Verbs**

****

As he was in a bad mood, I didn't dare **to ask** him about it.

(7) . His father shouted at him, 'Do you dare **to speak**
your mind ?'

. *may**

(1) . May I leave now? ⇐ formal permission/request

(2) . The machine may not start immediately. ⇐ possibility

(3) . What will you do on Sunday?
We <u>may travel</u> to York to visit some relatives.

indicating intention/prediction ↵

(4) . He <u>may be</u> a good doctor but he is a rude person.

admitting that something is true and then stating another point

(5) . Our club membership has been steadily growing.

Long may it continue to do so. ⇐ formal way of expressing
wishes/hopes

<u>In the formal context, it is used to state the purpose of something, e.g.</u>

(6) . We want a youth centre for our community, so that our
youths <u>may</u> have a place for social and sporting activities.

(7) . If I <u>may</u> say that he is always helpful.

politely asking for permission to speak

---

* Modal verb may is also used in an idiom: **be that as it may**
(formal), *meaning nevertheless or in spite of that:*

. I know John is really a very kind person; be that as it may, his
behaviour was unacceptable this afternoon.

. His references are very impressive; be that as it may, he
hasn't answered our questions satisfactorily.

. *might*

(1) . Why don't you rent a caravan? I might do that. ⇐ possibility

<u>In example(2), it is used to make a polite suggestion:</u>

(2) . You <u>might</u> try fish and chips shop for some hot food.

(3) . If I <u>might</u> add that she is a pleasant person.

politely giving information about a person – *she*

****

In example(4), in the formal context asking for information:
> (4) . How <u>might</u> students' performance be monitored?
> (5) . You <u>might</u> have at least telephoned us about this grim situation.

showing annoyance as someone could have done something to help
> (6) . Don't you think you <u>might</u> at least help John whose life in ruins?

showing annoyance as someone could do something to help

. *must*

> (1) . I must first speak to my parents about my release. ⇐necessity
> (2) . We must examine this plan carefully because it will have
>
>   some serious effects on our sales. ⇐ stressing importance
> (3) . I have been working since 6 am today. Well, it is 11 pm and
>
>   you must be tired by now. ⇐indicating certainty or truth
> (4) . I don't have any money as I am unemployed. Well, you must
>
>   find a job. ⇐ telling to do something to earn money
> (5) . You must process this batch of invoices before lunch. ⇐ order

. *need**

As a modal verb, it is used to say that something <u>is</u> or <u>is not necessary</u>:
> (1) . Thank you for your offer. <u>Need I pay a deposit now</u>?
>
>   Meaning: Is it necessary to pay a deposit?↵ = obligation
>
> (2) . You <u>needn't pay</u> a deposit. ⇐ not required/no necessity
>
> (3) . You <u>needn't have brought</u> so many presents. ⇐ no necessity
>
>   past form ↵

---

* **Need** as a main verb is used to mean:
> (4) . to want something, e.g.
>> . Do you need a red or white ball?
> (5) . to think or suppose that something is required or necessary, e.g.
>> . She said, 'Do you need any help?'
>> . It is already 1 pm, and I need to have my lunch.
> (6) . to be obliged to do something, e.g.
>> . German citizens need to show only their national identity
>> cards when entering France.
>> . Did you need a membership card to use the reference library?
>> I didn't need it as I went to read newspapers.

****

. *ought (to)*

(1) . Our local council <u>ought to build</u> a modern public library.

advice as you feel it is required ↵

(2) . The rain has stopped. Driving on the road <u>ought to</u> be better now.

suggesting possibility↵

(3) . We ought to be nicer to each other. ⇐obligation/advice

. *shall*

(1) . I shall spend my long summer holiday in Spain. ⇐ intention

(2) . What shall we do to help him? ⇐asking for advice/suggestion

(3) . You shall be the first person to lecture. ⇐ promise

<u>In formal circumstances, the use of **shall** can mean a rule for a future happen-ing</u> or action, e.g.

(4) . As I am now in charge of this commission, I shall send a copy
of today's minutes to all members ten days before the next

meeting. See ⇒ future tense for shall

. *should**

(1) . I should write to you soon from India. ⇐ prediction

(2) . I should study hard as I want to gain high grades. ⇐obligation

(3) . You <u>should not</u> park on double yellow lines.

 - negative form

criticizing in order to point out what is the right thing to do

(4) . You <u>should</u> respect elderly people.

used to emphasize what is appropriate

(5) . By that time there <u>should be</u> far less traffic on the M1.

used here to state what is expected to happen in the future

(6) . If I were* to pay so much to a lawyer, I <u>should**</u> represent myself.

⇑

it is used to say what I would to do if something else happened first

---

* For the first person singular 'I' in conditional expressions, when the
condition is assumption/supposition/doubt , we use the past subjunctive
'were' instead of the past indicative 'was'. For instance: If I were a king,
I should live in a palace.

** To mean what you would do if something else happened
first - **should** is used only with '**I**' or '**we**'. Here is another example:

(7) . If we were required to start work ten minutes earlier without pay,

we <u>should</u> strike.   ⟸ rather a formal style

It is often used in '**that clause**', i.e. after 'that', when something is
suggested, advised or arranged. Here are two examples:

(8) . My doctor advised me that I <u>should</u> not do any physical work.

(9) . I must add that a student's practical project <u>should</u> include
serving customers in some restaurants.

(10) . I/we <u>should</u> be most grateful for your help in this matter.

to show politeness when making a request formally

(11) . Ask them to pay (a) deposit now if they want to reserve it.
Is £100 is enough for a deposit? I <u>should</u> think so.

giving an opinion when someone is not sure about something

---

* The modal verb should is often used with '**why**', '**how**' and '**what**'
in order to indicate annoyance, refusal or surprise about something, e.g.

(12) . John Smith is leaving our department. Would you like to
contribute towards the present we want to give him?
<u>Why should I</u> contribute? I hardly communicate with him.

(13) . Do you know who has made this mess? <u>How should</u> I know
as I was in the meeting all morning?

(14) . We are facing a serious challenge? <u>What should</u> we do now?

Note it is used as such with 'I' and 'we'.

. *used to*

There is some controversy surrounding the status of **used to**. Some
people consider it as an ordinary verb, which expresses a past state or some
occurrence, meaning something was happening continuously over a period of
time, but not now, e.g.

(1) . We <u>used to</u> live in Lancaster for some years.

(2) . When I was young, I <u>used to</u> feel sick on a ship.

(3) . I am not as tall as I <u>used to</u> be some years ago.

(4) . She does not cook at home as much as she <u>used to</u>.

it can be used on its own↵

. In questions and negative forms, **did** and **did not/didn't** are used
respectively, e.g.
(5) . Did you <u>use to</u> travel by car to London from Birmingham?
(6) . Didn't you <u>use to</u> call her aunt?
(7) . What kind of book did you <u>use to</u> write?

. **Used to** is uncommon in negative sentences. In informal speech,
sometimes **didn't** is placed before **used to***, which is incorrect
construction. For example:
(8) . We <u>didn't used</u> to bother about his presence in our club.

incorrect ↵

This example is re-written correctly as:
(9) . We <u>didn't use</u> to bother about his presence in our club.

Here is another example of the correct construction:
(10) . Didn't she use to work with you?

---
* The correct form is use to not used to.

. You can replace **'did not/didn't'** before 'used to' by **never**.
For instance:
(11) . I <u>never used to</u> dine in that restaurant.
(12) . We <u>never used to</u> have such long delays as we do now.

. Some people place **'not'** between **'used'** and **'to'** mainly in writing.
This sort of construction is not only old-fashioned but also very formal.
Here is an example:
(13) . You **used not to*** work so late in those days.

. In questions placing of you between used and to is very formal and
old-fashioned. For instance:
(14) . What time **used you to*** get up in the morning?
(15) . What sort of alcoholic drink **used you to** like most?

---
* The structure of examples (13) – (15) should be avoided.

. *<u>will</u>*

****

(1). I will attend the annual office party this year. ⇐ intention

(2). We will travel to India next week, if we receive confirmation

of our arrangements by Friday . ⇐prediction

(3). <u>Will</u> you please do me a favour?

used here for asking someone to do something ⇒favour

(4). I asked him if he <u>wouldn't</u> mind opening the window.

used in negative form to ask someone to do something⇒opening---

(5). <u>Will</u> you leave the room now? ⇐ used to order to do something

(6). Indeed, she <u>will read</u> in bed.

used to state someone's habit

(7). This car <u>will</u> carry only four people in accordance with the law.

indicating what is possible

(8). You <u>will</u> not be admitted without a visa shown in your passport.

pointing out what is true

(9). You <u>will</u> have had a birthday party at home, I suppose.

expressing what you think is likely/probably true or has happened

See ⇒ future tense for **will**

. *would**

(1) . She <u>would</u> have gone to see me, if she had a day off from work.

used to indicate conditional intention/wish

(2). She <u>would</u> buy a mansion in Kensington, if she had married him.

condition/prediction

(3). You <u>would</u> look silly in this outfit.

pointing out the outcome of something imaginary/if it happens ⇒outfit

(4). You <u>would</u> regret very much to miss this golden opportunity.

used in this example in the same way as in the above example

(5). We <u>would</u> never have found out, if you had not informed us.

used to describe an <u>event</u> (**found out**) that happened because something else

had happened first ⟹ **informed us**

(6). If I had seen his CV, I <u>would</u> have never appointed him.

here it is used in the same way as in the above example, but relating to

<u>action</u> ⟹appointed him

(7). I asked Anne to accept John's apology, but she <u>wouldn't</u> do so.

here it is used to show someone's(Anne's) refusal to accept something
(apology)

(8). The shop manager <u>wouldn't</u> exchange or refund my money, despite
       the fact that I produced the required receipt of goods purchased.

Examples (7) and (8) are similar, but example (8) illustrates the
unwillingness of someone to do something.

(9). <u>Would</u> you like to sit by the window?

used here in order to make a polite offer

(10). <u>Would</u> you have lunch with me here at the same time tomorrow?

   used here to invite someone politely

(11). <u>I would</u> say he is genuinely interested in her.

used here to give an opinion to say what someone thinks

(12). <u>I would</u> imagine now they are about to land at Heathrow Airport.

used here to imagine/wonder about something happening ⟹landing

(13). I <u>**wouldn't**</u> argue with him, if I were you.

used here to give advice – it is used with ⟹ *if I were you*

<u>In example (14), it indicates the past occurrences that happened
frequently:</u>

(14). When we lived in London, we <u>would</u> often visit the
       British Museum.

(15). Peter told me about that nasty incident involving you.

<u>He would say that, wouldn't he?</u>

Here it is used to say disapprovingly that you think someone's (Peter's)
behaviour is typical

---

* would, would not /wouldn't - these are the past forms of the verb
will. These are used in reporting someone's statements, e.g.
(16) . They said they <u>would</u> be leaving Oxford for London today.
(17) . She told me that most likely she wouldn't refuse his offer of help.
(18) . They asked me if I would make a contribution.

See ⇒ will

. Verb aspects
Another important role played by two primary auxiliary verbs 'be' and
'have' is that they help to express the action, the state or condition referred to
by the lexical verb as:

    (1) . **progressive aspect** – an ongoing(continuous) action, the state
        or the condition referred to by the lexical verb; and
    (2) . **perfect aspect** - the completion of the action, the state or the

        condition referred to by the lexical verb has been completed. It
        implies that something has been completed.

. The progressive aspect of the verb is formed by using an
appropriate form of 'be' followed by the participle 'ing' form of the lexical
verb. In the following examples, the progressive aspect is shown in **bold**:
        (1) . She **is working** happily.
        (2) . They **were looking** very confident.

        (3) . He **was studying** hard for the exams.

<u>Note that here 'is', 'were' and 'was' are the appropriate forms of 'be'.</u>

. The perfect aspect of the verb is formed by using **has, have** or
had forms of 'have' followed by the past participle form of the
lexical verb. In the following examples the perfect aspect is
indicated in **bold**.
        (4) . John **has** sent Marion a bouquet of roses .
        (5) . They **had** some paintings to sell.
        (6) . We **have** some guests staying with us.

<u>You can also use both verb aspects (progressive and perfect) in a
sentence, e.g.</u>

(7) . Julia has been visiting her parents.

(8) . By that time, I had been living in China for ten years.

These aspect are expanded under tenses. See ⟹ tenses

. **Can we use both the progressive and perfect verb aspects in a sentence?** Yes, you can. This is demonstrated below:

(1). **He has been writing** for a living for the last ten years.

(2). She **had been visiting** her mother.

(3). Stewart **had been playing** cricket for England until he was 44 years old.

In summary, the verb is the most important element in a sentence. Without a verb, we cannot express action (working), condition, or state (alive).

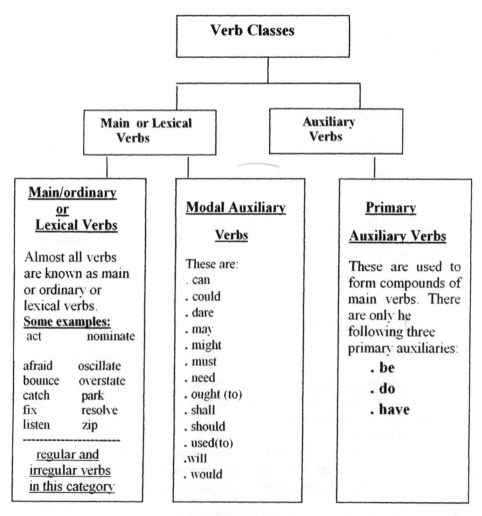

Verb Classes

Main or Lexical Verbs

Auxiliary Verbs

Main/ordinary or Lexical Verbs

Almost all verbs are known as main or ordinary or lexical verbs.
Some examples:

act   nominate

afraid   oscillate
bounce   overstate
catch   park
fix   resolve
listen   zip
----
regular and irregular verbs in this category

Modal Auxiliary Verbs

These are:
. can
. could
. dare
. may
. might
. must
. need
. ought (to)
. shall
. should
. used(to)
.will
. would

Primary Auxiliary Verbs

These are used to form compounds of main verbs. There are only he following three primary auxiliaries:

. **be**

. **do**

. **have**

Diagram 1

Chapter 2
Additional Verb Related Topics

. Linking or copular or copula verbs

A linking or copular or copula verb links the subject with a complement. The
Latin word *copula* means a 'bond', hence its derivative is linking. The basic
linking verb is '*be*' with its most used forms: *am*, *is*, *are*, *was* and *were*.
There are other linking verbs, which include:

---

appear, become, feel, get, go, grow, keep, look, make, prove, remain,
represent, seem, sound, stay, taste, turn

The following examples illustrate the role played by the copula verbs together with the complement is a sentence:

subject + linking verb + complement

Subject	Linking Verb	Complement
It	is	Monika. (noun)
They	remained	silent. (adjective)
She	became	a teacher. (noun phrase)
He	proved (may be followed by **to be**)	a helpful person. (noun phrase)
Our aim	proved	right. (adjective)
She	appears (**to be**)	intelligent. (adjective)
Our journey	looked	very long. (adjective phrase)
The old lady	feels	a lot of pain. (noun phrase)
This cake	tastes	delicious. (adjective)
You	got	it . (pronoun)
It	sounds	rather funny. (adjective phrase)

. Linking Verbs are also used to describe something other than action of
doing something. Here are some examples(linking verbs are in **bold**):

. His son **grew** <u>tall and handsome</u>.

adjective phrase ↵ - complement
. His wife **seems to be** <u>a very kind person</u>.

noun phrase ↵ - complement
. It **gets** <u>cold and windy</u>.

adjective phrase ↵ - complement

. **An adverbial phrase after a linking verb also relates to the subject:**
   linking verb + adverbial. Here are some examples:
. My chair was <u>here 10 minutes ago</u>.

adverbial phrase of place and time ↵
. She felt ill <u>before her meal time</u>.

prepositional phrase of time ↵

See ⟹ adverbial phrase

. Participles

The idea of present and past participles has been introduced in relation to regular and irregular verbs. See Tables 1 and 2. You know by now that the **present participle** and **past participle** are two important parts of the base form of the verb. For instance:

. **listen**   – base form of the verb as listed in a dictionary
. **listening** - present participle form
. **listened**   - past participle

Let's examine the following examples:
(1) . I <u>**listen**</u> to you.

base form of the verb↵
(2) . I <u>**am listening**</u> to you.

<u>auxiliary form of 'be' + participle-**ing** of 'listen'</u>

present participle form ↵
(3) . I <u>**have listened**</u> to you.

<u>auxiliary form + past participle –**ed**</u>

past participle form ↵

<u>Both present and past participle forms with the auxiliary verbs are used frequently as verbs.</u>
(4) . I <u>**listened**</u>.

past tense ↵

Example 4 demonstrates the difficulty associated with participles, as they can function in a variety of ways.

. Is listened functioning as the past participle in this example?

Here the verb **listened** is not functioning as the past participle, despite the fact that 'listened' is also the past participle form. To function as a past participle verb, the verb requires an auxiliary verb as illustrated by examples 2 and 3. Participles cannot work in their own rights as verbs. They can function as **verbals**. This is discussed below.

. Participles are frequently used in clauses. For example:

(5) . Flying in the air, he conceived the idea of his latest innovation.

participle clause↵ - phrase does not have a finite verb

(6) . She was at that bus stop for 30 minutes waiting for him patiently.

participle clause ↵

(7) . Smoking is prohibited in public places.

participle clause ↵ - clause has a finite verb

In example 7, smoking is functioning as a noun but it is a participle. When a participle functions as a noun, it is a gerund. It is getting somewhat complicated. Let's discuss gerunds because gerunds and participles are very close to each other.

. Gerunds

When a participle verb formed with *-ing* is used in a clause or a sentence as a noun, it is known as a *gerund*. In other words, a gerund is a verb form that functions as a noun. The following examples show that gerunds can function as the subject, object or form a phrase.

(1) . Running keeps you healthy.

unaccountable noun ↵ - *ing* form of the verb ⟹ *run*

In this example, Running is functioning as a noun, subject and *gerund*. In contrast, in example 2 below, running is only a participle(not a gerund).

(2) . He is running for his local charity.

present participle ↵ - *ing* form of the verb ⟹ *run*

(3) . Dancing is her favourite hobby.

gerund ↵ - stands alone as a noun - *functioning as* 'subject'

(4) . Washing is a burden.

gerund ↵ - stands alone as a noun - *functioning as* 'subject'

(5) . Antonia loves laughing.

gerund ↵ - *functioning as a noun and object*

(6) . I enjoyed <u>having</u> you.

gerund ↵ - *forming a noun phrase*
(7) . Hazel is very good at <u>cooking</u>.

gerund *forming a noun phrase   'at cooking'*↵
(8) . I wouldn't mind <u>waiting</u> for you.

gerund↵ - *forming a noun phrase*

waiting for you ↵

. Can a gerund be modified in a sentence?

Yes, it can be modified by only a possessive noun or a pronoun. This is exemplified below:

(9) . I don't like <u>Barbara's</u> *laughing* at the old lady*.

modifying gerund *laughing* ↵

---

* Here it would be grammatically wrong to say 'Barbara laughing'.

---

(10) . <u>We</u> choosing the colour won't be a good idea.

possessive pronoun↵ - modifying gerund – *choosing*

See ⟹ Modify

. Verbals

A verbal is derived from a verb. It may look like a verb, but it is never used in a sentence as a verb. In a sentence, it can function as a noun, adjective or adverb. There are three classes of verbals. These are participles, gerunds and infinitives. A gerund has the same form as the present participle. This can be a source of some confusion. Here are some examples of each class of verbals:

(1) . I find the show <u>*amusing*</u>.

participle ↵ - verbal
It is functioning as an adjective and modifying the noun *show*
(2) . We were given a talk by a very <u>interesting</u> speaker.

participle ↵ -verbal
It is functioning as an adjective and modifying the noun *speaker*
(3) . It was a <u>frightening</u> scene.

participle ↵ verbal as an adjective and modifying the noun *scene*
(4) . We sold our shop as a <u>going</u> concern.

participle↵ - verbal as an adjective and
modifying the noun *concern*

The above examples demonstrate that when a participle is functioning as an adjective, it is placed next to its noun.

. **The to-infinitive can be used to form noun and adverbial phrases.** For instance:

> (5). To take a train is the easiest means of transport tonight.
>
>   verbal ↵

Here the verbal is functioning as a noun phrase. It is also the subject of the sentence.

> (6). She wished to be the beauty queen.
>
>   verbal ↵

In this case, the verbal fulfils the function of both the object of the sentence as well as acts as a noun phrase.

> (7). To take a train, they didn't know the station whereabouts.
>
>   verbal ↵

Here the verbal is functioning as an adverbial phrase. It can also be called an infinitive phrase.

> (8). He telephoned me to break the news.
>
>   verbal ↵ - functioning as an adverbial phrase

These examples may not be easy to grasp. It will help you to understand these if you read about finite and non-finite clauses. See ⇒Clauses.

. **The gerund can be used as a verbal noun.** For instance:

> (9). Walking in the evenings is our daily routine.
>
> verbal noun ↵- functioning as a noun as well as the subject
>   of the sentence
>
> (10). Arriving late at work is not recommended.
>
>   noun phrase ↵ - verbal use of gerund forming a phrase

> (11). To run a small business is difficult.
>
>   noun phrase ↵ - verbal use of infinitive

In this example, the infinitive phrase is functioning as a noun phrase. It is also the subject of the sentence.

> (12). She wished to get another job.
>
>   noun phrase ↵- verbal use of infinitive

The infinitive phrase is functioning as a noun phrase. It is also the object of this sentence.

. <u>Should you always use **to-infinitive**?</u> The use of *to* with the base
  infinitive depends on the grammatical structure. For instance:

    (13) . I am pleased *to meet* you.

    (14) . I did not see Jane *enter* through this gate.

    (15) . She is always lucky *to be winning*.

    (16) . She likes **to touch** flowers. ⇐ It means that she likes to
                                      touch flowers, as a 'one-off'.

     (17) . I must say that helped being able *to talk* about it openly.

     (18) . She likes **touching** flowers. ⇐ it means that she always likes
                                  touching flowers, as a 'habit'.

. <u>Sometimes the omission of *to* is not considered as an error,
  but an ellipsis. It means shortening.</u> For instance:

     (19) . My husband helped Mrs. Williams(to) *carry* her shopping.

     (20) . They wanted us (to) <u>run</u> faster than we could.

               to is required ↲ -Without *to*, this is does not make sense.

     (21) . It is better if you do it now than (to) *leave* it till tomorrow.

. <u>Sometimes in informal and spoken English *to* is omitted,</u> e.g.

     (22) . Our aim is to help delegates (to) achieve their objectives.

     (23) . These tablets should help (to) reduce pain tonight.

     (24) . My advice will guide you in the future **(to)** <u>protect</u> yourself.

here without '**to**' it does not work – '**to**' is essential↲

. <u>Split Infinitives</u>

Placing of a word or words between the *to* and the *verb* creates a split infinitive. Some people do not like the idea of split infinitives. In fact, sometimes it
is desirable to use a split infinitive as it helps to show the verb is modified.
For instance:

    (1) . In order <u>to precisely reply</u> to your letter, I must consult my staff.

           split infinitive↲– precisely is causing a ⇒ **split**

<u>Adverb *precisely* is modifying the verb *reply*.</u>

      (2) . <u>To fully appreciate</u> your ideas, I must read your book.

      split infinitive↲ – appreciate is causing a ⇒ **split**

<u>Adverb *fully* is modifying the verb *appreciate*.</u> The writer of this sentence
may consider it necessary to use a split infinitive.

. <u>**Sometimes the use of split infinitives can result in a clumsy
  construction of a sentence.**</u> For instance:

      (3) . Caroline began *to slowly cry* until she became hysterical.

      (4) . The interview panel wanted *to again interview* me.

Examples 3 and 4 are re-written without split infinitives. The following re-constructions are simple and sound better:

> (5) . Caroline began *to cry slowly* until she became hysterical.
>
> (6) . The interview panel wanted *to interview* me again.

. There are no rules regarding the use of split infinitives. If you are sure that a split infinitive is needed, split the infinitive. If you think that it may create some ambiguity, re-write the sentence without it.

. Misuse or Omission of Infinitive, Participle and Gerund

When we write or talk about verbs, we refer to them as *to drink*, *to eat*, *to love*, *to go*, etc. Misuse of infinitives, participles and gerunds often happens. Here are some examples:

> (1) . Watching from the window, the procession got bigger and bigger.
>
> participle clause ↵   main clause ↵

This construction suggests that *the procession* was watching from the window. This is meaningless. It can cause misunderstanding. The reason for this misunderstanding is that the subject of the main clause is *the procession*, which is the implied subject of the participle.

In order to avoid the danger of misunderstanding, we can rewrite it correctly as:

> (2) . Watching from the window, *we saw* the procession getting bigger and bigger.

Here it means: *We were watching ....., we saw the ..... bigger.*

> (3) . Standing by the bus stop, the car hit a lamp post.
>
> participle clause ↵   main clause↵

This sentence implies: the car was standing...........stop, the car hit...........post.

The following re-construction is correct:

> (4) . Standing by the bus stop, *we saw* the car hit a lamp post.

. When using gerunds, writers often ignore the fact that a gerund can only be modified by *a possessive noun or pronoun*. For instance:

> (5) . Annemarie does approve of her husband buying another new car.

The correct statement of this example:

(6) . Annemarie does approve of her <u>husband's</u> <u>buying</u> another new car.

> possessive noun ↵   gerund↵

. The misuse of an infinitive happens, when it is separated from the word
  it is expected to modify. Sometimes an infinitive is placed in an
  inappropriate place in a sentence. For instance:

> (7) . All of us had electrical blankets to sleep when camping in the
>
> forest.   misuse ↵

In this sentence, the infinitive is connected with blankets instead of the subject. This is not the purpose of using it here. The following
re-construction is grammatically correct:

(8) . All of us had electrical blankets enabling us to *sleep* when camping
      in the forest.

(9) . The idea is that you use German to manage local branches.

>   inappropriate/incorrect use ↵

This construction suggests that you use a German person or the German language which will manage *(action)* local branches. This is ambiguous. This is
not the intention. The intended meaning is that you use the German language
to manage local branches *(action)*. The *action* of the verb is to be performed
by the subject. The following sentence is correct:

(10) . The idea is that you use the German language in order to manage
       local branches. (the language which enables you to manage)

This statement communicates the intended meaning.

---

*Some people feel strongly about the use of split infinitives as a
 contentious issue. This does not mean that you should avoid using them.

.Verb concord or agreement

Verb concord or agreement is a rule, which states that the form of the verb is
dictated by the person and number of the subject. Let's apply this rule to the
following examples:

> (1) . I travel today.
>   ⇑   ⇑
>   1   2

1 is a subject   *I* ⇒ first person and single (number)

2 is a verb   *travel* ⇒ it is the *base/infinitive* form of the verb

In this example, in accordance with the verb concord, the verb form is agreed
with the person and number of the subject.

****

(2) . She speaks German well.

    1↵   2↵

1 is the subject *she* ⟹ third person and single (number)

2 is a verb ⟹ It is *–s* **inflection** which marks the third person singular of the *present tense* as demonstrated above. This way, the verb form agrees with the third person singular.

(3) . They work in a restaurant.

    1↵   2↵

1 is the subject *they* ⟹ third person and plural

2 is a verb ⟹ it is the *basic/infinitive* present form of the verb. Here, the verb agrees with the third person and is plural (number).

(4) . I lived in London some years ago.

    1↵   2↵

1 is a subject ⟹ **I** - first person and singular

2 is a verb ⟹ it is the *-ed past or participle form* ⟹*regular form*

(5) . You left England yesterday.

    1↵   2↵

1 is the subject *you* ⟹ second person and singular

2 is a verb ⟹ it is the *-ed past/ participle form* ⟹ *irregular form*. Here, the verb agrees with the person and number of the subject. It is the *Past tense*.

. The essence of concord is that the subject controls the form of the verb. This rule is applied in all sixteen tenses discussed.

. Finite and non-finite verbs

In the following examples, the verb is marked for tense. When a verb is marked for tense, it is called a finite verb or a finite verb phrase. A finite verb may be the only verb in a sentence. You can have a finite verb in both main and sub-ordinate clauses. Here are some examples:

(1) . He breeds ducks.

     finite verb ↵ - present tense form

. The relationship between the verb *'breeds'* and the subject *'he'* is in concord (agreement).

(2) . Anne travels to Russia twice a year.

     finite verb ↵ - present tense form

. The relationship between the verb 'travels' and the subject 'Anne' is in agreement(concord).

>   (3) . I always <u>buy</u> some flowers for my wife.

>   finite verb ↵ - present tense form

. The relationship between the verb 'buy' and the subject 'I' is in concord (agreement).

>   (4) . We <u>love</u> their new cottage in the country.

>   finite verb ↵ - present tense form

. The relationship between the verb *'love'* and the subject *'we'* is in concord (agreement).

>   (5) . I <u>joined</u> your book club.

>   finite verb ↵ - past tense

. The relationship between the verb *'joined'* and the subject *'I'* is in concord (agreement).

>   (6) . You <u>interviewed</u> her the other day for a job.

>   finite verb ↵ - past tense

. The relationship between the verb 'interviewed' and the subject 'you' is in concord (agreement).

>   (7) . We <u>went to</u> Switzerland last year.

>

>   This verb phrase contains a finite irregular verb 'go'

The finite irregular verb *go* changes its form for the past tense by becoming **went**. This is equivalent to the past participle **-ed** form. There are many such irregular verbs. See ⟹Verbs

. The relationship between the verb *'went'* and the subject *'we'* is in concord (agreement).

. **A sentence must have one finite verb**. See ⟹ Clauses also Sentences

. **A non –finite verb is not marked for tense.** The non-finite verb phrase can contain one of the following verb forms:

>   . **infinitive** - the base form of a verb
>   . **gerund** - the –ing form of a verb
>   . **participle** – it has two forms:

>> >   (1) . the - **ing** from = the present participle or
>> >   (2) . the - **ed** from = the past participle

The non-finite phrase does not give information in the same way as the finite phrase gives on tense (time). It does not take a subject. All verbs except modal auxiliaries have non-finite forms. Here are some examples of non-finite verbs/ phrases:

(1) . serious <u>to study</u>

non-finite verb phrase ↵ - to- infinitive form

See ⟹ Phrases

(2) . slow <u>going</u>

non-finite verb ↵ - gerund form

(3) . <u>appearing</u> on screen

non-finite verb phrase ↵ - participle form

. <u>The past participle '–d' form, depending on the context, can function as finite and non-finite</u>:

(4) . Some young hooligans <u>attacked</u> Maria in the street.

finite verb ↵ - past tense

(5) . We saw Maria <u>attacked</u> by some young hooligans in the street.

non-finite participle verb ↵ – it has no subject and tense

. <u>A sentence can have both finite and non-finite phrases.</u> For instance:

(6) . We <u>wished</u> <u>to travel</u> together.

finite verb phrase↵   ⇑

non-finite verb phrase

(7) . The doorman <u>asked</u> us <u>to show</u> our tickets.

finite verb phrase↵   ⇑

non-finite verb phrase

See ⟹ Clauses and ⟹ Phrases

. Tenses

Tenses are mentioned above and in the last chapter. Now is the right time and place in this book to discuss these in detail. The word *'tempus'* is a Latin word, which means time. The word *tense* is a derivative of this Latin word. Therefore, the **present tense** means the present time (now). Similarly, the **past tense** means the past time (then). In precise terms:

. The tense is a form of a verb, which is either the present or past tense.

. As stated in the last chapter, the verb tense is marked by *inflection* - change in the form of a word, especially the ending for the *present tense* and *past tense* only.

. The future tense is expressed in different ways, as it can also be stated in the present tense form.

. There are sixteen tenses. These are summarised in Table 1.

1. Present Tense or Simple Present Tense

The present tense is used to express a present action or state that exists now. Let's first examine the following examples:

(1) . I <u>walk</u> all the way.

⇑ – subject ⇒ I singular first person

present tense formed from the base form of the verb ⇒ walk

(2) . You <u>talk</u> to him.

⇑ – subject ⇒ *you* second person singular/plural

present tense formed from the base form of the verb ⇒ talk

(3) . He/she <u>runs</u> fast.

⇑ –subject ⇒ **he/she** third person singular

present tense formed by an -s inflection on verb ⇒ run

(4) . They <u>sing</u> nicely.

⇑ –subject ⇒ **they** third person plural

present tense formed from the base verb ⇒ sing

. <u>These examples illustrate that the base form of the verb is used for all persons, except the third person singular. For the third person singular the verb form changes by – *s inflection*</u>. Here are some more examples of the present tense(used in verb phrases) :

(5) . He *lectures* on Russian literature. ⇒ indicates recurrence of event

(6) . We *arrive* the next day.   ⇒ *indicating future*

(7) . He loves his family very much   ⇒ *indicating feelings/state*

(8) . This car belongs to my brother   ⇒ *indicating relation/state*

(9) . Water is essential for our survival ⇒ *indicating fact true at all times*

(10) . I think it's a great idea   ⇒ *indicating opinion/state*

2 . Present Progressive/Continuous Tense

The present progressive tense indicates that the action is continuous. It is still happening. The present continuous can also be used for present states which last for some time. For permanent states, use the simple present tense. The following examples demonstrate the use of this tense:

(1) . I <u>am working</u> hard.

indicating action over a period of time↵

(2) . She <u>is cooking</u> our lunch.

someone in the middle of doing something ↵

****

(3) . They <u>are coming</u> tomorrow.

talking about some future happening ↵

(4) . We <u>are always dining</u> in this restaurant.

always shows that something has been happening for some time

(5) . After answering a telephone call, she <u>is feeling</u> depressed.

indicating a temporary state of one's mind

(6) . This afternoon our car sales <u>are looking</u> poor.

pointing to a temporary state of business ↵

In order to construct the present progressive tense, place the present form of the auxiliary **be** before the participle form 'ing'. It is easy to remember it as:

. **The present progressive tense = present form of be + participle form 'ing'**

3 . Past Tense

The past tense describes an event, which has already happened, or a state of something, which existed at a particular time **(then)** before the present time **(now)**. The following examples illustrate the construction of the past tense, which is also known as the **simple past tense**.

(1) . I <u>walked</u> to Chelsea.

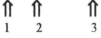

   1   2   3

Here:

    1 = subject first person singular. Also **I** is a *pronoun*

    2 = *verb* indicating the past tense formed from the past

       participle –ed (-ed inflection) the regular verb ⇒walk

    3 = noun phrase   The preposition *to* can occur before a noun

----

(2) . Robin <u>managed</u> his family business well.

⇑ - Robin ⇒ subject third person singular

verb indicating past tense formed from the past participle -ed form (**-ed** inflection)

(3) . You <u>led</u> your team successfully.

⇑ - You ⇒ subject second person singular

verb indicating the past tense formed from the past tense form of the

irregular verb ⇒lead

(4) . We <u>bought</u> a cottage in Wales.

Here, 'we' is the subject ⇒ first person plural. The verb 'bought' is

indicating the past tense formed from the past tense form of the irregular verb
⇒buy

. Examples 1 and 2 demonstrate that the past participle form 'ed'
  inflection of regular verbs is used to form the past tense.

. Examples 3 and 4 show that the past tense form of the irregular verbs is
  also used to form the past tense. Here are some more examples of
  using the past tense:

(5). She said that she was an actress. ⇐ reported speech

(6). They <u>announced</u> that <u>our train arrived on time</u>. ⇐ reported speech

(7). We <u>went</u> to school everyday by car. ⇐ describing past event

(8). Once upon a time we <u>lived</u> in that house.

   stating past circumstance ↵

(9). There <u>was</u> no rain. ⇒describes state or environmental condition

(10). <u>Was</u> he unconscious when you <u>arrived</u> at the scene? ⇐ inquiring

4 . Past Progressive Tense

The past progressive/continuous tense is used to express what was happening
at some point in time in the past. In order to express the past continuous state
such as feelings, normally the simple past tense is used. Sometimes for a
temporary state, one can use the past progressive tense. The following examples illustrate the use of this tense:

(1) . I <u>was swimming</u> in the sea.

   indicating action over a period of past time

(2) . He <u>was working</u> every day seven days a week.

   indicating action over a whole specific period

(3). We <u>were training</u> our staff when the fire broke out.

indicating sudden occurrence when in the middle of doing something

(4) . Due to an industrial strike, we <u>were working</u> from home that day.

indicating temporary action for a short period ↵

(5). She <u>was crying.</u> ⇒ indicating temporary feeling (cried = past tense)

. **To summarise its construction: the past progressive tense = past**
  form of be + participle form 'ing'

5. Future Tense

The future tense expresses actions or states which will happen in the future. It also describes the future in the past. The future tense is formed using an auxiliary verb with the bare infinitive form of the verb. We can summarise the construction of **simple future tenses** as:

. **Future tense = auxiliary will or shall + bare infinitive verb form**

Traditionally
shall *was used for the first person subject*
will *was used for the second and third person subject*
Present-day
For the first person subject use either **shall** or **will**
For other subjects use **will**

See ⟹ Shall and Will under Modal verb and see ⟹ Future time

Here are some examples of sentences with the future tense:

   (1) . I <u>shall visit</u> you soon in Germany.

will may be used with first person singular subject

   (2) . He will help you.
   (3) . They *will come* to see us next year.
   (4) . *We'll telephone* you on our arrival.
   (5) . It *will go* by airmail tonight.

. The future in the past is expressed by the future tense by using *would* form of the auxiliary *will*:

   (6) . Angelica *told* Thomas that he *would arrive* on time.

      past tense↵   future in the past↵

   (7) . You *promised* that we *would write* this article together.

      past tense↵   future in the past↵

The future can also be expressed in some other ways. Here we are discussing tenses rather than the future.

6 . Future Progressive Tense

The future progressive expresses an action that is continuous over a period in the future. It is constructed as:
   . **Future Progressive tense = shall/will + be + participle**
   form 'ing' form

Here are some examples of the future progressive tense showing the

****

relationship between the information conveyed by the verb phrase and time/tense, when these were uttered:

> (1) . I *shall/will be going* to see my mother soon.
>
> (2) . We shall/will be drinking in that pub over there.
>
> (3) . Everyone *will be cheering* when you appear on the stage.
>
> (4) . They *will be serving* us as soon as we take our seats.

7 . <u>Perfect or Present Perfect Tense</u>

The perfect or present perfect indicates that the action or state is complete in the near past up to the present time. This is just the opposite to the simple past, which denotes that the action or state ended in the past.

> (1) . Our guest <u>arrived</u>.

meaning the action was completed in the past ↵

. <u>**When did they arrive?**</u>

The only conclusion we can draw from this statement is that they arrived in the past time. It does not tell us that the past was a day ago, a month ago or whenever. It simply tells us that the action of arrival finished in the past.

> (2) . Our guests <u>have arrived</u>.

It means that the action was completed in the near past that is up to the present time.

. <u>**When have they arrived?**</u>

It signifies that our guests have arrived presently and that they are here

now. (⟹ present time)

> (3) . She <u>felt rotten</u> for leaving her children behind.

The action was completed in the past. We do not know when in the past.

> (4) . She <u>has felt rotten</u> for leaving her children behind.

It implies that the action was completed in the near past up to the present time.

The construction of the present perfect tense can be visualised as:

. <u>**Present perfect = present of auxiliary verb have + past participle**</u>

This is further illustrated below:

> (1) . He <u>has sheltered</u> his manager from criticism.

present perfect ↵

. In accordance with the concord, the verb is in agreement with the subject *he*. '*has*' is the singular form of the primary auxiliary verb *have*.

   (2) . We have written to them for a copy of the contract.

present perfect↵– irregular verb *write* its past participle form *written*

   (3) . Our hosts have shown us the area by car.

present perfect↵ - irregular verb *show* its past participle form *shown*

8 . Present Perfect Progressive Tense

The present perfect continuous/progressive is used to express an action over a period of time in the past and is continuing up-to the present time. Its method of construction can be stated as:

. **Present perfect progressive tense = present of have + been + participle form 'ing'**

   Here are some examples:
       (1) . She has been working with us for four years.

present perfect continuous ↵–repeated action/ working up to now
       (2) . We have been living in this building since it was built.

present perfect continuous ↵ - shows repeated action
       (3) . They have been singing on stage for a living for many years.

present perfect continuous ↵ - shows repeated action

9 . Past Perfect Tense*

The past perfect tense is used to express an action or a state that happened or existed some time/long time ago in the past**. It is constructed as:

. **Past perfect tense = past of auxiliary verb have + past participle**

The following examples exemplify the use of the past perfect tense:
   (1) . I had received many such requests before.

   past perfect ↵ - shows an action in the distant past
   (2) . This was a request for money. I had received such requests before.

                           past perfect ↵ - action in the distant past
   (3) . They had planned their trip some time ago.

   past perfect ↵ - action took place at some unspecified
                       time in the distant past/long time ago

(4) . They <u>had thought</u> about their own families.

past perfect tense↵- points to a state that existed in their
minds in the distant past

(5) . We <u>had admired</u> their courage.

past perfect tense ↵- shows a state 'approval' in the distance past

(6) . We <u>had had</u> a new car then.

past perfect tense↵-shows a state 'ownership/own' in the distant past

---

* Sometimes the past perfect is called the pluperfect
It is derived from Latin: Plūs quam Perfectum)

** Length of time can be specified by adding the time when something
occurred or existed.

(7) . She had found her future husband <u>only three years</u> before her death.

---

10 . <u>Past Perfect Progressive Tense</u>

The past perfect progressive is used to indicate a continuous action over a
period of time in the past. It is described as:

. <u>Past perfect progressive tense = past of have + been +
participle form – 'ing'</u>

This is illustrated below:

(1) . I <u>had been travelling</u> all day.

past perfect progressive ↵
It indicates a continuous action(**travelling**) in the past – it was happening in
the distant past.

(2) . We <u>had been running</u> early in the morning to get fit for this race.

past perfect progressive ↵ - in the distant past

(3) . In those days, our business <u>had been doing</u> very well.

past perfect progressive ↵

(4). When I met her, she <u>had been shopping</u> at Harrods.

past perfect progressive ↵

. This does not mean that I met her during her shopping at Harrods, but
after her shopping. If you wish to say that you met her during her
shopping period/time, use the <u>past progressive tense</u> as shown
below:

(5) . When I met her, she <u>was shopping</u> at Harrods.

past progressive tense ↵

(6) . When our guests arrived, I <u>had been cooking</u> for them.

> past progressive tense↲ **-** points to an ongoing action in the distant past

. In all these cases, it implies a continuous action in the distant past. The continuity in the distant past is at the heart of the past perfect continuous tense. A few more examples are:

(7) . We were in France. We <u>had been enjoying</u> our long weekend in Paris.

(8) . She <u>had been studying</u> at Warsaw University when I moved to Poland.

(9) . When we saw Daniel last time, he had been distributing leaflets for another musical show on the doorstep of the Carlton Club.

11 . <u>Future Perfect Tense</u>

The future perfect tense is used when the speaker or the writer is thinking about the future, and then looks back when something will be completed at a specific point in the future time. <u>It is future and perfect together</u>. It is constructed as:

. **<u>future perfect tense = will/shall + have + past participle (- ed/en/ other ending)</u>**

Here are some examples:

(1) . <u>By next month</u>, they <u>will have submitted</u> our report to the director.
      ⇑   ⇑

thinking about the future   <u>saying by next month, i.e.</u>
                                ⇑

> specific point in future time when

report will be submitted ↲ **-** looking back into the future

(2) . <u>Three days' stay is enough in Berlin</u>, as you <u>will have seen</u> its
                       | | main attractions within

projecting into the future ↲   ⇑   this time.

> saying in three days (specific point in future time) all main
>
> places will be visited ⇒ looking back into the future

(3) . <u>In two months' time</u>, we <u>will/shall* have gone to</u> Austria.
    ⇑   ⇑

projecting into the future   <u>saying in two months' time, i.e.</u>
                                ⇑

> specific point in future time

we will be in Austria ↲ **-** looking back into the future

> * You can use shall with the first person.

(4) . They <u>will have replied</u> to our letter <u>by now</u>.

⇑   ⇑

implying now (specific point in future time) projecting the future

12 . Future Perfect Progressive Tense

The future perfect progressive tense is used when the speaker or the writer is thinking about something and then looks back when something will be completed at a specific point in the future time. <u>It is future, perfect and continuous/progressive together</u>. It is constructed as:

. <u>future perfect progressive tense = will/shall + have +been + participle –'ing' ending</u>

(1) . At the end of January, I <u>shall/will have been living</u> in London.

(2) . Tomorrow night, we <u>will have been crossing</u> the English Channel by a night ferry.

(3) . She wants us to marry next summer, as we <u>will have been living</u> in our new home.

(4) . You <u>will have been staying</u> with us in three weeks' time.

<u>These tenses show continuity in the future.</u>

13 . Future in the Past

The future in the past is looking forward to the future from the past. You can imagine it as your intention of doing something in the future but in the past time. For instance:

(1) . I <u>should/would travel to</u> France to see Paris.

<u>simple future in the past</u>↵

⇑

travel in the future ahead of the present time but in the past time

(2) . I <u>should/ would be travelling</u> to France to see Paris.

<u>future progressive in the past</u> ↵

(3) . I <u>should/ would have travelled</u> to France to see Paris.

<u>future perfect in the past</u>↵

(4) . I <u>should/ would have been travelling</u> to France to see Paris.

<u>future perfect progressive in the past</u>↵

. Tenses show that there are many facets of verb phrases. When an **auxiliary verb** is added to the **lexical verb** (main verb) to construct a verb phrase, the auxiliary verb helps us to make a statement. Indeed, tenses contain verb phrases. Tenses enable us to express an extensive range of astonishing meanings. In Table 1, you can see at a glance the full working of all tenses. It is a summary of the information embedded in each statement, and the relationship between the **information** and the **time** (tense) when it was enacted or spoken.

. Future Time

We express future time in a variety of ways, depending on our
intention of doing something, predicting something to happen, making
a plan for achieving or doing something and so on. For instance:
(1) . Our seaside shop is to close/is closing in January.
(2) . Our council is going to repair our road next month.
(3) . The last train to Bridlington leaves Hull at 22.00 hours in
    two hours' time.
(5) . I will return to London tomorrow.
(6) . I will have to pay the full loan plus interest within 24 months.
(7) . Without you, it won't be safe to travel alone.
(8) . He will not find a job in the country and his wife and children
    will face financial hardship.
(9) . I will be leaving home as soon as I have finished this job.
(10) . She should have accepted the offer. ⇐ future in the past
(11) . If our company goes bankrupt today I am retiring. ⇐ Prediction

The above examples illustrate that the future time does not always refer
to certainty of events to occur in the future.

. some suggestions how you can refer to the future:

. When something is planned to happen, use the simple future tense, e.g.
    (12) . I will do it for you.

. When talking in general terms and you wish to say what you expect
  to happen in a given situation, use the simple future tense, e.g.

    (13) . At the next General Election, I will vote for you.

. When you are sure that something will happen because something
  has been planned, you can use the future continuous tense, e.g.

    (14) . I understand that your wife will be coming with you.

. When something has not happened until now, but it is expected to happen before a particular time in the future, use <u>the future perfect tense,</u> e.g.

   (15). When my grandson is 20 years old I will already have retired.

. When you want to state the duration of an occurrence/event in the future at a particular time, use <u>the future perfect continuous,</u> e.g.

   (16). She will have been living in Russia for two years in January.

. When you wish to state your future intention of doing something or some happening in the future, use **be going to** followed by the **<u>infinitive</u> form of the verb**, e.g.

   (17). She is going to have a bay soon.

. When referring to the future in a general way, you can use <u>the simple present tense,</u> as in examples (1) and (3) above.

. You can also use 'be due to' 'be about to', when talking about some future happening which is likely to happen as planned, e.g.

   (18) . I am due to start my new job at the Town Hall.

A Summary of Tenses

Present Simple	Past Simple	Future Simple	Future simple in the Past
I go	I went	I shall/will go	I should/would go
Present Progressive	Past Progressive	Future Progressive	Future Progressive in the Past
I am going	I was going	I shall/will be going	I should/would be going
Present Perfect	Past Perfect	Future Perfect	Future Perfect in the Past
I have gone	I had gone	I shall/will have gone	I should/would have gone
Present Perfect Progressive	Past Perfect Progressive	Future Perfect Progressive	Future Perfect Progressive in the Past
I have been going	I had been going	I shall/will have been going	I should/would have been going

Table 1

Chapter 3
Nouns

. Introduction

A large number of words are used as **names** of such things as:

- **People** - Anne, Blair, Clinton, John, Jane   (someone unique)
- **Places** - London, Frankfurt, Stockholm, Singapore, Manchester
        (a specific place)
- **Objects** - printer, table, book, pen, motor, computer   (an artefact)
- **Animals** - cow, horse, donkey, fox, rabbit
- **Nature** – star, earth, sea, sky, flowers, sun
- **Abstract** – it refers to ideas, concepts, qualities, a state of mind or
        intangible things., e.g.
        ability, desire, failure, reason, devotion, need, thirst,
        intimacy, sympathy, admiration, love, communism,
        unhappiness

The word **noun** is derived from the Latin word *nomen*. In Latin, it means *name*. Therefore, when a word is used as a name, it is called a **noun**. Nouns make up the biggest category of word classes. Every thing is given a name. Nouns are at the heart of our language as they are frequently used in speech and writing. For instance, in the following simple sentences:

(1) . James   loves   music.

noun ↵   noun ↵

proper noun↵ common noun↵

(2) . The capital of Scotland is Edinburgh.

noun ↵   noun↵   noun↵

common noun↵ proper noun ↵ proper noun ↵

. Types of Nouns

The above two examples illustrate that there are two types of nouns, proper nouns and common nouns. James, Scotland and Edinburgh are proper nouns. They are also proper nouns for the following reasons:

- . words Mary White refer to ⟹ someone unique

It is true to say that more than one person can be called **Mary White**, but still a particular person *Mary White* is unique.
> . the word Scotland refers to a specific country
> . the word Edinburgh refers to a particular city
> . Music and capital are common nouns. Why is it so?

The word music by itself does not refer to unique music. Similarly, the word capital by itself does not refer to a particular capital city of the world. There are many different types of music and a large number of capital cities in the world.

. Concrete and Abstract Common Nouns

Common nouns may be classified as concrete and abstract. This classification is based on the idea of tangible and intangible. One can see and touch tangible things. Such things may be concrete nouns. On the other hand, there are intangible things, which cannot be seen or touched, but they exist as ideas, concepts and qualities. Such non-material things may be abstract nouns. The following table shows some nouns of both types.

Some concrete and abstract nouns

Concrete Nouns	Abstract Nouns
park-	democracy
horse	freedom
floppy disc	falsehood
hammer	Buddhism
bed	anger
tree	liberty
officer	truth
woman	socialism
book	action

Table 1

. How can you know whether a word is a proper noun or a common noun? The following guide will help you to decide whether a noun is a proper noun or a common noun.

A Guide to proper and common nouns

Proper Nouns	Common Nouns
. Begin with a capital letter in writing	. Initial capital letter is not essential in writing unless

	it begins a sentence
Examples:	*Examples:*
Birmingham, Cairo, Thomas	coffee, bread, car, concept,
Friday*, July, Christmas,	method
India	
. Specific or unique names	. Group or member of group names
Examples:	*Examples:*
Einstein, Johnson,	girl, woman, man, people,
Cliff Richard, France	animal, train, club

---

* <u>Exception to the above rules - seasons :</u>
spring, summer, autumn and winter <u>do not </u>begin with a capital letter,
unless they start a sentence.

. <u>Noun Gender</u>

Another feature of common and proper nouns is that they have gender -
the fact of being male or female. In the English language, gender classification is based on a man and woman as natural creation. In accordance with
this idea, a **woman** is classified as **feminine** (female) and a **man** as **masculine**(male). A noun that relates to either a male or female is said to be of the
<u>common gender</u>. There is also the **neuter gender** that refers to things, which
are neither male nor female, such as a computer, a car and other similar
things.

However, there are some **exceptions,** in particular, to the neuter gender rule,
which should be observed. For instance, there are some artefacts(man-made
objects) such as **cars**, **ships** and **aeroplanes** and the like which are **<u>personi-
fied</u>** and given **<u>feminine gender</u>**.

Furthermore, there are some **<u>natural objects</u>** such as Sun and Moon, which
are also **<u>personified</u>**, particularly in poetry and sometimes in prose. The
<u>feminine gender</u> is given to things which are considered attractive or beauti-
ful, such as the Moon, Nature, Spring and the like. Some other objects such
as the Sun, Summer and Winter which are regarded as possessing power or
can cause some harm are given <u>male </u>gender.

. <u>How about countries?</u>

They are also referred to as feminine. It is worth mentioning that in many
other languages, such as German and French every noun is given a gender
form. In English sex corresponds to gender, but there are some exceptions as
outlined above. Even so, in English nouns are <u>not divided</u> into masculine,
feminine and neuter classification in the same way as nouns are classified in
some other languages.

. **How can you determine the gender of a noun?** The pronoun or
possessive adjective that goes with a noun determines its gender, e.g.

  (1) . **He** is such a nice **man**.
  (2) . That **woman** is honest because **she** did not hide her faults.
  (3) . There is an **animal**; **it** is black and huge.
  (4) . This **book** was published in England, but **it** is out of print.
  (5) . Our **ship** was so huge that **she** carried 3,000 passengers.
  (6) . **Spring** is already in the air, as you can feel **her** presence.

  Usually 'it' is used in informal English↵

. **Are there some nouns that do not fall into male and female
gender groups?**

Yes, indeed, a few nouns have their own gender class
known as **dual gender**. Here are some examples:

  . teacher man or woman ⇐ dual gender

  . singer   man or woman ⇐ dual gender

  . adult   man or woman ⇐ dual gender

  . player   man or woman ⇐ dual gender

  . student man or woman   ⇐ dual gender

  . doctor man or woman   ⇐ dual gender

  . dancer man or woman   ⇐ dual gender

. **Most animals have specific male and female forms:**
  For instance:

. dog	⇒ male	. bitch ⇒ female dog
. Stallion	⇒ male horse	. mare ⇒ female horse or donkey
. bull	⇒ male(cow family)	. cow ⇒ female
. cock	⇒ male(chicken)	. hen ⇒ female (chicken)
. drake	⇒ male(duck)	. duck ⇒ female duck
. lion	⇒male	. lioness ⇒female lion
. fox	⇒male	. vixen ⇒female fox
. tiger	⇒male	. tigress ⇒female tiger
. gander	⇒male goose	. goose ⇒female
. ram	⇒male sheep	. sheep/ewe ⇒female sheep

. In fact, most people use the same noun to refer to both male and female
animals* e.g. dog, cat horse, sheep and goose. There are many specialists
such as vets who have a special interest in animals. These specialists use

****

specific nouns to distinguish male and female animals.

---

* <u>You can refer to an animal as 'it'</u>. Some creatures such as fish, flies and the like are not given gender classifications.

Examples of proper nouns and their respective genders

Masculine	Feminine	Neuter
John Webb	Barbara Cartland	Russia
Robin Taylor	Rachel Berios	British Airways
Adam Shaw	Anne Kling	Microsoft
Daniel Shaw	Silvia Smith	Sweden

Table 2

Examples of common nouns and their respective genders

Masculine	Feminine	Neuter
king	queen	table
boy	girl	magazine
lion	lioness	banana
conductor	conductress (on a bus collects money)	post

Table 3

. Compound Nouns

A compound noun is made of two or more words. Here are some, e.g.

- . milkman ⟹ milk + man - is a compound noun
- . headache ⟹ head + ache - is a compound noun
- . postman ⟹ post + man - is a compound noun

A compound noun can be written as a single word, hyphenated word or as a pair of two words. Some compound nouns are shown in Table 4 below. A compound word may be listed in one dictionary as a hyphenated word and in another as one word or as a pair of two or more words.

<u>When some compound nouns are formed with **noun + gerund** (stamp-collecting) and **verb + adverb** (take-off), they are hyphenated.</u> Sometimes words which have prefixes such as **non**, **pre**, **anti**, **semi** and **ultra** are also hyphenated. Here are four examples: **pre-packed** sandwich, **anti-aircraft** missiles, **non-committal** reply, and **ulta-modern** design. It is best to be consistent with your own spellings and consult a dictionary when in doubt (sometimes two dictionaries may differ).

. **Some compound words are written as hyphenated words** – there
  are no exact rules about whether two or more specific nouns or words
  are hyphenated or not.

Some Compound Nouns

Single Words	Hyphenated words	A pair of words
postman	daughter-in-law	teddy bear
sportswoman	Anglo-American	blood bank
clergyman	non-fiction	shoe brush
housewife	major-general	blind spot
businesswoman	waste-bin	health food
policeman	window-shopping	wine bar
doorstep	father-figure	magic carpet
gamekeeper	ultra-modern	black box
standpoint	flight-recorder	court martial
teapot	X-ray	package holiday

Table 4

. Singular and Plural Nouns

As a noun is a name, it can be used for a single thing(singular) or a number
of the same things(plural),but plural nouns differ from singular nouns in their
endings. The following examples illustrate how in most cases plural nouns
are formed:

60   **Word Classes**   **Nouns**

****

. boat ⟹ singular and . boats ⟹ plural

. cake ⟹ singular and . cakes ⟹ plural

. chair ⟹ singular and . chairs ⟹ plural

. shop ⟹ singular and . shops ⟹ plural

. A large number of plural nouns end with 's' as exemplified in Table 5 below:

Examples of plural nouns with 's'

Singular	Plural	Singular	Plural
boat	boats	border	borders
bolt	bolts	bridge	bridges
candidate	candidates	car	cars
chop	chops	competition	competitions
corner	corners	date	dates
delay	delays	diplomat	diplomats
director	directors	dot	dots
effect	effects	effort	efforts
exhibit	exhibits	eye	eyes
farm	farms	fool	fools
jug	jugs	length	lengths
lip	lips	pedestrian	pedestrians

Table 5

. A large number of singular nouns end with a letter (-s, -ss, -sh, -tch, -x,-o) other than 'e' but their plural nouns end with 'es' as exemplified in Table 6 above.

. Singular nouns which end with ' e' also form their plural with 'es'. Here are some examples:

    . cabbage ⟹ cabbages   . cause ⟹ causes

    . cable ⟹ cables   . house ⟹ houses

    . shade ⟹ shades   . vegetable ⟹ vegetables

Word Classes   **Nouns**   **61**

****

Examples of plural nouns end with 'es'

Singular	Plural	Singular	Plural
boss	bosses	box	boxes
cargo	cargoes	bus	buses
crash	crashes	coach	coaches
loss	losses	sandwich	sandwiches
gas	gases	pass	passes
patch	patches	scratch	scratches
sex	sexes	blemish	blemishes
stitch	stitches	trench	trenches
torpedo	torpedoes	tomato	tomatoes
watch	watches	wish	wishes

Table 6

. If you carefully study Table 7, you will learn that all singular nouns <u>end</u> with '**a consonant + y**'. Therefore, their corresponding plural nouns are formed by changing the last letter y to '**ies**'. <u>Many plural nouns end with 'ies'</u>.

Examples of plural nouns end with 'ies'

Singular	Plural	Singular	Plural
body	bodies	category	categories
cavalry	cavalries	cemetery	cemeteries
community	communities	country	countries
currency	currencies	duty	duties
energy	energies	entry	entries
family	families	glory	glories
hobby	hobbies	humanity	humanities
itinerary	itineraries	liberty	liberties
penalty	penalties	story	stories
remedy	remedies	territory	territories

Table 7

. <u>All singular nouns, which end with a vowel (a, e, i, o, u) and 'y', do not always form their plural with 'ies'</u>.

Here are some examples of such singular nouns and their corresponding plural nouns:

         . way   ⇒   plural noun ⇒ ways

         . turkey   ⇒   plural noun ⇒ turkeys

. ray	⇒	plural noun	⇒ rays
. journey	⇒	plural noun	⇒ journeys
. toy	⇒	plural noun	⇒ toys
. holiday	⇒	plural noun	⇒ holidays
. essay	⇒	plural noun	⇒ essays

. Irregular Nouns

There are some smaller groups of nouns, which form their plurals in some different ways. These are illustrated below.

Examples of a smaller irregular group of nouns which form their plural by replacing their 'f' with 'ves' (v+es)

Singular	Plural	Singular	Plural
scarf	scarves	leaf	leaves
hoof	hooves	knife	knives
life	lives	loaf	loaves
thief	thieves	scarf	scarves
wife	wives	wolf	wolves

Table 8

Examples of another smaller irregular group of nouns which form their plural in some peculiar ways

Singular	Plural	Singular	Plural
child	children	criterion	criteria
goose	geese	foot	feet
man	men	mouse	mice
penny	pence **or** pennies	stimulus	stimuli
tooth	teeth	woman	women

Table 9

Examples of nouns which have two plural forms

Singular	Plural	Singular	Plural
appendix	appendixes appendices	formula	formulae formulas
focus	focuses foci	trauma	traumas traumata

Table 10

****

. A very small group of nouns has two forms of plurals. These plurals are formed in their own specific way as shown in Table 10.

Examples of nouns surrounded by inconsistencies

Noun	Singular verb	Plural verb
economics use as singular	The economics of the Third World is in need of help from the First World.	
premises use as plural		The premises were locked up when we arrived.
mathematics use as singular or plural	Mathematics is the science of numbers, quantity and space.	Her mathematics are good.
litter use as singular	Her room was a litter of dirty crockery and old clothes.	
Media it is often used as singular, but some people think it should be used as plural only.	The media has shown keen interest in this murder trial. (The Internet is the modern **medium** of communication - here medium is **singular**)	The media have shown keen interest in this murder trial. **(debatable use)**
news plural form but its use is singular	No news is good news.	
jeans plural and its use is singular with 'a pair'	He was wearing a pair of blue jeans.	
scissors plural and its use is singular with 'a pair'	Here is a pair of steel scissors for you.	
wrinkle use as plural		He is beginning to get wrinkles around his eyes.

Table 11

.

****

. A small group of nouns can be troublesome to some writers, as they have their own peculiarities. In this group, some singular nouns have <u>no</u> plural forms. On the other hand, some nouns are used only as plural. Furthermore, some nouns can be used in singular or plural forms. These forms are illustrated in <u>Table 11</u>.

. <u>Countable Nouns</u>

A noun is considered as countable if it meets the following requirements:

(a) . <u>**It has both singular and plural forms.**</u>
For instance:

    . dog $\Rightarrow$ singular form . dogs $\Rightarrow$ plural form

    . ship $\Rightarrow$ singular form . ships $\Rightarrow$ plural form

(b) . <u>It is countable, i.e. can be counted (how many).</u>
For example:
three men, two problems, ten books, etc.

(c) . <u>**It can be preceded by such determiners as listed below**</u>:
the, a, an, every, many, one, two, three, four, etc.
For instance:

  . a company $\Rightarrow$ two companies . a shop $\Rightarrow$ many shops

  . an egg $\Rightarrow$ two eggs   . a student $\Rightarrow$ a group of ten
                                          students

  . a coach $\Rightarrow$ a fleet of coaches **or** 10 coaches **or** many coaches **or**
              every coach, etc.

  . a singular form agrees with a singular form of the verb, e.g.
            . A dog **<u>is</u>** in their factory yard.

singular form of the verb 'be' ↵
  . a plural form agrees with a plural form of the verb, e.g.
          . Two dogs **<u>are</u>** in their factory yard.

    plural form of the verb 'be'↵

. <u>Uncountable (Uncount or Mass) Nouns</u>

These nouns have the following attributes:
        (a) . they cannot be counted – refer to qualities or mass
        (b) . they do <u>not</u> have a plural form – use a singular form only
        (c) . they can be used with or without a determiner
        (d) . some uncountable nouns are preceded by a <u>**partititive**</u>
            <u>**phrase or words**</u>. A partitive phrase or word refers to
        a part or quantity of something. For instance:

(1) . <u>I have a piece of</u> **information**

partitive phrase↵   uncountable noun ↵

This partitive phrase contains a partitive noun – **piece**. The reason is
that information is not countable. However, you can refer to any amount
of information as a part of the whole mass of information. It may be that you
want to refer to the whole mass of information (no matter how little is the
whole mass of information). Here are some examples of
uncountable nouns:

(1) . There <u>**is**</u> still ***some* milk** in the jar.

singular form of the verb ↵   ⇧

some is a determiner
Since **milk** not counted as an individual thing, it is
preceded by **some**.

(2) . There <u>**are**</u> ***three items of*** <u>equipment</u> for you.
                 1   2   3

1 =   plural form of the verb 'be'

2 =   since equipment is not counted as an individual thing, it is

      preceded by the actual number of items, i.e., ***three items***
      three items of is a partitive phrase

3 =   uncountable noun

(3) . <u>Chemistry is</u> her favourite subject at school.

uncountable noun ↵

In this sentence, there is no need to precede the uncountable noun with any
determiner.

(4) . It is common <u>knowledge</u> already.

uncountable noun ↵ - it is not preceded by '**a**'

(5) . The tutor spoke in <u>praise</u> of her class.

uncountable noun ↵ - it is not preceded by '**a**'

. <u>Sometimes, in accordance with the context, a noun may be</u>
<u>either countable or uncountable.</u> The following examples
illustrate this feature of nouns:

(1) . In the hall, all **lights** are switched on.

in this context - countable↵ - preceded by ⟹ *all*

(2) . Have you got a **light***?

countable↵ - preceded by ⟹ *a*

---

* Someone may ask you for a light, i.e. a match/device with which one
can light a cigarette.

(3) . This box contains a bedside **light**.

                                countable↵ - here it means a lamp

(4) . **Light** travels faster than sound.

uncountable↵ - here it is used as uncountable not preceded
                    by an article/determiner (see determiners)

(5) . Would you like to have ***two pounds* of** sugar?

        Partitive phrase ↵

                               uncountable noun

(6) . Do you take **one sugar** or more?

        determiner ↵   ⇑

                    countable noun

(7) . There is no personal ***sympathy*** * between John and Jill.

        uncountable noun ↵

> * In this context *sympathy* means understanding between people with
>   similar interests.

(8) . Sandra has no **sympathy***for Barbara; it was her wrong idea

        countable noun ↵

> * In this context *sympathy implies* the feeling of being sorry for Barbara

(9) . You can have ***two slices of*** **bread**.

        partitive phrase ↵   ⇑

                  uncountable noun

. Collective Nouns

A collective noun is a singular word, but it refers to a group of things. These
things or objects in a group can be people, animals, animated things, ideas or
concepts. In most cases, a collective noun takes a singular verb.

. Some examples of collective nouns agreeing with **singular verbs**:

(1) . Our team has 10 members in it.
    ⇑   ⇑   ⇑

    collective singular   more than one person
    noun   form of   in this group
          the verb

(2) . The council has 30 elected members.
       ⇑   ⇑   ⇑

    collective   singular form more than one person
    noun   of the verb   in this group

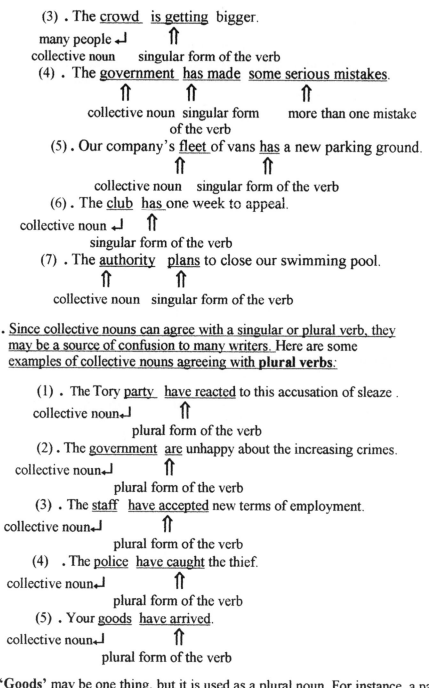

(3) . The <u>crowd</u> <u>is getting</u> bigger.

many people ↵   ⇑

collective noun   singular form of the verb

(4) . The <u>government</u> <u>has made</u> <u>some serious mistakes</u>.

⇑   ⇑   ⇑

collective noun singular form   more than one mistake

of the verb

(5) . Our company's <u>fleet</u> of vans <u>has</u> a new parking ground.

⇑   ⇑

collective noun   singular form of the verb

(6) . The <u>club</u> <u>has</u> one week to appeal.

collective noun ↵   ⇑

singular form of the verb

(7) . The <u>authority</u>   <u>plans</u> to close our swimming pool.

⇑   ⇑

collective noun   singular form of the verb

. <u>Since collective nouns can agree with a singular or plural verb, they</u>
<u>may be a source of confusion to many writers.</u> Here are some
<u>examples of collective nouns agreeing with</u> **plural verbs**:

(1) . The Tory <u>party</u> <u>have reacted</u> to this accusation of sleaze .

collective noun↵   ⇑

plural form of the verb

(2) . The <u>government</u> <u>are</u> unhappy about the increasing crimes.

collective noun↵   ⇑

plural form of the verb

(3) . The <u>staff</u> <u>have accepted</u> new terms of employment.

collective noun↵   ⇑

plural form of the verb

(4)   . The <u>police</u> <u>have caught</u> the thief.

collective noun↵   ⇑

plural form of the verb

(5) . Your <u>goods</u> <u>have arrived</u>.

collective noun↵   ⇑

plural form of the verb

'Goods' may be one thing, but it is used as a plural noun. For instance, a parcel may contain one item only. We still say, *goods have arrived*.

. **When should you use either singular or plural verbs with a**

collective noun?

Usually, when one is thinking of the whole group or body of objects as a single unit, the singular form of the verb is used. On the other hand, if one refers to individuals or components, which make up the body or group, the plural form of the verb is applied.

(1) . The jury has/have returned a verdict of guilty.

collective noun↵   ⇑

either singular or plural form

. How can you test that a word is a noun?

The following tests can help you to determine whether a word is
a noun:
. **A noun has a determiner in front of it.** If you can justify placing one
of the determiners such as **a, an, any,** or **the** in front of the word, then
you know that it is a noun. For instance:

(1) . She was walking with **_a_** dog.

determiner ↵

The determiner is in front of the word dog. This indicates that the word
dog is a noun.

. When you can justify placing one of the partitive words or phrases
in front of a word, you can conclude that the word is a noun:

(2) . I have **_three pieces of_** information that might be of some use to you.

partitive phrase ↵

Here the partitive phrase before the noun points to an uncountable noun in-
formation.

. Nouns can point to ownership. For instance:

(3) . I do not know about his **sister's** marriage.

indicating ownership/possession ↵

The word **sister's** is a **possessive form**. Now, isolate the word marriage and
then place the determiner in front of it to read: **a marriage**. This is indeed
another noun in this sentence. For instance:

(4) . Our registrar will conduct a marriage ceremony today.

. Possessive Forms

When we add an -**'s** to a singular noun, we change its form to the
possessive form. Here are some more examples:

****

(1). brother ⟹ This is my br<u>other's</u> hat.

　　　　　possessive noun↵

(2). team ⟹ Our <u>team's</u> brilliant victory is good news.

　　　possessive noun↵

(3). shop ⟹ Someone has smashed our <u>shop's</u> front glass door.

　　　　　　possessive noun↵

(4). car ⟹ This is my <u>wife's</u> car.

　　　possessive noun↵

. <u>When proper nouns end with –s, you have a choice of adding</u>
　<u>apostrophe s, or placing an apostrophe after the 's'.</u> For instance:

　　(1). I have been invited to stay in the ***Jones's*** new
　　　　home for the weekend.
　　(2). They went to ***James'*** office to see a demonstration of new
　　　　office equipment.

. <u>When a common plural noun ends with –s, just add</u> ***an apostrophe*** <u>to</u>
<u>convert it into its possessive form.</u> For instance:

　　(1). Our history tutor often does not remember his ***friends'*** names.
　　(2). You can use our ***customers'*** car park until 17.00 hours every day.
　　(3). The idea of socialism was to make ordinary ***workers'*** lives easy.

See ⟹ Noun Phrases

In summary, nouns are words that we use to give names to people, animals, natural and man-made objects. They are also used to name abstract things. Common and proper nouns are the main groups of nouns. The other two groups of nouns are collective and abstract nouns. Nouns are also classified as countable and uncountable.

In order to use nouns correctly in both written and spoken English, it is important to understand noun gender (male, female and neuter) and number (singular or plural) of the same gender.

Chapter 4
Pronouns

. Introduction

A word used instead of a noun or a noun phrase is called a pronoun. Diagram 1 contains types of pronouns. Personal pronouns occur more frequently than any other types of pronouns. In fact, pronouns do the work of a noun in naming a person or a thing. They take the place of a noun.

Diagram 1

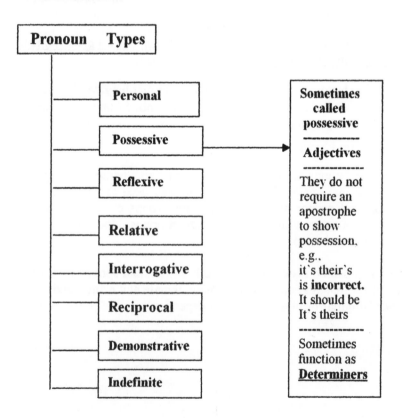

Pronoun   Types

- Personal
- Possessive
- Reflexive
- Relative
- Interrogative
- Reciprocal
- Demonstrative
- Indefinite

Sometimes
called
possessive

Adjectives

They do not require an apostrophe to show possession, e.g., it's their's is **incorrect.** It should be It's theirs
----
Sometimes function as **Determiners**

****

. <u>Personal and Possessive Pronouns</u>

Consider the following examples:

(1) . <u>I</u> would like a cup of tea.

personal pronoun – refers to ⟹ **first person**

I stands for a single <u>first person</u> who would like (action) a cup of tea. The first person is used by a writer or a speaker about himself/herself. It is the <u>subject</u> of this sentence, and for this reason, it is called a <u>**subjective pro-noun**</u>. The subjective pronoun occupies the subject position in a sentence. <u>The subjective pronoun comes before the verb.</u>

(2) . <u>You</u> went home at about 11 p.m.

⇑

personal pronoun – the second person

You is the <u>second person</u>. The second person in a sentence is the person to whom he/she writes or speaks. <u>You</u> can be singular or plural. Here, <u>you</u> is in the subject position. It also comes before the verb. Therefore, it is the <u>subjective pronoun</u> in this sentence.

(3) . John has already informed **me**.

personal pronoun ↵

objective form ↵

<u>me</u>* represents a single person. Here, <u>me</u> is the <u>**object**</u> of this sentence. Thus it is known as an <u>**objective pronoun**</u>.

---

* The pronoun **me** occurs after the verb informed.

---

* It is worth mentioning that an objective pronoun may be in the subject position. This can happen in informal writing, as shown by the following example:

(4) . <u>**Me***</u> and John have agreed to work together in out mutual interest.

⇑

<u>objective pronoun used in the subject position in this sentence</u>

* <u>This is not recommended as it is not standard English.</u>

(5) . <u>They</u> want to go to the cinema in <u>**my**</u> car.

⇑   ⇑

personal pronoun   <u>possessive pronoun*</u>

plural form   ⇑

indicating that the car belongs to
the person who writes or speaks this sentence

In this example, the possessive pronoun <u>my</u> comes before the noun <u>car</u>. Here, the possessive pronoun is used with a noun. <u>If a possessive pronoun is used with a noun, then it is in the **dependent form**.</u> In this example, <u>my</u> is a possessive pronoun in the dependent form.

<u>They</u> is in the <u>third person plural form</u>. A <u>third person</u> is the person or thing/object/abstract idea about which the first person speaks or writes. A third person can mean things, or objects or abstract ideas, as well as persons.

See ⟹ Person and number for the third person

(6) . Here are two copies of 'The Sunday Times' newspaper.
One is **mine** and the other is **hers**.

⇑   ⇑

possessive pronoun   <u>possessive pronoun</u> - independent form

indicating noun's **gender** ↵

In this example, the possessive pronoun **hers** is used <u>without</u> any noun. In fact, it is independent of any noun. <u>When a possessive pronoun is used instead of a noun phrase then it is in the **independent form**.</u>

(7) . <u>**Theirs**</u> is the red car parked in row A. <u>**Ours**</u> is parked in row C.

⇑   ⇑

possessive pronoun   possessive pronoun **
plural independent form   plural independent form

---

* Possessive pronouns indicate that something belongs to someone.
** An apostrophe is not required in writing a possessive pronoun.
For instance, it is wrong to write **your's**.
. <u>Is there any exception to the rule?</u> Yes, there is one exception worth mentioning:
. One must look after *one's* elderly parents.

<u>Here one's implies people in general – not one person.</u>

The classification of personal and possessive pronouns is given in <u>**Table 1**</u>.

Classification of Personal & Possessive Pronouns

Person/ Number	Subjective Pronouns	Objective Pronouns	Possessive Pronouns*	
Singular			De-pendent form used with nouns	Independent form used instead of nouns
1st person	I	me	my	mine
2nd person	you	you	your	yours
3rd person	he, she, it, they	him, her, it, them	his, her, its	his, hers, its
Plural				
1st person	we	us	our	ours
2nd person	you	you	your	yours
3rd person	they	them	their	theirs

Table 1

. The above examples illustrate that personal and possessive pronouns perform a number of following <u>functions</u> in a sentence:
  (a) <u>show the person</u>:

   . **first person** - person (s) speaker (s) or writer (s)
    . **second person** - the person or thing being addressed
              It does not refer to the speaker or the writer.
   . **third person** - it is the person or thing about which
              the first person is writing or speaking.
  (b) <u>indicate the gender of the noun which it renders</u>
  (c) denote the number - **singular or plural**
  (d) substitute for the proper noun, e.g. **Johnson**
  (e) point to the case of a sentence, e.g. **possessive case -**
    case refers to subjective, objective or possessive of a noun or
    pronoun when indicating relation to some other word
  (f) identify a belonging , or belonging to, or a possession, e.g. **our**

. <u>Reflexive Pronouns</u>

A reflexive pronoun refers to the subject. Consider the following examples:

(1) . I cut **myself** last night with a kitchen knife.
　　⇑　　　⇑
personal pronoun   reflexive pronoun

Here myself is a reflexive pronoun because the subject's action comes back on the person (pronoun) concerned. In this example, the person concerned is the subject 'I', i.e. personal pronoun – singular.

(2) . **John** has found new employment at a computer shop **himself**.
　　⇑　　　　　　　　　　　　　　　　　　　　　　　⇑
　　Noun　　　　　　　　　　　　　　　　reflexive pronoun

(3) . **They** earn a great deal of money for **themselves**.
　　⇑　　　　　　　　　　　　　　　⇑
　personal pronoun　　　　　　reflexive pronoun
　　　　　　refers back to the subject 'they' ↵

. These examples illustrate that a reflexive pronoun refers back to the subject of a sentence, which may be a noun or a pronoun. In List 2, you can find all reflexive pronouns.

. Sometimes a reflexive pronoun is used for emphasis or clarification. When a reflexive pronoun is used for this purpose, it is labelled as an **intensifying pronoun**. This is illustrated below:

(4) . I designed my web site **myself**.

functioning as an intensifying pronoun ↵ - placing emphasis

(5) . Did you see the accident **yourself** ?

functioning as an intensifying pronoun ↵ - clarifying/emphasising

(6) . The parked car started rolling down the hill **itself**.

intensifying pronoun - indicating no interference ↵

Reflexive Pronouns

Person	Singular	Plural
First Person	myself	ourselves
Second Person	yourself	yourselves
Third Person	himself, herself, itself, themselves*	themselves

Table 2

****

The following style is not recommended in this book. It is incorrect grammatically.

* **Themself** is not recognized in standard English. It is used when someone does not want to specify the sex of the person, or when the gender is unknown. In this case, the word **they** is treated as a singular personal pronoun without any sex-marking. Its reflexive pronoun is derived from them and self as **themself**. It is a modern idea, which is disliked by many people. Its use is illustrated below:

> (1) . If any of you are bored, **he or she** can quietly leave the room now
>   for ten minutes for some fresh air for himself or herself.

In order to avoid the use of he or she in the above sentence, it is stated as:

> (2) . If any of you need some fresh air, **they** can quietly leave the room
>   now for ten minutes for some fresh air for **themslf**.

incorrect↵

To rewrite it correctly: replace 'they' by 'you' and 'themself' by 'yourselves:

(3) . If any of you need some fresh air, **you** can quietly leave the room
      now for ten minutes for some fresh air for **yourself**.

If you write **they** and **themselves** for a singular personal pronoun, most of your readers will find this use repellent.

. Relative Pronouns

A relative pronoun is a word, which links a subordinate clause to a main clause. These words
are *that, who, whose, which,* and *whom*. The following examples illustrate their application:

> (1) . He inherited a great deal of money, *which* he has used to set up
>   a new business.
> (2) . This is the same person *who* sent us so many threatening letters.
> (3) . Joan is the lady *whose* son was tricked by the perpetrator.
> (4) . The car *that* I was to purchase was in poor condition.
> (5) . He is a man *whom* you can trust.

See ⇒ Clauses

. Interrogative Pronouns

Interrogative pronouns are used to ask questions. These words are also called **wh-words**. There are only five of them. These are exemplified below in *bold* characters:

(1) . *Who* are you?

(2) . *Which* of these bicycles do you wish to order?

(3) . *What* is your prime aim now?

(4) . *Whose* are those birds in a cage left in our front garden?

(5) . By *whom* were you interviewed last week?

These interrogative pronouns also function as relative pronouns.

. Reciprocal Pronouns

Reciprocal pronouns express a mutual relationship. They are like a two-way communication mode: one message going in one direction and one coming back from another direction. There are only two such pronouns: *each other* and *one another**. Here are some examples:

(1) . They wrote to *one another* for a number of years.

each person wrote to the other persons ↵

(2) . Jack and Jill always help **each other**.

each member helps the other person↵ - a group of two persons

(3) . They can use *each other's/ one another's* **cars.

use in possessive form ↵

(4) . Sometimes they stay at *one another's/each other's* country homes.

use in possessive form ↵

---

* . **When more than two persons use**: **one another**, e.g.

(5) . It was a very friendly gathering, as we got on very well with one another.

It means that each person who was at this gathering was friendly with other members of the gathering/group.

. **When only two persons in a group use: each other**, e.g.

(6) . Beata and Philip love each other.

(7) . John and Jane seem to enjoy each other's company.

Now-a-days, each other and one another are interchangeable.

** Note the use of the apostrophe before the –s in the possessive form

---

. Demonstrative Pronouns

Demonstrative pronouns are those pronouns which indicate, show, or point to things. They are also used to refer to a particular person or people. These pronouns consist of :

. **this** ⟹ singular demonstrative pronoun - indicates something within close reach

. **that** ⟹ singular demonstrative pronoun - points to something further way

. **these** ⟹ plural demonstrative pronoun - shows something nearby

. **those** ⟹ plural demonstrative pronoun - refers to something further away

The following examples illustrate their usage:

(1) . **This** is our car.

indicates <u>here</u> near the speaker <u>now</u> ↵

(2) . **These** chairs are needed in this room.

shows a <u>present</u> situation in a <u>nearby place</u> ↵

(3) . **These** are our friends from Germany: Anne and Wolfgang.

refers to people <u>now</u> and <u>nearby</u>

(4) . In my view **that** contract should be renewable.

refers to people's action <u>backward in time and space</u> - a contract is between people

(5) . **These** are slightly faulty goods for our next summer sales.

refers to things <u>forward in time and space</u>

(6) . **That** was Margo sitting at the end of the second row.

refers to a <u>person</u> <u>farther away in time and space</u>

(7) . **That** was our sales forecast revealed by our sales manager.

refers to a <u>thing</u> <u>farther away in time and space</u>

(8) . **Those** suitcases were found unattended by the airport police.

refers to <u>things</u> <u>farther away in time and space</u>

(9) . Sarah hasn't written to us from Sweden during the last six months. **This** is a worrying situation.

⇑

<u>refers</u> to a person's action mentioned earlier on - person's action (Sarah's action) rather than just a person

(10) . The motorways were very busy.

That's why our coach arrived two hours late.

⇑

refers to 'traffic' on the motorway to tell why their coach arrived late

    (11). I'd like to say **this**. Our team displays enthusiasm but lacks

⇑   a real talent to win tonight.

use this construction when you are going to explain something

This way you **refer forward**. Note **that** is not used this way.

In the above sentences, the meaning is relative to the context. The reader can understand the meaning from the **context** of each sentence.

. During a conversation, the speaker can also point to something without mentioning the noun or noun phrase. The following examples illustrate that the meaning is relative to the **speaker** who points to things without mentioning the noun or the noun phrase:

    (12) . I will take **this**.

a speaker picks up a basket of strawberries without mentioning it –leave out the noun phrase

    (13) . She prefers **those**.

a speaker points to a pair of shoes in a shoe shop

    (14) . Was **that** John on the telephone?

⇑

it is used here to refer to a particular person ⇒John

    (15) . **These** will do.

a speaker buys a bunch of flowers

. Indefinite Pronouns

Indefinite pronouns are those words which do not refer to any particular person or thing. There are a large number of words which can be used as indefinite pronouns. **Table 3** shows some commonly used indefinite pronouns.

. Some of these indefinite pronouns have exactly the same meaning. This is illustrated by the following examples:

(1) . In this room, **everyone** is aware of the class test this afternoon.

    it means all persons↵

(2) . In this room, **everybody** is aware of the class test this afternoon.

    it means all persons ↵

. **Therefore: everyone = everybody** ⟹ all persons in the context in
                                                which it is spoken or written

(3) . <u>**Someone**</u> has removed my spectacles from the table.

meaning a person

(4) . <u>**Somebody**</u> has removed my spectacles from the table.

it means a person

. **Therefore: someone = somebody** ⟹ a person in the context in which
                                                it is spoken or written

(5) . <u>**Nobody**</u> has given me any message for you.

it means no person

(6) . <u>**No one***</u> has given me any message for you.

⇑

it means not a single/no person

. **Therefore: nobody = <u>no one</u>** ⟹ no person

Note that **no one** is usually written as a two-word pronoun. Some people may write it with a hyphen. All other indefinite pronouns listed above are compound words.

---

* **No one** is more common than nobody in written English.

---

(7) . The <u>council</u> has postponed <u>**its***</u>general meeting until next week.

collective noun↵

---

* Here, the collective noun <u>council</u> is viewed as a whole
  (the whole council) and thus the correct form of the pronoun
  corresponds to the singular number - **its**

If you view the council as a collective noun <u>comprising of individual
members</u>, in this case, the pronoun for it must be of plural number, e.g.

(8) . The **council** will announce **their** decision at next month's meeting.

(9 . The <u>**jury**</u> **have*** not yet returned **their** verdict.

collective noun↵

---

* Here collective noun <u>jury</u> is considered as <u>consists of individual</u>
<u>members</u> constituting the jury as a single unit/group. Thus, the
correct form of the pronoun is the plural number **their**. If you view the jury
as a **whole group** – collective noun , in this case, the correct form should correspond to singular number, e.g.

  (10) . **The jury** has returned **its** guilty verdict.

. Often there is some confusion about the correct use of 'each'* as a
pronoun. As it is a singular pronoun, it should be used with a singular
from of the verb. Here are some examples:

  (11) . Each of the players was awarded the same medal.
  (12) . Each guest was accommodated in a separate single room.
  (13) . Each woman has her own terrifying experience to tell.

---

* When 'each' comes after a plural noun, the verb should be plural, e.g.
  (14) . The players each have won a medal.
  (15) . We each have our own car.

Each also functions as a determiner. See ⇒ determiners

Some commonly used indefinite pronouns

all	anyone	either	every-thing	little	no-body	several
any	anything	enough	few	many	none	some-body
an-other	both	every-body	least	much	no one	some-one
any-body	each	everyone	less	neither	noth-ing	some-thing

Table 3

. Numerals

Numerals often function as pronouns. These are discussed under determiners.

See ⇒ determiners

In summary, a pronoun is a word used instead of a noun. It is a
substitute for a noun when you <u>do not</u> wish to name someone or something
directly, e.g. we, they, she, it, each, everyone, etc.

Chapter 5
Adjectives

. Introduction

Adjectives are words used with a noun or a pronoun to modify the noun or the pronoun. In doing so, they qualify the noun, i.e. give more information about the noun. They tell us what something is like. There are many thousands of words that are classed as adjectives and function as adjectives only. In addition, many more thousands of words which function as nouns, adverbs and so on also function as adjectives. Adjectives change their forms when a comparison is made. They <u>do not</u> do so for a gender or number (singular or plural). Some adjectives are shown in
List 1 below.

Some Adjectives

awful, beautiful, big, busy, cheap, clear, clever, dangerous, dark, difficult, easy, expensive, extraordinary, famous, foreign, gloomy, glorious good, happy, harmful, harmless, huge, inaccessible, inaccurate, incapable, jealous, jobless, jolly, kind, lovely, loving, low, mean, medium, mental, native, nice, noble, nosy (or nosey), obnoxious, obscene, opportune, painful, passionate, popular, quick, quiet, quizzical, recent, relentless, religious, short, smooth, straight, tall, three-quarters, tiny, ugly, unfit, unfriendly, vain, vast, vivid, weary, wedded, wide, yellow, young, youthful, zonal.

List 1

Let's consider first the following two examples:

    (1) . I can see a **tall** man standing in front of our house.

        adjective ↵

In this sentence, the word <u>tall</u> gives some information about the man by describing him as tall. Since it is used with the noun <u>man</u>, its function is considered as modifying or qualifying the noun <u>man</u>. Here the adjective is a modifier. If you wish, you can think of modifying as defining the noun <u>man</u>. The adjective in this position in this sentence is giving us information about an attribute (tall) of the noun man.

      (2) . I can see a <u>very</u> <u>tall</u> <u>man</u> jumping up and down.

        intensifier ↵

Here very is preceding the adjective tall and thus functioning as an intensifier. The reason for placing it in front of the adjective is to grade the height of that particular man who is jumping up and down. By placing very in front of tall, we have graded the adjective on an imagined scale. Very is an adverb of degree that tells us about the measurement on an imagined scale as it does not specify the height in any recognised unit of measurement. This example shows that adjectives are gradable.

Here are some more examples:

(3). She is a **most generous person**.

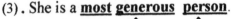

    intensifier ↵   ⇑   ⇑

                     adjective   noun

(4). You are **kind** to me.

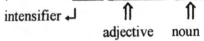

  ⇑   ⇑   ⇑

  1   2   3

In this example:

          1 is personal pronoun – subject form
          2 is adjective
          3 is personal pronoun – object form

In this example, the adjective kind refers to the personal pronoun you. This way, it is modifying the personal pronoun by giving information (kind) about the pronoun.

    (5). It is a **nice new** car for us.

In this example, nice(adjective) is modifying the adjective *new*. The adjective *new* is modifying the noun car. When two or more adjectives occur before a noun, their position is fairly fixed as above.

. The following examples further illustrate that adjectives modify
  pronouns. Both adjectives and pronouns are highlighted:

    (6) . **She** was **happy** to hear the news about her son.
    (7) . **They** arrived home **hungry** and **angry** due to traffic congestion
        on the M1 motorway.
    (8) . **It** is a **cold**, *wet* and *stormy* night.

. The Position of Adjectives

Most adjectives can occur in two particular positions in a sentence or a clause. Certainly, some adjectives can be placed in one particular position, but not in the other position in a sentence or clause. These rules are explained below:

. **An adjective can occur before a noun**. Here are some examples:

      (6). John lives in an **old** house.

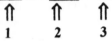

    adjective before the noun ↵

****

The adjective old relates to the house. In fact, it defines or modifies the noun
'house' in terms of its age. The word age as an attribute is giving information
about the house. When an adjective modifies or defines a noun and it comes
before the noun, such a word is called **attributive adjective**. This is further
illustrated by the following examples:

> (7) . We are having a **lovely** time.

> attributive adjective ↲

> (8) . It is certainly a **big** day for all of us.

> attributive adjective ↲

> (9) . This is an **expensive** property.

attributive adjective ↲

> (10) . I do not like **loud** music.

attributive adjective ↲

In the following examples attributive adjectives are underlined:

> (11) . It was a memorable holiday for all of us in France.
> (12) . It is a beautiful garden to visit and enjoy.
> (13) . They have two lovable daughters.
> (14) . A number of countries of the former Soviet Union are now
> independent states.
> (15) . The proposed new road will link the principal cities in our
> part of the country.
> (16) . Her bank overdraft upper limit is £2500.

. **An adjective can occur in the predicate.** For instance:

> (1) . This **crime** is the **worst** in our city's history.

noun to which the ↲   ⇑
adjective relates   adjective

In this sentence, the adjective occurs between a noun and a verb. Here the adjective is in the predicate. **Why?** In this example, crime is the subject. The
remainder of this statement is the predicate. Since after the subject, the remainder of the sentence describes the crime (subject) as the worst (adjective),
and thus the adjective occurs in the predicate.

See ⇒ predicate

> (2) . The **house** in which John lives **is** **old**.

noun to which the ↲   verb ↲ ⇑
adjective relates   adjective occurs in the
                                               predicate position

When an adjective occurs in a sentence in the predicate as illustrated above,
it is called **predicative adjective**. In each example, the adjective is placed
after the noun. An adjective can also be placed after a pronoun in the

predicative position. Here are some more examples, illustrating the position of the adjective in the predicative position (and underlined):

    (3) . I am very sorry that he is <u>unwell</u> and will not be able to come to work today.

    (4) . He lives <u>alone</u> in a big house.

    (5) . He was a <u>contented</u> person.

    (6) . She is afraid of UFO.(<u>U</u>nidentified <u>Fl</u>ying <u>O</u>bject)

    (7) . He looked <u>scared</u> of verbal test.

    (8) . Our winter usually is <u>wet and cold.</u>

and can be between two adjectives ↵

    (9) . This car is small <u>but economical to run.</u>

but can be placed between two adjectives when you refer to two opposing qualities attributable to a noun/pronoun

In each of the above examples, the adjective is used after a linking verb. Thus, adjectives in examples (1)–(9) are used as <u>complements after linking verbs</u>. **A complement is** an adjective or a noun, which comes after a linking or copula or copular verb.

. Can you place adjectives in either the attributive position or the predicative position? Most adjectives can be used both in attributive and predicative positions. There are some adjectives, which can be placed in one position but not in the other. <u>Here are some examples of adjectives used</u> **only in the attributive position:**

    (1) . This is the <u>indoor</u> swimming pool in our town.

    (2) . The Queen waved to the <u>adoring</u> crowds.

    (3) . Scarborough is a <u>neighbouring</u> town.

    (4) . What is your <u>main</u> reason for objecting to her presence so strongly?

    (5) . He is the <u>only</u> person who knows her whereabouts.

    (6) . She felt an <u>utter</u> fool! (**fool** is used here as noun)

    (7) . I was in <u>Western</u> (or western)France last year.

    (8) . It was a <u>punishing</u> journey on the back of a donkey in Egypt.

    (9) . Our team is now in the <u>commanding</u> position.

       have a commanding lead ↵ - lead ⇒ noun

    (10) . The chairman said, 'A <u>remedial</u> action must be taken now.'

<u>Some examples of adjectives used only in the predicative position**</u>:

    (1) . You mustn't be <u>afraid</u>.

    (2) . Where is Jane ? She is <u>ill</u> and couldn't come.

    (3) . He is <u>unable</u> **to** attend this meeting <u>due</u> to illness.

    adjective↵   adjective↵ - followed by ⇒ to

(4). In this office, I am <u>answerable to</u>* sales director

adjective⏎ - followed by ⟹ preposition **to**

(5). Ministers are <u>answerable **for**</u>* their actions.

adjective⏎ - followed by ⟹ for

---

* The difference between **answerable to** and **answerable for**:
answerable to means you have to explain your actions to someone who
is higher than you in some official capacity. On the other hand,
answerable for something means responsible for something one has
done and ready to accept any criticism and punishment for it. Both are
followed by prepositions **to** and **for**.

** A tricky situation: Some adjectives which are used in the predicative
position only can also be used in the attributive position if they are
modified by an adverb, e.g.

. She was an **<u>extremely</u>** <u>difficult</u> woman to deal with.

adverb⏎   adjective⏎ - used here attributively

---

(6). She felt something was <u>lacking</u> **in** her life in this area and left it

adjective⏎ - followed by ⟹ preposition **in**

(7). I am <u>ashamed</u> **to** see you dressed in rags.

adjective⏎ - followed by ⟹ preposition **to**

. <u>Comparison of adjectives</u>

The only time adjectives change their forms is when a comparison is made.
There are three comparative forms of adjectives, namely:

. **Descriptive or Positive**   . **Comparative**   . **Superlative**

These forms are graded by degree, which shows the extent of comparative
qualities. The **<u>descriptive form</u>** is the form of the adjective as listed in dictionaries. It is also known as the **<u>positive form.</u>** The **<u>comparative form</u>** is
used for comparing two objects, and the **<u>superlative form</u>** is for comparing
three or more objects. Objects are people, animals, animated and natural
things . The following examples illustrate these forms of adjectives:

(1) . He is a **<u>tall</u>** person.

descriptive (or basic) form of adjective – no comparison is intended here

(2) . He is **<u>taller</u>** than you.

comparative form of adjective - a comparison is made

(3) . He is the **tallest** in our group of 10 persons.

superlative form of adjective - compares a person with more
than two other persons

Some examples of adjective forms

Descriptive (Positive)	Comparative	Superlative
beautiful	more beautiful	most beautiful
black	blacker	blackest
big	bigger	biggest
cold	colder	coldest
difficult	more difficult	most difficult
endearing	more endearing	most endearing
few	fewer	fewest
great	greater	greatest
intelligent	more intelligent	most intelligent
large	larger	largest
long	longer	longest
loud	louder	loudest
lovely	lovelier	loveliest
many	more	most
nice	nicer	nicest
noisy	noisier	noisiest
old	older	oldest
poor	poorer	poorest
quiet	quieter	quietest
short	shorter	shortest
sunny	sunnier	sunniest
tall	taller	tallest
ugly	uglier	ugliest

List 2

Descriptive	Comparative	Superlative
good	better	best
little	less	least
bad	worse	worst
many/ much	more	most

List 3

. There are some adjectives that have **irregular forms.** The adjectives shown in <u>List 3 above</u> with their comparative and superlative forms are among the most commonly used irregular adjectives.

. **Intensifiers** are words like *extremely*, *fairly*, *incredibly*, *quite* and *very*. Sometimes an adjective can be preceded by an intensifier to emphasise the quality of the adjective. By means of intensifiers we can strengthen the meaning or the quality of the adjective to a desirable varying low or high degree of comparisons. The following examples illustrate the use of intensifiers:

(1) . You can say about someone:
> . He is *very* clever.
> . He is *fairly* clever.
> . He is *quite* clever.
> . He is *extremely* clever.
> . He is *incredibly* clever.

(2) . You can describe a place as:
> . It is a *large* cricket ground.
> . It is *quite* a large cricket ground.
> . It is a *fairly* large cricket ground.
> . It is a *very large* cricket ground.
> . It is an *incredibly* large cricket ground.

(3) . You can compare one person or thing with another:
> . James was *more* intelligent than John.
> . Today the crowd was *much* bigger than any other crowd I have ever seen.
> . His speech proved <u>*less*</u> formidable than yours.

lower degree comparison↵
> . Europe's Express Coach Network is the <u>least</u> expensive travel system in Europe.

lowest degree of comparison↵- cheapest mode of travel
> . He is the <u>*least*</u> successful in our group.

. Absolute Adjectives

There are some adjectives that cannot be graded by degree in the same way as shown above. Such adjectives exist only in their basic form. The following examples demonstrate this characteristic of some words used as adjectives:
> (1) . You are <u>right</u> this time.

descriptive/basic form ↵ - no other forms exist

It means that you cannot be more or less right if you are right. It is the

88   **Word Classes**   **Adjectives**

****

highest degree of quality implied by this adjective. Just the opposite is wrong. For instance:

(2) . Robert is <u>wrong</u> to suggest that John is guilty.

descriptive/basic form ↵ - no other forms exist

It means what it implies is no more, no less. It cannot be graded. <u>It is incorrect to say *very wrong*</u>.

(3) . This is a <u>unique</u> occasion in our lives.

descriptive/basic form ↵ - no other forms exist

It means one specific occasion. <u>It is wrong to grade it as a *very unique* occasion or *more unique* than other occasions.</u>

(4) . It is <u>impossible </u>to reach Manchester now by car before 10 pm.

 descriptive form↵

You cannot say *less impossible fairly impossible* or add any thing else to it in order to grade it, as it an absolute adjective.

As illustrated by these examples, you cannot compare absolute adjectives. The following words are also examples of absolute adjectives:

---

absolute, dead, eldest, infinite, like, only, perfect, real

. When can a word function as an adjective?

There are a great many words, which can function as adjectives. A noun can be used as an adjective. Similarly, an adverb can function as an adjective. Pronouns can do the work of adjectives. Furthermore, some words can be used as participles and adjectives. Indeed, you can also create many adjectives by adding suffixes to many words. For the sake of understanding words that can function as adjectives, we can discuss them as follows:

. **Descriptive** - These are descriptive words and easily recognised. For instance:

  handsome, good, beautiful, green, black, ugly, bad, rough, smooth.

. **Demonstrative** – *this*, *these*, *that* and *those*. They indicate the noun , which they modify. For instance in phrases:

  . This ship - the noun ship is modified by <u>this</u>

  . those books - the plural noun books is modified by <u>those</u>

  . that car – the singular noun car is modified by <u>that</u>

In the following examples, 'that' and 'this' are modifying nouns <u>car</u> and <u>house </u>respectively:

(1) . That car is mine.

(2) . This house belongs to John's sister.

****

. When *this, that, these* and *those* are used with nouns as shown above, they are known as **demonstrative adjectives**; otherwise they function as **relative pronouns**. In the following examples relative pronouns are underlined:

> (1) . You can have <u>this</u>.
> (2) . I have already told you <u>what</u> you should not do.
> (3) . Yesterday I agreed that you can have <u>those</u>.
> (4) . <u>What</u> made John so angry was Jill's refusal to forgive.

In the last example, the relative pronoun is used to place emphasis.

. **Interrogative Words** - **What ? Which?** These words are used with nouns to ask questions. For instance:

> (1) . <u>What</u> time was it when you saw her?

interrogative adjective⏎   ⇑

            noun

> (2) . <u>What</u> arrangements have you made for Easter?
> (3) . <u>Which</u> newspaper do you normally read?
> (4) . <u>Which</u> car did you buy the other day?

In examples 1 – 4, both **what** and **which** as adjectives are connected with one attribute of a noun that is next to them in each sentence. By asking a question, the speaker is inquiring about the quality/ attribute of a noun. This is how they function as adjectives when they are next to a noun.

. **These interrogative words can perform different functions under other word classes as illustrated below:**

> (5) . <u>What</u> went wrong ?

pronoun⏎

> (6) . <u>What</u> job will you do first?

determiner⏎

> (7) . I have several products. <u>Which</u> do you want?

            pronoun⏎

> (8) . <u>Which</u> teacher is your tutor?

determiner⏎

In examples 6 and 8 *what* and *which* are before nouns and thus they are functioning as determiners. On the other hand, in examples 5 and 7, *what* and *which* are not used with nouns next to them and thus these are functioning here as pronouns.

. **Adverbs used as adjectives** – Some words can function as adjectives as well as adverbs. For instance:

90   **Word Classes**   **Adjectives**

****

(1). She talks <u>fast</u>.

     adverb ↵ - modifying verb ⇒ talks

(2). It is a <u>fast</u> train.

     adjective ↵ - modifying noun ⇒ train

<u>**Fast** can also function as a verb and as a noun.</u>

(3). We will most <u>likely</u> miss* her now.

     adverb ↵ - modifying verb ⇒ miss**

---

* The word miss also functions as a noun

** The word likely means expect or probable

. <u>When **likely** is functioning as an **adverb**, it must be preceded by any</u>
<u>of these intensifiers: **most, more**, or **very**. For instance:</u>

(4). The most <u>likely</u>* outcome is a draw.

     adjective ↵ - modifying noun ⇒ outcome

---

* <u>When **likely** is used as an **adjective**, it is usually preceded by **more** or</u>
<u>**most**, e.g.</u>

(5). She seems the <u>most likely</u> winner.

(6). It is <u>more likely</u> that he still does not know the final outcome.

. **Nouns** – Some nouns can function as adjectives. Conversely,
adjectives can also function as nouns. The following examples show
how this happens in practice:

(1). From my <u>past</u>* experience I'd say it is more likely to happen.

     adjective ↵ - modifying noun ⇒ experience

(2). During the <u>past</u>* month I was in Italy.

     adjective ↵ - modifying noun ⇒ month

---

* In both examples, past means gone by in time.

---

(3). He often looks back on the <u>past</u> with a mixture of regrets and joys.

     functioning as a noun ↵

(4). I have travelled on this route in the <u>past</u>.

     functioning as a noun ↵

In examples 3 – 4, past means the time that has passed away; and things that
you have done in an earlier time. The context of these examples illustrates in

what capacity a word is functioning in a sentence.

. <u>**Sometimes adjectives can function as nouns if they are preceded by**</u>
a definite article 'the'. Here are examples:

    (5) . Our government must do more to help the <u>homeless</u>.

                      functioning as a noun ↵

    (6) . There have been many failed attempts to help <u>homeless</u> people.

                     functioning as an adjective ↵

. <u>**Participles used as adjectives**</u>– Some participles
(verb + -' ing' ending) can function as adjectives:

    (1) . The current international political crisis is <u>worrying</u>.

                    functioning as an adjective ↵

    (2) . Marion's forthcoming travel to Siberia alone is <u>worrying</u> us.

                    functioning as a participle ↵

See ⇒ Participles

. <u>**How can you recognise an adjective?**</u>

Words such as **cold, good, bad** and *wonderful* are descriptive adjectives.
Such adjectives are easily recognisable. The English language has thousands
of adjectives. There are some common word endings that help you to recognise adjectives. Some of these word endings, together with some adjectives,
are listed below:

– able	breakable , fashionable, desirable, comparable
– al	commercial, brutal, dismal, natural
– ar	circular, perpendicular, popular, solar
– ed	worried, excited, subdued, inexperienced
– ent	intelligent, excellent, urgent, negligent
– ful	joyful, wonderful, harmful, careful
– ible	incredible, sensible, compatible, horrible
– ic	alcoholic, athletic, classic, idiotic
– ing	dying, laughing, charming, encouraging
– ish	Irish, foolish, childish, selfish
– ive	decorative, demonstrative, adhesive
– less	meaningless, harmless, childless, defenceless
– like	childlike, warlike, businesslike, ladylike
– ous	dangerous, courageous, nervous, marvellous
– some	awesome, troublesome, handsome
– worthy	newsworthy, praiseworthy, roadworthy

. A Word of Warning

Words ending with –*ly* and –*y* often cause confusion as many adverbs and adjectives have these endings. For instance: **holy** is an adjective but **yearly** is both an adjective and an adverb.

In summary, some adjectives only identify the noun as in the phrase **first chapter**. Many adjectives describe nouns as in the phrase **a green coat**. It is telling us about the noun which is of a green colour. There is a widespread tendency to use adjectives, when they do not add any information to the meaning of the nouns they modify, i.e. in *serious crisis*, both words mean the same.

Chapter 6
Adverbs

. Introduction

An adverb is a word that modifies or qualifies another word, which may be a verb, an adjective or another adverb. It can also modify or extend an adverbial phrase, prepositional phrase and conjunctions. Indeed, the adverb has the largest range of functions of any part of speech/word class.

Adverbs can be difficult to identify. However, the most common function of adverbs is to modify the main verb in a sentence. Therefore, it is reasonable to assume that this is a reason for giving it this name. There is a large number of adverbs for expressing reason, time, manner, place, order, etc.

Some Adverbs

abruptly, absolutely, accordingly, afterwards, again, aggressively, carefully, early, easily, frightfully, fully, gently, ghastly, heavily, here, however, just, nevertheless, nervously, now, quickly, quietly, perfectly, roughly, slowly, so, softly, sometimes, successfully, suddenly, then, there, therefore, too, truthfully, unintelligently, unintentionally, vaguely, vastly, very, violently, why, wholly, widely, willingly, worriedly, yearly, yearningly, yesterday, yet

List 1

The following examples illustrate the use of adverbs:
>   (1) . We walked <u>slowly</u>.

>   adverb of manner↵ – modifying the verb ⟹ walked

It tells us how we walked. The adverb **slowly** has affected the meaning of this short sentence.
>   (2) . <u>Soon</u> we will leave home.

adverb of time ↵ - informing us **when** we will leave in the future

>   (3) . He said <u>almost</u> nothing new to protect his reputation.

>   adverb of degree↵ – meaning scarcely (scarcely anything)

In this example, <u>almost</u> is modifying the quantifier <u>nothing</u>
(= no single thing = not anything)

        (4). Some people go to bed <u>early</u>.
                adverb of time↵
        (5). Have you anything <u>else</u> to do this afternoon?
adverb modifying the question ↵

Here <u>else</u> means in addition to something already known.
    (6). If you <u>ever wish to</u> visit Berlin, you must come and stay with us.
adverb of frequency ↵ - modifying the verb ⟹ wish
    (7). You knew where I was. <u>Moreover</u>, you knew who had done it.

    adverb supporting the previous statement (moreover = in addition)
    (8). <u>Somehow,</u> I do not feel she can convince them of her honesty.
    ⇑ - somehow = unknown reason
    adverb of reason – related to an unspecified reason
    (9). During the boring seminar, he answered the question <u>drowsily</u>.

          adverb of condition – indicating sleepy state
    (10). That red car could <u>easily</u> be our motor.
      adverb of possibility↵ – indicating possibility
    (11). There was a road accident but <u>luckily</u> no one was injured.
          adverb – expressing wish↵
    (12). Silvia spoke <u>very</u> quickly.
         adverb↵ - modifying another adverb ⟹quickly
    (13). That little girl looks <u>very</u> pretty.
           adverb↵ - modifying adjective ⟹pretty
    (14). I rang <u>twice,</u> but no one answered.
adverb of number↵ - modifying the verb ⟹rang

The above examples demonstrate that adverbs are useful words to enhance
the meaning of both written and spoken statements. Many adverbs give information about <u>when, where, how and the extent of something</u> . In addition,
there are many other adverbs of other meanings. Some of these are exemplified above and more examples are given later.

. <u>Position of adverbs</u>

You can see in the above examples that adverbs can be positioned at the beginning, in the middle or at the end of a sentence. However, if you place an adverb without thinking about which word the adverb should modify, you can change the meaning of the sentence unintentionally. For instance:

(15). John explained <u>clearly</u> the situation.

adverb of quality↵ - modifying the verb⟹ explained

It is suggesting that John explained the situation in a way that was easy to hear or see.

(16). John explained the situation <u>clearly</u>.

adverb of quality ↵- modifying ⟹ verb

Here the <u>adverb clearly</u> means that John explained the situation in a way that made sense as it is easy to understand.

(17). <u>Clearly</u>, John explained the situation.

adverb of quality↵ - clearly = certainly

In this sentence, the adverb is modifying the whole sentence. It refers to the entire context of this sentence. It is emphasizing that <u>without doubt John explained the situation, i.e. what you are saying is obvious and true.</u>

(18). He visited them <u>once</u> on the weekend.

adverb of number↵

It means on <u>one time</u> on the weekend. It also implies that he might have done so on a number of individual weekends. On the other hand, in the following example, the position of <u>the adverb</u> **once** in the sentence gives a different meaning:

(19). He <u>once</u> visited them on the weekend.

adverb of number↵

Here, the <u>adverb</u> **once** means at some time in the past, he visited on the weekend. It does not imply more than one weekend.

These examples demonstrate that an adverb can modify different parts of the sentence. It is, therefore, important to position it correctly in order to avoid ambiguity. You may come across some rules of placing the adverb in a sentence. There are no universally laid down rules. In general terms, you can place an adverb before the word it is modifying. This rule is not workable in many cases. However, before using an adverb, make sure that it does not lead to unnecessary ambiguity of meaning.

. <u>Adverb forms</u>

1. <u>Many words exist as adverbs</u>

These adverbs are not related to adjectives or any other classes of words.

Many adverbs of this group are commonly used. Here are some examples
of such adverbs:

again, always, ever, else, here, however, perhaps, quite, soon

2. Many adverbs have the same form as adjectives

List 2 contains some words which can function as adjectives
as well as adverbs.

Some words perform duel function

Adjective	Adverb
backward(s)	backward(s)
early	early
enough	enough
fast	fast
forward(s)	forward(s)
full	full
further	further
hard	hard
late	late
long	long
next	next
only	only
straight	straight
weekly	weekly
well	well

List 2

. The following examples illustrate the application of such words:

(20). It is a straight street.

    adjective↵

(21). I went straight home as we were expecting a guest.

    adverb↵

(22) . You must cook it for a further 3 minutes.

    adjective↵

(23) . I had walked further than I had planned.

    adverb↵

(24) . It is hard work for me.

  adjective↵

(25) . You must try <u>hard</u> to pay back my money.

           adverb⏎

(26) . From London to Edinburgh by coach is a <u>long</u> journey.

                     adjective⏎

(27) . You can stay here as <u>long</u> as you like.

           adverb⏎

(28) . How far is it to the <u>next</u> underground station?

          adjective⏎

(29) . Who will jump *next*?

         adverb⏎

(30) . He was the <u>only</u> person at the scene of the accident.

        adjective⏎

(31) . I <u>only</u> arrived a few minutes before the meeting started.

adverb⏎

(32) . Since the car accident, she is not a <u>well</u> woman.

           adjective⏎

(33) . Nothing was going <u>well</u> without him.

        adverb⏎

3 . <u>Many adverbs are formed from adjectives as:</u>
adverb = adjective + ly

Adjective	Adjective + ly = Adverb
articulate	articulately
bold	boldly
certain	certainly
descriptive	descriptively
excessive	excessively
glorious	gloriously
honest	honestly
jealous	jealously
legal	legally
mental	mentally
obvious	obviously
quick	quickly
serious	seriously
unconditional	unconditionally
unconscious	unconsciously
violent	violently

<u>**List 3**</u>

Examples in List 3 illustrate how adverbs are created by
applying this rule stated above.

. In addition to the above, the following spelling rules for
  converting adjectives into adverbs are applied:

4. **To form an adverb from an adjective ending in a consonant
   and 'y': insert 'i' after the consonant and replace 'y' by 'ly'**

List 4 contains some examples of adverbs generated by applying
this rule:

Adjective	Adverb derived from adjective
bloody	bloodily
bloodthirsty	bloodthirstily
cheery	cheerily
drowsy	drowsily
dry	drily (also dryly)
easy	easily
gloomy	gloomily
haughty	haughtily
hearty	heartily
lazy	lazily
lucky	luckily
patchy	patchily
risky	riskily
shy	*shyly* (exception as it does not obey the rule)
sly	*slyly* (another adverb formed against the rule)

List 4

It is worth mentioning that the adjective **gay** has a vowel 'a' before 'y'. It
becomes an adverb **gaily** in the same way as adverbs derived above. This is
another **exception** to the above rule.

5 . **To form adverbs from adjectives ending in 'll', just add 'y'
   to the word.** For instance:

> . full ⇒   fully (also full)) . shrill ⇒ shrilly

There are not so many adjectives which end in double -*ll*.

6 . **To form an adverb from an adjective ending in a consonant
   and 'le' , replace 'e' with 'ly'.**

****

In List 5, you can see how adverbs are created by applying this rule:

Adjective	Adverb derived from adjective
agreeable	agreeably
able	ably
ample	amply
credible	credibly
debatable	debatably
equable	equably
humble	humbly
laughable	laughably
probable	probably
possible	possibly
reasonable	reasonably
simple	simply
subtle	subtly
terrible	terribly
understandable	understandably
vulnerable	vulnerably

List 5

Adjective	Adverb derived from adjective
apologetic	apologetically
artistic	artistically
basic	basically
bureaucratic	bureaucratically
characteristic	characteristically
dramatic	dramatically
frantic	frantically
heroic	heroically
historic	historically
idiotic	idiotically
intrinsic	intrinsically
optimistic	optimistically
organic	organically
periodic	periodically

List 6

7. To form an adverb from an adjective ending in 'ic', add

'ally' to the word.

The above examples in List 6 illustrate how adverbs are created by applying this rule. Indeed, there are some exceptions. Here is an example of an exception to the above rule: **public ⟹ publicly**

The word public also functions a s a noun, meaning ordinary people.

**8 . To form an adverb from an adjective ending in 'l',
just add 'ly' to the word.**

 The following examples illustrate how adverbs are created by applying this rule:

Adjective	Adverb derived from adjective
awful	awfully
beautiful	beautifully
boastful	boastfully
careful	carefully
eventual	eventually
material	materially
meaningful	meaningfully
medical	medically
punctual	punctually
respectful	respectfully
successful	successfully
wonderful	wonderfully

List 7

. Adjunct word or phrase

An adverb or phrase that adds meaning to the verb in a sentence or part of a sentence is called an adjunct. When additional information is given by the adjunct in a sentence, it is called modifying or qualifying. For instance:

(1) . He came fast.

fast is an adverb and adjunct (adjunct verb)

(2)   . He telephoned us in a great hurry.

adjunct phrase↵

In these examples, both the adverb and the phrase add further information to the verbs came and telephoned respectively.

****

. Functions of adverbs

. **The most common function performed by many adverbs is to modify the verb.** Here are some examples:

(1) . She drives <u>safely</u>.

adverb modifying the verb drives by adding further information **- safely**

The adverb <u>safely</u> enhances the central meaning conveyed by this statement.

(2) . He walks <u>gently</u>.

adverb modifying the verb walks

Here the adverb adds further information by way of highlighting *how* this particular person walks.

(3) . We are <u>very</u> pleased to meet you.

⇑

adverb modifying the verb pleased

Here the adverb <u>very</u> places emphasis on the meaning of the whole sentence.

(4) . <u>Due to noisy people in the room,</u> I could <u>hardly</u> hear you.

phrase ↵   adverb modifying the verb hear ↵

In this sentence, the adverb <u>hardly</u> adds meaning to the verb - **could** in the clause(part of a sentence).

(5) . She was seen <u>recently</u>.

adverb modifying the verb was seen ↵

Here the adverb adds further information to the meaning of this statement by pointing out the time (recently) when she was seen.

. An adverb modifies another adverb:

This is exemplified below:

(1) . Police arrived at the accident scene <u>very</u> <u>quickly</u>.

first adverb ↵   ⇑

second adverb

In this sentence, quickly modified the verb <u>arrived, and</u> <u>very</u> modified the second adverb - <u>quickly</u>. In this case, the adverb <u>very</u> acted as <u>an</u> <u>intensifier</u>. It is one of the adverbs of degree. Its use in this sentence has graded the adverb <u>quickly,</u> and thus placed greater emphasis on the meaning of the other adverb.

(2) . He has performed <u>unexpectedly</u>   <u>well</u>.

first adverb ↵ first adverb ↵

****

In this sentence, the adverb <u>well</u> modified the verb <u>performed, and</u> the
adverb <u>unexpectedly</u> modified the adverb <u>well</u>. Here the adverb <u>unexpect-
edly</u> is a <u>descriptive adverb</u>. Its function is similar to that of an
adjective when it is modifying a noun. It adds an extra layer of meaning to
the central meaning of this statement.

(3). He left home <u>most</u> <u>resentfully</u>.

first adverb↵   ⇓

second adverb

. resentfully ⇒ adverb modifies verb ⇒*left*

. most ⇒ adverb modifies adverb ⇒resentful*y*

(4). We visited John <u>quite</u> <u>often</u>.

first adverb ↵   ⇓

second adverb

. often ⇒ adverb modifies verb ⇒ visited

. quite ⇒ adverb modifies adverb ⇒ often

Here the adverb <u>quite</u> adds extra meaning conveyed by <u>often</u> which is an <u>ad-
verb of time</u>.

(5). Sarah answered questions <u>more</u> <u>fully</u> than Jane did.

first adverb↵   ⇓

second adverb

. fully ⇒ adverb modifies verb ⇒ answered

. more ⇒ adverb modifies adverb ⇒ fully

In this example, <u>more</u> is acting as an intensifier by placing emphasis on the
meaning of the adverb <u>fully</u>. Here the adverb <u>fully</u> is used as an
<u>adverb of comparison</u>.

. An adverb can modify an adjective:

The following examples illustrate this action:

(1) . He is <u>fairly</u> <u>happy.</u>

adverb ↵   ⇓

adjective

. fairly ⇒ adverb modifies happy ⇒ adjective

The adverb <u>fairly</u> is placed before the adjective <u>happy</u> in order to
intensify the meaning of this adjective.

(2). This suitcase is <u>really</u> <u>nice</u>.

adverb ↵   ⇓

adjective

. really ⇒ adverb modifies adjective ⇒ nice

****

The use of the adverb <u>really</u> adds further information to the meaning of the adjective nice.

> (3). This car is <u>too</u> <u>long</u>.
>
> adverb ↵   ⇓
>
>   adjective

> . too ⇒ adverb modifies adjective ⇒ long

> (4). You're <u>absolutely</u> <u>right</u>.
>
> adverb ↵   ⇓
>
>   adjective

> . absolutely ⇒ adverb modifies adjective ⇒ right

> (5). This is a <u>quite</u> <u>small</u> office.
>
> adverb ↵   ⇓
>
>   adjective

. quite* ⇒ adverb modifies adjective

. small ⇒ adverb modifies ⇒ noun ⇒office

> * when quite is used with an adjective, before a noun , it must be preceded by a, or an as above.

. **<u>An adverb can modify a preposition:</u>**

This is exemplified below:

> (1). He is *sitting* <u>right</u> <u>beside</u> his father.
>
> adverb ↵   ⇓
>
>   preposition

. right (right = exactly) ⇒ adverb modifies preposition beside
(beside = next to)

> (2). The car <u>just</u> <u>in front of</u> me stopped suddenly causing this accident.
>
> adverb ↵   ⇓
>
>   preposition

. just (= exactly) ⇒adverb modifies preposition ⇒ in front of
(in front of = ahead but near)

> (3). I was <u>really</u> <u>in</u> the garden shed without my mobile phone.
>
> adverb ↵   ⇓
>
>   preposition

. really (= truly or in reality) ⇒ adverb intensifying the meaning of

the preposition ⇒ in

> (4). They are <u>always</u> <u>at</u> home in the evenings.
>
> adverb ↵   ⇓
>
>   preposition

. always (= at all times) $\Rightarrow$ adverb modifies preposition$\Rightarrow$ at

(5) . He entered the hall <u>quietly from</u> the back door, which was unlocked.

       adverb↵   ⇓

           preposition

. quietly (= without any sound or noise) $\Rightarrow$ adverb modifies

  preposition $\Rightarrow$ from

. <u>Adverbs can also modify prepositional phrases:</u> See $\Rightarrow$ phrases.

. Types of adverbs

The prime function of an adverb is to support the central meaning of a statement by supplying further information. Indeed, the inclusion of an adverb in a sentence can enhance the meaning of a statement. The examples given above illustrate this role played by adverbs in sentences. The following kinds of adverbs cover a wide range of functions performed by adverbs according to their meaning:

. Adverbs of manner

The adverbs of manner describe how something happened or was done. Similarly, adverbs can be used to tell us about someone's feelings, i.e. 'sorry' or 'happy' state of mind and the circumstance or situation that has led to this state of mind. Thus, adverbs of manner can tell us how something is done and the circumstance in which it has happened. For
instance:

    (1) . Andrew approached Jane <u>calmly.</u>

        adverb of manner ↵ modifying the verb - **approached**

It gives us information about <u>how </u>Andrew approached Jane (calmly). It also tells us the <u>feelings </u>of Andrew at the time when he did something – approached Jane.

      (2) . He drives <u>carefully</u>.

     adverb of manner ↵ modifying the verb – **drives**

It is enhancing the meaning of the statement, by indicating the way he does something – driving.

      (3) . We talked <u>frankly</u> about our political views.

     adverb of manner ↵ modifying the verb – **talked**

How we talked? <u>Frankly</u> – describing the way talking was done.

    (4) . We signed the document <u>jointly</u>.

        adverb of manner ↵ modifying the verb – **talked**

In this case, the adverb <u>jointly</u> is indicating the circumstance in which something was done - jointly

        (5) . They married each other <u>happily</u>.

              adverb of manner ↵ - informing us about their feelings

. Most adverbs of manner end in '*ly*' as illustrated by the above
  examples. Some adverbs of manner do not end in '*ly*' as
demonstrated below:

        (6) . Cars were running <u>fast</u> on the motorway.
        (7) . Robert walks <u>straight</u>.
        (8) . She told him the <u>loudest</u>* in front of their guests

---

* Louder, loudest are used in *informal style.*

. In List 8, you can find some commonly used adverbs of manner:

---

accidentally alone angrily anxiously awkwardly beautifully bitterly
bodily boldly carelessly casually cheaply collectively comfortably
dangerously differently directly effectively enthusiastically explicitly
fluently gently gladly happily hastily hopefully illegally
intelligently incredibly intently legally mutually meticulously
nervously nicely oddly openly passionately peacefully politically
professionally proudly rapidly regardless reluctantly roughly sadly
secretly sensibly smoothly softly specially tenderly truthfully
uncomfortably unhappily urgently warmly wearily willingly---

List 8

. Adverbs of time

Adverbs of time state <u>when</u> something or some action has taken place or
will take place. As an adverb of time is an adjunct not the tense of the verb, it
dos not refer to the tense but the time. What does it mean ?
The tense carries time reference such as simple present or past perfect, but as
adverb of time refers to time irrespective of the tense. For instance:

        (1) . we are leaving <u>tomorrow</u>.

           adverb of time ↵

In this example, the adverb of time is used with the present tense to refer to
the action of leaving in the future, i.e. tomorrow.

        (2) . We arranged to meet <u>finally</u>.

           adverb of time ↵

In this case, the adverb of time is used with the past tense, but referring
to future time in the past. Here are some more examples:

(3) . We discussed this matter <u>yesterday</u>.

(4) . She is ill <u>now</u>.

(5) . This news programme is broadcast <u>nightly.</u>

(6) . <u>Soon</u> I will finish this job.

(7) . We enjoyed a group discussion <u>afterwards</u>.

adverb of time ↵

It answers the question:

.When did you enjoy a group discussion? ⇒ afterwards

. Adverbs of place (or position)

Adverbs of place tell us ***where*** something occurs, exists or happens. The following examples demonstrate the use of adverbs of place:

(1) . We will meet <u>here.</u>

adverb of place ↵ - it modifies the verb ⇒ will meet

(2) . They live <u>upstairs</u>.

adverb of place ↵ - it modifies the verb ⇒ live

(3) . We parked our car <u>somewhere</u>.

adverb of place ↵ - it modifies the verb ⇒ parked

(4) . Silvia is <u>abroad</u> for her friend's wedding.

adverb of place ↵ - it modifies the verb ⇒ is

(5) . The bad weather kept us <u>indoors</u> over the weekend.

adverb of place ↵ - it modifies the verb ⇒ kept

Here are some more examples in which adverbs are underlined:

(6). All our stock items were manufactured <u>in</u> Yorkshire.

(7). We all joined hands and danced <u>round.</u>

(8). She was standing <u>far away</u> <u>from us</u>.

adverb of place/position↵   ⇑

prepositional phrase modifying the adverb

(9). He said, 'Haven't we met before <u>somewhere</u>?'

(10). I said, '<u>Nowhere</u>* have we met as I have just arrived from
the USA.'

---

* When **nowhere** begins a clause/sentence, the subject of the verb comes
after an auxiliary verb. In this case, 'met' is the verb of the subject 'we'
and the primary auxiliary is 'have'.

. In <u>List 9</u> below, you can see some of the words used as adverbs of place:

. Adverbs of reason and purpose

abreast, ahead, about, above, anywhere, around, apart, ashore, away,
below, beneath, beside, globally, here, in indoors, inland,
internationally, locally, nationally, nowhere, off, opposite, outdoors,
outside, over, overseas, somewhere, there, together, underground,
universally, up, widely, worldwide

List 9

Adverbs of reason and purpose inform us why an action or something has
happened. The following examples show their application:

> (1) . He said it <u>deliberately</u>.

> adverb of purpose ↵ - it modifies the verb ⇒ said

It tells us the reason why he said it and thus answers the question:
Why did he say it?

(2) . <u>Inevitably</u>, our journey was cancelled because of late payment.

⇑

adverb of reason - meaning something certain to happen/occur

Why inevitably?. The reason is given in this statement.

Here are some more examples in which adverbs are underlined:

> (3) . I broke it <u>accidentally</u>.
> (4) . You made it difficult for us <u>purposely</u>.
> (5) . I did not hurt your feelings <u>intentionally</u>.
> (6) . She <u>therefore</u> walked out of the room.

Adverbs of frequency

Adverbs of frequency tell us about the repetition or occurrence of
something. Some adverbs of frequency are used in the following
examples:

> (1) . The class <u>always</u> begins at 9.15.

> adverb of frequency ↵ - How often ? always
> > (2) . I come to this park <u>often</u>.

> > adverb of frequency ↵ - How often? often
> (3) . It's <u>usually</u> the manager's responsibility.

adverb of frequency ↵ - How often? usually
> > (4) . I eat rice <u>rarely</u>.

> adverb of frequency ↵ - How often? rarely (seldom = rarely)

In the following examples adverbs are underlined:

(5) . I have been to Paris <u>twice</u>.

(6) . We met <u>once</u> in London.

(7) . She <u>seldom</u> writes to me.

(8) . I did not call <u>again</u>.

. <u>Adverbs of degree</u>

Adverbs of degree show the **extent** to which something has happened. These adverbs include words like: easily, enough, forever, somewhat, and twice. The following examples show how to use such adverbs

(1) . He visited us <u>fairly</u> <u>recently</u>.

adverb of degree ↵   ⇓

adverb of time

In this example, <u>fairly</u> is intensifying the meaning of the adverb - recently

(2) . I <u>hardly</u> knew his intention.

adverb of degree ↵ - modifying the verb ⇒ knew

(3) . This pair of shoes is <u>rather</u>   expensive.

adverb of degree modifying expensive ↵ adjective↵

(4) . She fell <u>right</u>   <u>to</u> the bottom of the stairs.

adverb of degree modifying to↵   ⇓

preposition

(5) . The lecture hall was <u>half</u>   <u>full</u>.

adverb of degree full↵   ⇓

adjective

In the following examples adverbs are underlined:

(6) . She knew that she was <u>altogether</u> mistaken.

(7) . The arrangements were good <u>enough</u> for me.

(8) . Indeed, you have <u>almost</u> reached it.

<u>Adverbs of degree can also be a fraction (half) or percentage, e.g. thirty per-cent wrong. These examples illustrate that adverbs of degree are used to indi-cate how much, or in what degree or to what extent is something.</u>

. <u>Adverbs for other functions</u>

In addition to the above types of adverbs, there are adverbs for indicating a wide range of meanings including the following:

. *<u>Adverb of Viewpoint</u>* expresses a particular view concerning a particular state or situation. Some adverbs of viewpoint are: financially, economically, personally and strictly. Here are some examples:

(1) . This trip is <u>financially</u> bearable.

adverb of viewpoint ↵ - expressing financial state

****

(2) . Economically, the USA is the strongest country.

adverb of viewpoint ↵ - expressing economical status/state

. *Adverb of Focus* is used to highlight the word or a phrase which the
writer or the speaker wants to focus on. Some adverbs of focus are:
*alone, also, chiefly, entirely, even, exclusively, just, largely, mainly,
mostly, notably, only, particularly, partly, primarily, purely,
principally, simply* and *specifically* .
Here are some examples:

(1) . I only visited him once in London.

adverb of focus ↵ - focusing on the verb *visited*

Only is before the word, i.e. **visited** we want to focus on.
(2). Only* you can help us now.

When we want to **focus on the subject,** the adverb comes before the
subject as shown in example 2. Similarly, the adverb **even** is before the subject in example 3:

(3). **Even**** the managing director could not confirm the firm's closure.

    adverb of focus   subject

---

* Usually in written official English, the focusing adverb **only** is placed
after the word or phrase it is modifying, e.g.
(4) . Your visa is valid for six months **only**.

** In informal English, both **only** and **even** can be placed in the middle
of the sentence:
(5) . I am not suggesting that your mother **even** cannot cook.
(6) . she told me that she **only** met him once in a night club.

---

(7) . She especially loves his wealth.

adverb of focus ↵ - focusing on the phrase ⟹ *his wealth*
(8) . Just add one tea spoon of honey.

adverb of focus ↵ - focusing on the whole phrase
(9) . We chatted up all afternoon about the party mostly.
(10) . I don't like coffee particularly.

Examples 9 and 10 illustrate that in informal English, focusing adverbs can
be placed after the phrase or word they are focusing on.

. *Adverbs of different attitudes* relate to a comment on someone's
behaviour, feeling, truth, falsity and similar attitudes. Some relevant

****

adverbs are: *curiously, fortunately, honestly, possibly, naively,*
surprisingly and *wisely*. Here are some examples:

>> (1) . He was in the lecture hall, but curiously, I did not see him.

>> adverb of attitude ↵

In this sentence, the adverb curiously (= strangely*)* indicates the truth the
writer/speaker knows.

>> (2) . She naively trusted the caller.

> adverb of attitude ↵ - indicating behaviour

>> (3) . Honestly, I have no idea where he has gone for his lunch.

adverb of attitude ↵ – emphasizing that what I am saying is true

>> (4) . Possibly, they will reject our invitation.

adverb of attitude ↵ – predicting feelings of some people

. *The linking adverb* relates to the previous sentence or clause. They
show the kind of link there is between one sentence and another. For
instance:

> (1). You say the balance is nil. However, I think you owe us £12.50.

>>

>> linking two sentences together by way of contrasting the
>> statement of the previous sentence

> (2) . We are late for the meeting. Anyway, we must attend it.

>>

>> linking two sentences and enforcing action, i.e. attend

> (3). You must talk to them now. Alternatively, send them an e-mail.

>>

>> linking two sentences and giving another point of view

> (4) . Our records reveal that your membership fee was received on
>> 1st July. Therefore you are entitled to use the club facilities.

>>

>> linking two statements and indicating the relationship between
>> them as inter-dependent, i.e. entitlement due to the fact
>> mentioned in the first statement

> (5). What are the advantages of an advance booking? Firstly, you get
>> 40% discount. Secondly, your seats are reserved. Thirdly, you
>> will get free refreshment on arrival.

The above examples show that linking adverbs are used for a wide
variety of situations. The following words can function as linking
adverbs:

> *accordingly, also, again, anyway, besides, consequently,*
> *equally, further, furthermore, hence, however, instead, likewise,*

****

moreover, nevertheless, rather, similarly, thereby, thus, too, yet

. **The comparison of adverbs** It is similar to the comparison of
adjectives. Some adverbs have the same form as adjectives. Adverbs
take the comparative and superlative forms with such endings:

er/est, more/most, farther / farthest, further, furthest
and *better/best*. For instance:

(1) . Tomorrow you should come to work ten minutes earlier than usual.

comparative form of adverb ↵

(2) . She likes him more than his wife.

comparative form of adverb ↵

(3) . Friday is the soonest I can contact you by telephone.

superlative form of adverb ↵ - it means here as soon as possible

(4) . Which car do you like best?

superlative form of adverb ↵ - superlative of *well*

(5) . The railway station is farthest from where our car is parked.

superlative form of adverb far ↵ - (*farthest = very long distance*)

(6) . His complaint was the worst I had heard.

superlative form of adverb badly ↵ - *(badly, worse, worst)*

As you have already noticed adverbs are single words. In addition, there are
many groups of words that can function with and without adverbs as ***adverbial elements***. These adverbials form phrases and clauses. These are discussed and exemplified in Part 2. For instance:

. Yesterday morning, I saw him.

adverbial element ↵ - or adverbial phrase as it has no finite verb

See ⟹ Phrases

. **When is a word an adjective or an adverb in a sentence?**

Both adjectives and adverbs have some common features and differ in some
respects. In order to understand adverbs as a word class, it is vitally important
to appreciate their specific characteristics. Certainly, there are many adjectives and adverbs, which perform the same function of describing something
in a sentence. However, from the context of a sentence you can find whether
it is an adjective or an adverb.
For instance:

(1) . She had a long wait at Heathrow due to an industrial strike.

adjective ↵-long is placed before the **noun** ⟹ modifying **wait**

(2) . She had to wait long at Heathrow due to an industrial strike.

adverb ↵- long is positioned after the

verb wait ⟹ modifying **wait**

Sometimes, it can create some confusion in recognising when a word is an adjective or an adverb. Furthermore, this may lead to the incorrect use of a word.

In summary, adverbs can enhance the overall meaning of a statement. Even so, most of the time, they are not essential components for structuring sentences. You can construct a meaningful and grammatically complete sentence or statement without any adverb. However, there are occasions when the inclusion of an adverb in a sentence is vital.

Chapter 7

Prepositions

. Introduction

A preposition is a word or a group of words used before a noun, pronoun or noun phrase. It also shows the relation of a noun, pronoun, noun phrase or clause to the rest of a sentence. There are many simple words and groups of words which function as prepositions. Some of these are listed below:

Simple prepositions

about, above, abroad, across, along, alongside, among, around, astride, at, bar, before, behind, below, beside, between, beyond, by, circa, down, during, except, for, from, in, inside, into, minus, near, notwith-standing, of, off, on, onto, opposite, out, outside, over, per, past, plus, round, since, through, throughout, to, towards, under, underneath, up, with, within, without,

Group prepositions*

according to, afraid of, ahead of , all over, apart from, as far as, away from, because of, close by, close to, due to, fed up with, in between, in accordance with, in addition to, in front of, instead of, for the sake of, in favour of, in front of, in a hurry, in terms of, in view of, near to, next to, on behalf of, on top of, out o f, with reference to, with regard to

----

* Two or three word prepositions may be considered as prepositional phrases. In some other publications, you may find them under idioms ,e.g. in stead of something---See ⇒prepositional phrases

List 1

As shown above, the basic form of a preposition is just one word. This form is known as a <u>simple preposition,</u> e.g. <u>at</u>. A <u>group</u> or <u>compound</u> or <u>complex preposition</u> consists of two or more prepositions, e.g. <u>in accordance with</u>. It is worth mentioning here that sometimes two or more simple prepositions merge together to form a complex word preposition, e.g. <u>onto</u>. See List 1.The following examples illustrate their specific feature of coming before a noun, pronoun or noun phrase:

(1) . **Anne left the office** <u>before</u> <u>lunch</u>.

preposition before a noun ↵   noun↵

In this sentence, the preposition **before** joins the first part of the sentence (highlighted) with its second part. This is how it shows the relationship between these two parts of the sentence. It also meets the specific requirement of a preposition, e.g. a preposition comes before a noun **lunch**. Similarly:

(2) . **They shouted my name** <u>across</u> <u>the road</u>.

preposition before a noun phrase ↵noun phrase↵

(3) . **We live** <u>next to</u> <u>him</u>.

preposition ↵pronoun↵ - personal pronoun

Prepositions express a variety of relationships between a noun, pronoun, noun clause or noun phrase and the rest of a sentence. They cover a wide range of meanings. The most typical are the relationships of *place* and *time*. Some of these relationships are illustrated below:

. Prepositions of place

This is illustrated by the following examples:

(1) . You will find it <u>near</u>   <u>the door</u>.

preposition of place ↵noun phrase↵ - near refers to the door/place

(2) . I will meet you <u>at</u> <u>Piccadilly Circus.</u>

preposition of place ↵ noun phrase↵ - at refers to a place

(3) . Anne saw me <u>opposite</u>   <u>the main post office</u>.

preposition of place ↵   noun phrase ↵ - opposite referring to a
                                                    place/main post office

Here are two more examples:

(4) . The car park is <u>in front of</u>   <u>the post office</u>.

preposition of place ↵   noun phrase ↵

(5) . At the meeting I was sitting <u>next to</u> <u>John</u>.

preposition of place ↵ noun ↵

In example 5, John is a person who was sitting in a certain place. Thus, *next to* refers to the place where John was sitting.

. Prepositions of time

We use prepositions of time in a variety of ways. For instance:

(1) . We arrived here <u>on</u>   <u>Monday</u>.

preposition of time ↵ noun↵ - on referring to the time/today

(2) . Roads were deserted <u>during</u> <u>the World Cup matches</u>.

preposition of time ↵   noun phrase↵

Preposition *during* refers to a period of time - the World Cup matches, a definite time.

> (3) . We have lived in France <u>for</u> ten years.

>> preposition of time↵ - *for* indicating time – how long

> (4) . You should arrive <u>before</u> the weekend.

> preposition of time ↵

Preposition *before* refers to the time which is <u>no later than the weekend</u>.

> (5). My contract will not expire <u>until</u> the end of next month.

>> preposition of time ↵

Preposition *until* refers to the time when something ends 'contract'.

. <u>A sentence can have both place and time prepositions.</u>

This is exemplified below:

> (1). We will meet you <u>at breakfast</u> <u>in our hotel</u>.

>> <u>preposition of time</u>↵   ⇑   ⇑   ⇑
>> <u>refers to breakfast</u>   noun <u>preposition</u> noun phrase
>>   ⇓   ⇓
>> 'at' a particular time   refers to a place - our hotel

> (2). We have been living <u>for</u> three years <u>in</u> this house.

>> preposition of time ↵   ⇑
>> referring to a period of time   preposition of place referring to this house

> (3). We lived <u>close to</u> their shop <u>in</u> 1995.

>> preposition of place ↵   ⇑
>> refers to a place = shop   preposition of time referring to 1995

. <u>Prepositions of other meanings</u>

Here are some other prepositions related to other meanings. These are discussed under some appropriate headings below.

. <u>Prepositions of cause, reason and purpose</u>

These are described below with the aid of the following examples:

> (1) . I am happy <u>because of</u> <u>a return to normal working hours</u>.

>> ⇑   ⇑
>> <u>preposition of **cause**</u>   noun phrase – describes an event
>>   ⇓
>> indicates the effect of an event described by the noun phrase on
>> *I* (subject) as 'happy'

(2) . His lateness was <u>due to</u> <u>a traffic jam in the town</u>.

         ⇑   ⇑

<u>preposition of **cause**</u>   noun phrase describing an event

               ⇓

indicates the effect of an event stated by the noun phrase on
his (subject) 'lateness'

Note that *a cause* produces *an effect*, e.g. an event or something that happens. On the other hand, a reason has a much wider scope. For instance, you
can give a reason for something which is done. A reason can be a justifica-
tion for something happening. The following examples illustrate the use of
some *prepositions of reason*:

    (3) . The brutal crime was committed <u>without</u> <u>a motive</u>.

           preposition of reason ↵   ⇑

                                     noun phrase

The preposition *without* is followed by the noun phrase, which points to *a
motive* - reason

    (4) .Our Prime Minister is anxious <u>about</u> the predicated election result.

           preposition of reason ↵

. It is worth mentioning that the word *purpose* means an intention or
  determination to do something. Here are two examples of using
  prepositions of purpose:

    (5) . <u>Despite</u> the rain, we will travel to London for Jane's wedding.

    ⇑

preposition of purpose - pointing to travel without being deterred by rain

    (6) . She went to work <u>contrary to</u> her doctor's advice.

preposition of determination↵- showing the determination to work

. <u>Prepositions of exception, addition, support, opposition---</u>

Consider the following examples:

    (7) . We have paid the loan <u>except for</u> interest charges.

      preposition of exception ↵- except* refers to an exception

---

* <u>The word except can also be a verb meaning *exclude* or *exempt*</u>.
  It can also be used as a conjunction, e.g.
. Our car is the same make except that it has a sunroof.

---

    (8) . All guests have left <u>except</u> John Smith from England.

preposition of exception↵ - implying that only John Smith is still here

(9) . We have no close friends in this area <u>other than</u> Jack and Jill.

preposition of exception↵ - implying only or except

Here is another example to demonstrate its further use:
(10) . Jane seldom seems <u>other than</u> cheerful.

preposition of exception ↵ - implying only or except (seldom)
(11) . She is beautiful, <u>apart from</u> her height.

preposition of exception↵ - implying that height is excluded
(12) . I have completed all orders <u>apart from</u> this new order.

preposition of exception↵ - implying new order uncompleted

. In examples 11 and 12, *apart from = except for.* In examples 13 and
14, *apart from* has a different meaning. In these examples:
apart from = in addition to = as well as
(13) . <u>Apart from</u> his inherited wealth, he has built up

<u>preposition of addition</u>↵   his own large multi-national enterprise.
⇓

meaning here in addition to inherited wealth
(14) . <u>Apart from</u> his well-paid full-time job, he

<u>preposition of addition</u>↵   also has a part-time job.
⇓

implying in addition to his ------job
(15) . Our trainer was **with** us throughout the race.

preposition of support*↵

---

* Also see example 18, in which the preposition **with** is used twice in
order to illustrate its applications as preposition of **accompaniment** and
preposition of **possession**.

---

(16) . His age is <u>against</u> him for this travelling salesman's job.

preposition of opposition ↵

. <u>Among the most common prepositions are **of** and **with**. These are</u>
<u>used to denote possession or belonging as demonstrated below:</u>

(17) . Sarah is a young pianist <u>of</u> rare talent.

preposition of possession ↵
(18) . I saw Eric walking <u>with</u> a girl <u>with</u> red hair.

preposition of accompaniment ↵   ⇑

preposition of possession

Example 18 shows that sometimes prepositions can express different meanings in the same statement. In this sentence 'with red hair' means 'who has
red hair'.

. There are some prepositions for almost all kinds of meanings*.
   Here are some examples:

    (19). You can pay <u>for</u> your travel <u>by</u> cheque or <u>by</u> card.

In this example: **for** $\Rightarrow$ preposition of purpose and **by** $\Rightarrow$ preposition of
manner. Here 'by card' implies any card – credit or debit

    (20). Some parents stay together <u>despite</u> their differences
        <u>for the sake of</u> their children.

In this case, **despite** $\Rightarrow$ preposition of concession and

for the sake of $\Rightarrow$ preposition of reason/purpose

    (21). My bank charged me interest <u>at</u> 8 per cent.

                preposition of rate↵

    (22). <u>In spite of</u> his world –wide fame, he is not content.

preposition of contrast↵

    (23). This is a quotation <u>from</u> our prime minister's last speech.

  preposition of source/origin↵

. Some prepositions are not easy to recognise, e.g. via and vis-à-vis.
   These are exemplified below:

    (24). We came to know about your success <u>via</u> your sister.

            preposition of manner ↵

    (25). It is claimed that Microsoft has an unfair commercial
        advantage <u>vis-à-vis</u> other software companies in the world.

preposition of comparison - (French origin)

The preposition *vis-à-vis* means in comparison with or in relation to something. Here is another example of its use:

    (26). Nurse's earnings <u>vis-à-vis</u> the national average are very low.

preposition of comparison/relation↵

. Prepositional idioms

Many prepositions are used with idioms. You have to learn the use of idioms.
Here are a few examples of prepositional idioms.

    (27). John and Jill began to argue loudly, and I thought it was time
        I <u>stepped in</u>.

        ⇓

    prepositional idiom meaning *to intervene*

(28). She is <u>at heart</u> a very kind person.

prepositional idiom meaning *really*

(29). He thanked us <u>from the bottom of his heart</u> for all our help.

prepositional idiom meaning *very sincerely*

(30). The manager wants to talk to all of us <u>one by one</u>.

⇑

prepositional idiom meaning *individually*

(31). The resolution was passed by the board of directors
<u>on the nod.</u>

prepositional idiom meaning *all agreed without taking a vote*

. <u>When is a word a preposition, adverb or conjunction?</u>

A word can function as a preposition, adverb or conjunction. The main feature of a preposition is that it is followed by a pronoun, noun or noun phrase.
If you apply this rule to a sentence, you should be able to find any preposition in a sentence. The following three examples illustrate the use of the word
before.

(1). John had left home <u>before</u> <u>his wife's arrival</u>.

Preposition of time ↵ noun phrase ↵

. <u>The adverb modifies a verb, an adjective, another adverb or an</u> <u>adverbial phrase.</u> For instance:

(2). That happened <u>before</u>.

adverb of time ↵ - modifying the verb *happened*

. <u>The function of a conjunction is to join clauses to form compound and</u>
<u>complex sentences.</u> For instance:

(3). <u>It may be a long time</u> <u>before</u> <u>we meet again</u>.

clause 1 ↵   conjunction ↵ clause 2 ↵
clause 1 + conjunction + clause 2 = complex sentence

You have to examine the context in which the word is used in a sentence to
determine if the word is a conjunction, adverb or preposition.

In summary, prepositions have a wide range of meanings and many different
uses. They can be a source of confusion. For example, *by* can express time,
place, manner and action. For instance: The computer was repaired *by*
me.(Preposition of *action*). It must arrive *by* next day. (Preposition of *time*).
It is laying *by* the table. (Preposition of *place*). They went away *by* taxi.
(Preposition of *manner*). In accordance with the way a preposition is used, it
can be placed under several headings to yield different meanings.

Chapter 8
Determiners and Interjections

Groups of Determiners

Definite Determiners	Indefinite Determiners

. Definite article:
    the
	. Indefinite articles:
	    a, an

. Possessive determiners:
  my, your, his, her, their, our
  its
- when qualifying nouns or
  pronouns these are
  possessive determiners
  These are also called
  possessives or possessive adjectives
- When standing in for nouns they
    are **pronouns:** mine ,his, hers,
    yours, ours, theirs
	. Indefinite determiners:
	    all, almost, another,
	    any, both, each,
	    either, enough,
	    every, few, fewer,
	    fewest, little, less, least,
	    many, more, most, much,
	    no, neither, other,
	    several, some

. Demonstrative determiners:
    this, that, these, those
    There are often called
    demonstrative adjectives
	. Interrogative determiners:
	    what, which, whose

. Numerals:
 	
    - **cardinal:** one, three, ten,…
    - **ordinal:** third, fourth seventh …
    - **fraction:** a quarter of, a seventh of…	

List 1

. Introduction

A determiner is a word that comes before a noun or a noun phrase. It is used
to determine which person (s) or thing(s) are being referred to in a statement.
Let's consider two examples:

(1). The <u>chancellor</u>.

determiner ↵   noun↵

There are chancellors' posts in many countries. In this sentence, it refers to a unique chancellor in one country. Here the determiner indicates a unique position.

(2). The House of Commons.

determiner ↵   noun phrase↵

The United Kingdom has only one place called the ***House of Commons***. This is the only recognised place of this name in the country. In this case, the determiner refers to a unique status for a unique building.

The above examples show that some words are called determiners because they determine how nouns and pronouns are being used. In the above examples, it determines how the noun the ***chancellor*** and phrase ***House of Commons*** are used. A determiner by itself does not make much sense, but when it is used with nouns and noun phrases it amplifies their meaning. <u>In order to identify different determiners, in List 1 the most commonly used determiners are shown under major groups.</u>

. **The Definite Article**

Its usage is exemplified below:

(1). It is <u>the </u>house where I was born.

the definite article before a noun ***house*** indicates
the uniqueness of the house

Here its function is to place emphasis on the noun (house), which comes after it.

(2). I will buy a **car** tomorrow. <u>The </u>car will make my life easy.

definite article before a noun ↵

In this example, <u>definite article *the* refers to a noun a *car* already mentioned in the previous sentence.</u> Here its function is to attach an attribute to a car: "*will make my life easy*"

(3). We developed interactive timetable software.
    <u>The </u> software is licensed to schools.

refers back to the software mentioned previously

(4).   Some members of <u>the </u>Royal Family attended the celebration.

denoting a distinct family ↵

****

(5). The French nation was pleased when France won the World Cub.

⇑   ⇑

pointing to a distinct group of people   specifying the unique award

(6). The promised letter is in the post.

↵

indicating that the noun *post* is a communication organisation

Here the *post* is not thought of as a particular post office, but as an organisation in the communication business.

(7). *The* highest mark in the history examination was gained by Anne.

noun phrase↵

the precedes the superlative adjective *highest*

(8). June 21st is *the* longest day each year.

noun phrase↵

the preceded the superlative adjective l*ongest*

In this example, *the* is modifying the superlative adjective *longest.*

(9). Margaret Thatcher has been *the only British* female prime minister.

the preceded the adjective **only** in this noun phrase ↵ – modifying *only*

(10). Now is *the* turn of *the* next person.

1↵   2↵

In this case: 1 is modifying a noun and 2 is modifying an adjective.

(11). It was *the* summer of 2000, when I went to Poland.

phrase of time ↵

It is not preceded by an adjective but by *the.* A phrase of time containing a noun begins with *the* as illustrated above. The condition is that the noun must not be preceded by an adjective. Some more examples to illustrate this rule are:

(12). We visit our parents at *the* weekend.

phrase of time without an adjective before the noun ↵

(13). They married *the* following Saturday.

the preceded the phrase of time ↵

. Use *the* before the name of a country, if its name ends with kingdom or republic. For instance:

(14). This book was published in *the United Kingdom*.

(15). *The Republic of Ireland* is in Europe.

. Use *the* before a plural name of countries. For example:

(16) . In 1958, *the Netherlands* became a founding member of the EEC.

(17) . *The United States of America* consists of 50 administrative states.

. If the name of a region is not modified by another word (an adjective), *the* comes before it. For instance:

(18) . Birmingham is situated in *the Midlands.*

. The definite article can be used to express how something is measured. This is illustrated below:

(19) . In these days, potatoes are sold by *the* **kilogram**.

. The definite article precedes the names of entertainment places, trade and similar centres, galleries and museums.
Here are a few examples:

(20) . We met in *the* Tate Gallery some years ago.

(21) . *The* World Trade Centre is situated near London Bridge*.

the is not needed before this name ↵

---

* Many bridge names are without *the*, but there are exceptions to this rule. For example, the River Humber in East Yorkshire, England, has a bridge over it. This bridge is called *The Humber Bridge*. It is the second largest suspension bridge in the world.

---

(22) . I have been to *the* Albert Hall several times.

an entertainment hall in London ↵

(23) . *The* Dorchester is a well-known hotel.

. A definite article comes before a noun, if it indicates a unique position/status. For instance:

(24) . As *the* secretary of this club, I am responsible for administration.

. *The* is used with an unaccountable noun, providing an unaccountable noun refers to some particular person(s) or object(s). For instance:

(25) . *The* petrol in the United Kingdom is more expensive than in

unaccountable noun↵ – preceded by *the*   France.

(26) . Their cat loves *the* music played on radio.

unaccountable noun↵– preceded by *the*

. _**The**_ is used with a plural noun when a noun refers to some
specific meaning. For instance:
   (27) . Michael Jackson and _**the**_ children were shown together in a

         plural noun⤶   documentary programme.

In this case, it means some particular children

 (28) . _**The**_ books we received from Poland are not in English.

plural noun⤶ - refers to some specific books

. _**The**_ is used in front of a noun to emphasize that someone is special or
best or something is the best of its kind. For example:
   (29) . I went the see the show as it is the event of the year in our town.
   (30) . Once I shook hands with Clinton when he was in London.
         Do you mean **the** Clinton who was American president?

In speech, the word **the** is stressed in order to emphasize it.

. **Indefinite articles**

The indefinite article has two forms: _a_ and _an_. Their functions are exemplified below:
   (1) . Yesterday was _**a**_ _**bit**_ warmer day.

      indefinite article⤶   ⇑

            noun phrase

. When a noun phrase describes something or a person, the indefinite
article precedes the noun phrase as shown above. In example (1) the
indefinite article _a_ is required. On the other hand, in example (2), _**an**_ is
essential as explained below.

. The article _an_ precedes the noun if a singular noun begins with a vowel
(a, e, i, o, u). For instance:
         (2) . _**An**_ elephant from India has ears like **the** map of India.
            ⇑   ⇑

      indefinite article   definite article

In example 2, four nouns (elephant, India, ears, map) are mentioned five
times. Only on two occasions indefinite and definite articles are used respectively. On the other three occasions, there is no need to insert any of these determiners. Both examples show that the indefinite article stands for _**one**_ or in
other words, **a** and _**an**_ function as one.
         (3) . My son is _**a**_ student.

      indefinite article⤶ - preceded a singular noun _**student**_

(4) . She is *a* nice girl, isn't she?

indefinite article⤸   ⇑

noun phrase with a singular noun *girl*

. A phrase of time begins with *a* if a noun is preceded by an adjective.
This is illustrated below:

(5) . *A* very cold* winter day is here. Or : *A* very cold winter day!

⇑   ⇑

phrase indicating time   phrase of time forming no sentence

In both cases, winter noun is preceded by the adjective *very***

(6) . *A* wonderful day when England won the World Cup.

phrase of time ⤸ - noun day is preceded by the adjective *wonderful*

---

*   *cold* is both an adjective and a noun. Here it is used as an adjective.

* * *very* is both an adjective and an adverb. Here it is functioning as an
   adjective of degree.

See ⟹ adjectives

Here is another example:

(7) . *A* remarkable *day!*

In this phrase, the noun is preceded by the adjective. For this reason, the indefinite article *a* started this phrase.

. The indefinite article comes before a noun if it does not indicate
a unique position/status: For instance:

(8) . As *a* member of this union, I am entitled to free admission.

a is essential in this phrase ⤸

Since a union has many members, the status of a member is not unique.

. The indefinite article a/an precedes a noun expressing prices and similar
rates: For instance:

(9) . Bananas are eighty pence a kilogram.

essential in this phrase ⤸

. The indefinite article can come before a noun in place of one.
For example:

(10) . I would like to buy **a** car.

here a = one ⤸

. The indefinite article is used to indicate someone's job or profession or any attribute that describes the person: For instance:

> (11) . Jane is *a belly dancer* in Cairo.
>
> *a* is essential here ↵
>
> (12) . Before he joined the Labour Party, he was a communist.
>
> *a* is essential ↵

. The indefinite article can be used instead of *any.* For instance:

> (13) . Just buy a book on psychology.
>
> a book = any book ↵

. Many idiomatic phrases embody both definite and indefinite articles. Here are some examples of idiomatic phrases:

(14) . *an* angel of mercy	(15) . *a* bag of nerves
(16) . *a* fair crack of the whip	(17) . *the* top brass
(18) . *the* iron curtain	(19) . *the* golden rule

. When can you omit the article?

The article is **not** required in the following cases:

. When referring to relatives in phrases and clauses, e.g.

> (20) . Mother has just finished baking.
>
> (21) . Father smiles!
>
> (22) . Uncle lives here.

. When referring to an activity that goes on in places like educational situations, religious buildings, health organisation and the like*, e.g.

> (23) . Where is John? Shamefully, my husband is in **prison**.
>
> (24) . My wife was still in **hospital** when you rang.
>
> (25) . I went to **teacher training college** in London..
>
> (26) . I don't go to **church**.

---

* On the contrary, the definite article comes before the names of buildings/places when referring to them as definite places, e.g.

> (27) . I wanted to go to the hospital in our town.
>
> (28) . The university is situated about 5 miles away.
>
> (29) . The art gallery is in the north of the town.

. When referring to meals* in general terms, e.g.

> (30) . I usually have lunch between 13.00 – 14.00.
>
> (31) . What's for supper?

(32). Anne does not eat much breakfast.

---

* 1. If there is <u>an adjective</u> before breakfast, lunch, dinner and
supper the indefinite article **a** comes before the adjective, e.g.
  (33). We had <u>a delicious lunch</u> yesterday.
  (34). Madam, dinner is ready.
* 2 . You can use **the** if it is desirable to place emphasises on 'meal', e.g.
  (35). **The breakfast** I had with her was at her parents'
    holiday villa in the South of France.

. <u>For names* of most individual mountains, hills, rivers, lakes, islands,
continents, countries, cities, town, etc.</u>, e.g.
  (36). Mount Everest is in Asia.
  (37). Lake Balaton is in Hungary.
  (38). Thames is a river in England.

---

* for <u>plural names of countries</u> – see definite article as the is placed
before them.

. <u>When countable nouns are used in their plural form* without referring
to something in particular</u>, e.g.
  (39). They sell cars.
  (40). We have books.
  (41). She loves biscuits.

---

* When you use a <u>countable noun</u> in its plural form in order to specify
a particular circumstance, situation or to convey a particular meaning,
<u>a determiner</u> comes before it, e.g.
  (42). <u>The</u> computers in Room5 are for students' practice.
  (43). Where are <u>the</u> students this afternoon?
  (44). <u>Our</u> children are at my mother's home.

. <u>When you use an uncountable noun without a qualifying adjective</u>
before it, or state something in general terms, e.g.
  (45). I admire his <u>courage.</u>
  (46). <u>Justice</u> has been done.
  (47). <u>Sugar</u> is no good for lowering your cholesterol level.

<u>On the other hand, if the uncountable noun is preceded by an adjective, then
the is required,</u> e.g.

****

(48) . I will not forget <u>the extreme poverty</u> I saw in Africa.

(49) . She remembers well <u>the pleasant time</u> she spent with you.

. <u>If you use an uncountable noun in a specific situation, use the before it,</u>
<u>e.g.</u>

   (50) . We <u>demonstrated</u> our anger as <u>the freedom</u> is valued by us.

a particular situation↵

                 (51) . <u>Would you pass me the salt/sugar/milk?</u>

a particular situation when eating ↵

. <u>When referring to someone's status or job held by them previously, e.g.</u>

     (52) . Once she was <u>administrator</u> of this region.

     (53) . She became <u>chief psychologist</u> at the local hospital before
          her early retirement.

. <u>Possessive determiners</u>

Possessive pronouns function as determiners if they <u>qualify a noun</u>.
The following examples illustrate their function as determiners.

    (1) . This is <u>my</u> book .

possessive determiner qualifies a singular noun **- book**

    (2) . This is <u>his</u> car.

possessive determiner qualifies a singular noun - *car*

    (3) . That house is <u>our</u> property.

possessive determiner(plural form) qualifies a noun **- property**

    (4) . This is <u>her</u> handbag.

possessive determiner qualifies a singular noun **- handbag**

    (5) . Where are <u>your</u> horses?

possessive determiner qualifies a plural noun **- horses**

    (6) . They are <u>their</u> parents.

possessive determiner *their* qualifies a plural noun - *parents*

. <u>Indefinite determiners</u>

Indefinite determiners function as determiners if they modify a noun. Here are some examples of their use:

(1). <u>All</u> things work well here.

indefinite determiner qualifies a plural noun - ***things***

(2). Can he be <u>another</u> Ali in boxing?

indefinite determiner qualifies a singular noun - ***Ali***

(3). He doesn't eat <u>any*</u> meat.

indefinite determiner qualifies ***meat*** - an unaccountable noun

---

* The determiner <u>any</u> is usually used with negative sentences.

---

(4). <u>Both*</u> students are brilliant.

indefinite determiner ↵ - qualifies ***students*** - a plural noun

---

*Strictly speaking, the word **'both'** functions as adjective, adverb and pronoun.

---

(5). <u>Each</u> article is priced.

indefinite determiner qualifies a singular noun - ***article***

(6). <u>Either</u> place is suitable for our purpose.

indefinite determiner ↵ – qualifies ***place*** - a singular noun

(7). You can take a seat on <u>either*</u> side of the table.

indefinite determiner ↵ – qualifies ***side*** - a singular noun

---

* Note that ***either*** is also a pronoun and an adverb. It is often used with *or* as ***either ...or*** to indicate a choice between two alternatives.

Here are some more examples:

(8). I have recorded *every* item I found.

(9). *Several* men refused to show their passes.

(10). <u>Few*</u> players have shown an interest in this tour.

qualifies ***players*** - a plural noun

> * The word *few* (= not many). It also functions as an adjective and pro
>
> noun. Its attributes are fewer and fewest. See ⟹ pronouns

. <u>Demonstrative determiners</u>

A demonstrative pronoun becomes a demonstrative determiner <u>only if it pre-</u>
<u>cedes a noun.</u> You can leave out a noun, if you think that a sentence makes
clear sense. The following examples illustrate how a possessive word becomes a demonstrative determiner:

(1) . Please come to my office to see <u>this</u> invoice from the suppliers.

   demonstrative determiner ↵

This indicates that the invoice is near the speaker. *These* is the plural form
of **'this'**. Its use is illustrated below:

   (2) . <u>These</u> bags are full of bank notes.

demonstrative determiner ↵ - precedes bags - a plural noun

On the other hand, *that* and *those* imply that a person(s) or thing (s) are not
so near but further away:

   (3) . <u>That</u> man looks suspicious.

   precedes man ↵ - a singular noun
      (4) . <u>Those</u> eggs were hardly boiled.

   precedes eggs ↵ - a plural noun

. <u>Demonstrative determiners can also be used to imply space of time</u>
   <u>in terms of:</u>
   now = near in space of time indicated by *this* and *these*
   then = further away in space of time indicated by *that* and *those*

For instance:
      (5) . I will be in France <u>this</u> month

precedes month a singular noun↵ - *this* = now at present
      (6) . The only thing I do in my spare time <u>these</u> days is reading.

         precedes days - a plural noun↵
      (7) . During 1999, I lived far from here and travelled to work
         by car in <u>those</u> days.

   precedes a plural noun ↵

      (8) . When you telephoned me <u>that*</u> time, I was having a shower.

         some time elapsed ↵

> * *that/ those = then* implying time elapsed.
> *those* is used with a plural noun.

. Interrogative determiners

What, *which* and *whose* function as interrogative determiners if they precede
a noun. Their use is shown by the following examples:

. The word **that** as an interrogative determiner is used when one wants to
ask someone to specify something from an indefinite number of
possibilities. For instance:

(1) . <u>What</u> time is it?

determiner preceded the noun ↵

(2) . <u>What</u> politician did you see at Harrods of Knightsbridge?

⇑

interrogative determiner preceded the noun - politician

. The word **which** as an interrogative determiner is used when one wants
to ask someone to specify or identify something from a limited number
of possibilities. Examples 3 and 4 show this use.

(3) . <u>Which</u> lecturer did you see in our department?

⇑

Interrogative determiner precedes the noun — **lecturer**

(4) . <u>Which</u> library do you often visit in this area?

⇑

interrogative determiner precedes the noun — **library**

. **Whose** is an interrogative determiner of whom when it comes
before a noun. Here are some examples:

(5) . <u>Whose</u> book is this ? determiner precedes the noun - book

(6) . <u>Whose</u> car is parked in my place? ⇐ determiner precedes the
noun - car

(7) . <u>Whose</u> idea is this ? ⇐ determiner precedes the noun - idea

. Numeral determiners:

As shown in List 1 in this chapter, numerals are divided into cardinal
numbers, ordinal numbers and fractions. These are explain with examples below:

. **Cardinal numbers** - in both numbers and words:

. 1 - one   . 2 - two   . 3 - three   . 4 - four

- 20 - twenty
- 100 - hundred
- 400 - hundred
- 1000 - thousand
- etc.

The following examples show how cardinal numbers are written in words and numbers:

(1) . I have ordered ten bottles of French quality red wine.

(2) . They have bought two new cars in the last 12 months.

(3) . 5 million people voted for our party at the last local election.

4) . In 1999, I met her in London.

. The following phrases illustrate the use of commas in cardinal numbers:

(4) . 3,580 full-time students and 500 part-time students.

read it as three thousand five hundred and eighty

(5) . 1,000,000   read it as ⟹ a million or one million

(6) . 123,000,590 people.

read it as one hundred and twenty three million five hundred and ninety.

. You can make phrases with cardinal numbers: For instance:

(7) . Three of us together.   ⟸ cardinal number used in a phrase

(8) . approximately two thirds full.

modifying the number - about 2/3 full (not exactly 2/3)

(9) . Over 100 guests.

modifying the number – more than 100

. **Ordinal numbers** - these are in both words and numbers:

- 1st first . 2nd second . 12th twelfth
- 20th twentieth   . 100th hundredth . etc.

Here are two examples:

(10) . On my 60th birthday, I invited my parents for a meal at the Bombay Restaurant.

(11) . 1st and 2nd prizes were won by two brothers.

. **Fractions** - these are:

quarter, half, third, fourth, two and a third, etc.

. If the number is less than one, the noun phrase is preceded by *of.*
  For instance:

(12) . <u>One third of</u> our products is for export to the USA. (1/3 = one third)

(13) . Our company is entitled to <u>half of the rebate</u> paid this year.

Here are some more examples:

(14) . It is only <u>four fifths</u> full.   (4/5 = four fifths)

(15) . It should be <u>four and three quarter metres*</u> long.

(16) . The length of this stick is <u>only three quarters of a metre.</u>

(17) . She was <u>an hour and a half</u> late. Or alternatively you can say:

(18) . She was <u>one and a half hours*</u> late.

---

* When a fraction is greater than one, a plural noun comes after it.

In summary, the most common determiners are the definite and the indefinite articles. Other parts of speech such as adjectives and pronouns also function as determiners.

. Interjections (Exclamations!)

Interjections are considered as a minor class of words. These are exclamations. Interjections are useful for expressing feelings such as excitement, surprise, etc. They are not essential for the construction of sentences. Some of these are listed below:

Aha! Alas! Damn! Gosh! Hey! Ooh! Ouch! Phew! Ugh! Wow! Yuck!

Here are some examples:

    (1) . <u>Oh!</u> How is he now?

indicating someone's reaction to something that has been said
It also points out that one did not know it before.

    (2) . *Phew! it is stuffy in here!*

      showing disapproval
(possibly the place is warm in an unpleasant way and
  without enough fresh air)

. <u>Some of the most commonly used exclamatory phrases are as follows:</u>

      (3) . Good heavens!

      (4) . Oh dear!

(5) . Marvellous!

(6) . Great!

You can see from the above examples that some interjections are made
from certain groups of words in order to express some sudden feeling or
emotion . Here are some more examples:

(7) . Good gracious!

(8) . Good show!

(9) . Well done!

. There are some interjections in which verb forms are used.
For instance:

(10) . Watch out!

(11) . Cheers!

(12) . Look out!

(13) . Shut up!

(14) . What lovely flowers !

(15) . How warm it is today!

(16) . <u>Thanks a lot!</u>

a sarcastic remark suggesting just the opposite of what you mean

. <u>An exclamation mark(!) is also discussed under punctuation.</u>

See ⇒Punctuation

****

Chapter 9
Conjunctions

. Introduction

A word that joins other words, phrases, clauses or sentences is known as a conjunction.
For instance:

> (1) . She is called Mary and* she is my student.
>
> clause 1↵ conjunction↵   clause 2 ↵

> * Commas are usually omitted between short main clauses.

In this case, **and** joins two main clauses or two simple sentences into a compound sentence. This is a simple conjunction. It has no other function except to combine parts of a sentence. In this example, clause 1 and clause 2 can exchange places without altering the meaning of this sentence. We can classify conjunctions into the following two classes:

- coordinating conjunctions or coordinators
- subordinating conjunctions or subordinators

. Coordinating conjunctions or coordinators

The most common coordinating conjunctions or coordinators are:
and, but, or, so, nor , than and **yet.**

Nor is the negative counterpart of **or** coordinator. It is less used than other coordinators. A coordinating conjunction is a linking element. For this reason, it comes between two clauses. It cannot be placed anywhere in the sentence. It performs the following functions:

. To join two or more clauses of equal status in a sentence. The use of the coordinator generates a compound sentence in which clauses are independent. This is illustrated below:

> (1) . Ralf cleaned the car and Silvia prepared lunch.
>
>   ⇑   ⇑   ⇑
>
> clause 1 +   coordinator + clause 2 = *compound sentence*

This is a compound sentence. It consists of two main clauses joined together by the and coordinator. The clause on the left of the coordinator and is of the same status. We can analyse clauses in this sentence as shown below:

<u>Clause 1</u>		<u>Clause 2</u>		
Ralf $\Rightarrow$ subject $\Rightarrow$ s		Silvia $\Rightarrow$	subject $\Rightarrow$ s	
cleaned $\Rightarrow$ verb $\Rightarrow$ v		prepared $\Rightarrow$	verb $\Rightarrow$ v	
the car $\Rightarrow$ object $\Rightarrow$ o		lunch $\Rightarrow$	object $\Rightarrow$ o	

svo (clause 1) = svo (clause 2) are grammatical units of equal class status

Both clauses have an equal grammatical status.

We can reverse the order of clauses in this sentence without changing their meaning or the meaning of the sentence. Thus, the sentence becomes:

(2) . Silvia prepared lunch and Ralf cleaned the car.

coordinator is still between the two clauses ↵

It should be noted that *and* does not add any new information to the meaning, except that it tells us that there are two parts in the sentence. The sentence consists of two independent clauses. Since it is not a long sentence, the use of a comma between the clauses is unnecessary. If you prefer to place a comma, in accordance with the rules of punctuation for a main clause, you can do so. See $\Rightarrow$ punctuation

(3) . Anne* did the gardening and cooked a meal.

coordinator↵

---

* In this sentence, both clauses have the same subject *Anne*.

Examples 4-5 below show the use of the coordinator *but*:

(4) . Barbara likes to travel abroad (/Barbara/she)* but hates flying.

(5) . She was in the car (she)* but was unhurt.

The coordinator *but* suggests that there is an obvious contrast between the meaning of clauses on both sides of it.

( )* When two clauses have the same subject as in examples 4 and 5, there is no need to repeat the subject in the second clause. No comma is required when the linked clauses are short.

---

(6). The shop was closed **so*** I could not buy anything.

clause 1 ↵   coordinator ↵   clause 2 ↵

(7). I was tired last night **so*** I went to bed early.

clause 1 ↵   coordinator ↵   clause 2 ↵

---

* Here **so** means therefore.

So* as a conjunction is used to indicate a reason or result of some-thing. In these two examples, it is pointing to the reason given in clause 1 and the result in clause 2. In fact, it is coordinating the verb in clause 1 with the verb in clause 2. Both clauses are units of equal grammatical status. In other words: svo clause (1) = svo clause (2)

---

*   The word *so* also functions as an *adverb*.

. The coordinator *or* introduces an alternative to the meaning conveyed by the first main clause. For instance:

(8). You mustn't stay so* near the fire **or** your trousers will catch fire.

coordinator ↵

Since both clauses are of the same/similar grammatical status:

svo clause (1) = svo clause (2)

---

* *so* is functioning here as an adverb of degree.

See ⟹ adverbs

Another example of the use of *or* :

(9). You can collect it tonight *or* your son can collect it now.

⇓ coordinator ↵   ⇓

svo clause (1)   =   svo clause (2)

. Often we use coordinators in pairs in order to join:

    . units of equal status – clauses in compound sentences, and

    . words and phrases.

. When coordinators are used in pairs, they are known as
       correlative conjunctions or coordinators.
Some common correlative coordinators are:
both … and, but … also, either … or, neither … nor, whether … or
Here are some more examples:

(10). Either you will drive the car to London or we will travel by coach.

     main clause 1↵   main clause 2↵

Both clauses start with one of the pair of either ---or correlative coordinators. Main clause 2 implies an alternative to the first suggestion in main clause 1.

> (11). **Either** <u>you do the gardening</u> **or** <u>we ask someone to do it.</u>
>
> main clause 1↵   main clause 2 ↵

Examples 10 and 11 illustrate that *either* comes at the start of the first clause in a compound sentence. It is also shown that the pair of *either...or* joins clauses of similar status in a compound sentence.

. <u>In order to render negative meaning, we can use</u> *neither ... nor* <u>in phrases.</u> For instance:

> (12). **Neither** <u>the public library</u> **nor** <u>the main post office</u> were open.
>
> noun phrase ↵   noun phrase ↵
>
> (13). Due to heavy snowfall, we could turn *neither* <u>north</u> *nor* <u>south</u>.

In example 13, neither ---nor joined two single word phrases, i.e. <u>north</u> and <u>south</u>. Strictly speaking, a phrase may be a single word. <u>The pair</u> *neither ... nor* <u>does not join clauses but phrases.</u> See ⟹ phrases

Here are some examples of coordinators joining words of equal status:

> (14). Slow <u>and</u> steady.
>
> joining two words together ↵
>
> (15). fast *or* slow.
>
> coordinator ⟹ joins two words together
>
> (16). The room was narrow *yet* long.

. *Or* <u>has its negative counterpart</u> ***nor***. <u>One can use</u> ***nor*** <u>to coordinate</u> clauses providing the first clause in a compound sentence relates to a negative idea or thought. It can also coordinate words as well as phrases. For instance:

> (17). She can't dance <u>nor</u> can she speak.
>
> coordinates negative clauses↵
>
> (18). The car could not move backward <u>or</u> forward.
>
> coordinates words/phrases ↵
>
> (19). Unfortunately, he <u>neither</u> hears <u>nor</u> speaks.
>
> (20). She is <u>neither</u> rich <u>nor</u> poor.

. <u>The correlative pair of</u> *but ... also* <u>shows a mutual relationship, e.g.</u>

> (21). **Both** Jack **and** Jill are likely to be present at the wedding.

(22) . He was a great **Prime Minister,** but also the winner of the

phrase1↵   Nobel Prize for Peace.

phrase 2↵

. Subordinating Conjunctions or Subordinators

Like the coordinators, subordinating conjunctions also join parts of a sentence. They perform the following functions:

- . to link two clauses of unequal status in complex sentences
- . to introduce subordinate clauses (often adverbial clauses)
- . to link sentences - many subordinators can do so
- . to indicate the relationship between a subordinate clause and a main clause

Complex sentences have clauses of unequal status. Subordinating conjunctions such as *when, although, if, until, etc.* join subordinate clauses to a main clause in compound sentences. Therefore, they link unequal grammatical units in compound sentences. Sometimes, a subordinator can add meaning of its own to the overall meaning of a subordinate clause. A subordinating conjunction introduces a subordinate clause, which is a less important component of a compound sentence than its main clause. There are many subordinating conjunctions. There are also multi-word subordinators. These include: *so that, as long as, in order that, etc.* Some of these are listed in List 1 below:

Some Subordinating Conjunctions

after, although, as long as, as quickly as, as soon as, as if, as though, as to, assuming that, because, before, even if, even though, except, except that, excepting that, if, in case, in order to, lest, more ... than, rather ... than, provided that, since, so that, sooner than, such, such as, till, unless, until, when, whenever, where, whereas, wherever, whether ,while

List 1

. Coordinating conjunctions **and, but** and so can also be used as subordinators. The following examples illustrate the use of some main subordinators:

(1) . Our train arrived after the other train had left the platform.

main clause ↵subordinate clause introduced by the subordinator↵

Here the clause introduced by the subordinator after is an **adverbial clause**

of time. The use of the subordinator has linked two clauses in this compound sentence. Furthermore, it has established a relationship between these clauses which helps us to understand the meaning of the whole sentence. Without the subordinator, the meaning of the sentence would not be clear. The subordinator **after** has preciously enhanced the intended meaning of this sentence by indicating the time factor between the arrival of one train and the departure of the other train.

See ⇒Clauses

(2). You must have lunch with us before you leave.

subordinator indicating time ↵   ⇑

subordinate adverbial clause introduced by the subordinator - **before**

(3). She is upset as her son hasn't won the first prize.

subordinator of cause ↵   subordinate clause↵

pointing to a cause/reason

(4). He ran fast because the last bus was about to depart.

main clause ↵ subordinator↵   subordinate clause ↵

of reason

(5). Because the last bus was about to depart, he ran fast.

subordinator ↵ subordinating clause↵   main clause ↵

Here the subordinator started the sentence. It has enhanced the meaning of the sentence by expressing the reason for **running fast**. This way, it has established the relationship between the main clause and its subordinate clause.

(6). If you eat too much, you will get fat.

subordinator ↵   main clause ↵

In this example, the subordinator is indicating a condition and a predictable outcome.

(7). **If** you come late, **you will not be allowed to enter the lecture hall.**

main clause ↵

In this case, the subordinator if is indicating predictable possibility, which is given in the subordinate clause(not highlighted).

(8). **As long as** you are here we will care for you.

⇑   main clause↵

subordinator indicating condition

(9). I wouldn't travel by sea even if the passage was free of charge.

subordinator indicating condition ↵   conditional clause↵

(10). He spends his small inherited fortune **as if** it was a large fortune which could last forever.

****

The subordinator(**highlighted**) is introducing the subordinate clause and indicating comparison/contrast.

(11). He says he is penniless, **_although_** * we are sure he has
considerable savings.

In this case, the main clause comes after the subordinator(**highlighted**) because the fact is stated in it.

---

* although = though here it implies **but** or **yet**

---

(12). He works seven days a week **so that** he can payback his loans.
    subordinator indicating purpose↵   subordinate clause↵
(13). He teaches youngsters cricket <u>so that</u> they can play for the club.

subordinator indicating result/purpose ↵
(14). He ran fast *lest* he might be recognised by the policeman as the wanted man.

Here, the subordinator(**highlighted**) is indicating result – for fear that ... (negative outcome). *lest* is usually used to express fear of something.

(15). I have written to some friends in Paris <u>in order to</u> invite
    them to the wedding.   ⇑
                subordinator indicating purpose

(16). Our television works <u>except that</u> <u>the picture is poor</u>.
subordinator indicating exception ↵   ⇑
                subordinate noun clause

See ⇒ Clauses

(17). She would visit the hospital <u>except</u> she has little time to spare.
            ⇑
        subordinator indicating exception
(18). I'd prefer to walk to my hotel <u>rather than</u> travel in his car.
        subordinator indicating preference ↵
(19). You should find out <u>where</u> the car was stolen.
    subordinator indicating place ↵
(20). He travels by car <u>wherever</u> he goes for his business in Europe.
    subordinator indicating place↵

(21). We will decide soon <u>whether</u> we can buy that car from you.
subordinator indicating possibility ↵

(22) . I don't know <u>whether</u> I will be able to fly from Humberside
                Airport to Berlin.
subordinator indicating possibility/alternative

(23) . Our sales will decline <u>unless</u> we advertise our products.
⇑

subordinator indicating negative possibility

(24) . <u>Their house doesn't have a back garden</u> **unless** you call a
backyard a back garden.

In this example, the subordinator adding afterthought to the main
statement/main clause(underlined).The afterthought is introduced by
the subordinator(highlighted).

(25) . <u>You can send it by e-mail</u> <u>so that</u> <u>they can receive it immediately</u>.
sentence 1 ↵   ⇑   ⇑
subordinator linking two sentences   sentence 2

(26) . <u>Can we have lunch together?</u> <u>If</u> <u>you wait until 1 pm.</u>
sentence 1 ↵   ⇑   ⇑
subordinator linking two sentences   sentence 2

. <u>Some subordinating conjunctions also function as prepositions</u>
<u>and adverbs.</u> For instance:

(27) . I haven't seen you <u>since</u> last December.

functioning as preposition of time↵

(28) . I haven't seen you <u>since</u> you moved away .

functioning as subordinating conjunction↵

(29) . You have moved away and I haven't seen you <u>since</u>.

functioning as adverb↵

(30) . You should have asked for it <u>before</u>.

functioning as adverb↵

(31) . The matter was brought <u>before</u> the tribunal.

functioning as preposition ↵

(32) . You must do it <u>before</u> you forget.
⇑

functioning as subordinating conjunction

In summary, conjunctions are widely used in phrases, clauses and
sentences. There are ample examples of their usage in the next part of the
book.

Part 2
Analysis, Transformation and Synthesis

. Introduction

<u>**Analysis**</u> is concerned with the identification of different components in grammatical structures namely, phrases, clauses, and sentences. On the other hand, <u>**synthesis**</u> is the opposite of analysis, meaning the combination of different parts in the construction of phrases, clauses and sentences.

Knowledge of word classes lays the foundation for comprehending the English grammatical system, and seeks to help you to analyse and synthesize, i.e. construct phrases, clauses and sentences. One often finds long sentences in some official documents, newspapers and in the work of well-known writers. By means of analysis and synthesis of grammatical structures, you can appreciate and understand different types of phrases and clauses in both short and long sentences. Furthermore, it will enhance your skills of using word classes and express your thoughts more confidently. Here are two examples:

. This is my wife Anne.

You can analyse this simple sentence by dividing it into its two main parts namely, subject and predicate:

This   **is my wife Anne**.

subject↵   predicate ↵

Here the **subject is** the person about whom something is said. The **predicate** is what is said about the person.

. Over there is my wife. ⇐ simple sentence

. Her name is Anne. ⇐ simple sentence

. Over there is my wife Anne. ⇐ synthesis by transforming/combining two
                                           sentences into one sentences

By means of synthesis, you can eliminate unnecessary words and compose a new meaningful sentence. This is an example of **transformation of** two sentences into one meaningful sentence. Similarly, by transformation, one can change the sentence without changing its meaning. For instance:

. He ran too fast for me to catch.

. He ran so fast that I could not catch him. ⇐ new sentence/by transformation

The concepts of sentence, clause, phrase, subject, object and predicate are already outlined on pages 8-10. In accordance with the ideas already introduced, a sentence has a group of words that makes complete sense.

****

One method of analysing a sentence is to divide it into two main parts
namely, the subject and the predicate, For example:

(1) . <u>It</u> <u>rains</u>.
⇑   ⇑
subject predicate

(2) . <u>My sister</u> <u>lives in London</u>.
subject↵   predicate↵

(3) . <u>I saw some</u> <u>naughty boys in the park</u>.
subject↵   predicate↵

(4) . <u>A policeman</u> <u>was walking along the road</u>.
subject↵   predicate↵

(5) . <u>John and Graham</u> <u>are not in today as they are on sick leave</u>.
subject↵   predicate↵

This is the simplest way of analysing a sentence, which illustrates that the
subject may consist of one or several words. Similarly, it also indicates that
the predicate may consist of one or more words. **The subject** is usually a
noun or a group of some words, which does the work of a noun:

(6) . <u>His **mother**</u> was my aunt.
(7) . <u>That tall **building**</u> is my old school.

In examples (6) and (7), <u>**the subject**</u> consists of two or more words, of
which one word is the most important word. This word is the **subject-word**.
In these examples, the subject-words are mother and building respectively.
In the following examples, the <u>subject-words</u> are
highlighted:

(8) . <u>A divided **nation**</u> cannot win against a united nation.
subject ↵

(9) . <u>My **manager**</u> is not in the office this morning.
subject ↵

(10) . <u>In Paris, many **streets**</u> are usually washed during the day.
subject ↵

. <u>Often the subject of a sentence is modified/qualified by an **attribute**,
which may be a word, such as an adjective or a group of words, e.g.</u>

(11) . My uncle is a fairly tall person.
(12) . His attempt to cross the English Channel failed once again.
(13) . That man wearing a black jacket is also travelling with us.

We can analyse these sentences as follows:

	Subject		Predicate
	Subject-word ⇓	**Attribute** ⇓	⇓
(11)	uncle	My	is fairly tall person
(12)	English Channel	His attempt to cross	failed once again
(13)	man	That wearing a black jacket	is also travelling with us

. In fact your knowledge of word classes enables you to identify each **attribute** as follows:

. In example (11) . my – possessive pronoun's dependent form used
with nouns. Some people call it possessive
adjective.

. In example (12) . His – possessive pronoun/possessive adjective
attempt – noun – it can be used both as countable
or uncountable.
to cross – to-infinitive verb form (see page 12)

. In example (13) . that – determiner used for the noun that is not near
the speaker
wearing – gerund/ present participle form of the verb
ending in *-ing*
a- indefinite article
black – adjective
jacket – noun

You can also identify different elements in a predicate. In order to do so, you require the knowledge of word classes as well as the grasp of the structures and different types of phrases, clauses and sentences.

. **Why is it so?**

The reason for these requirements is that a predicate may be just one word as in example (1) above, or a group of words as illustrated above. This group of words may be a complex grammatical structure containing, objects, phrases, clauses in a complex sentence. The next three chapters are aimed at exploring these topics in detail with the aid of examples. The following sketch shows types of grammatical structures which are discussed in this part of the book.

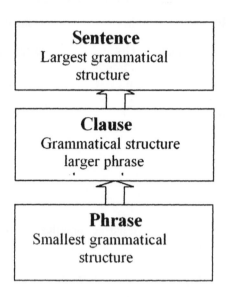

Chapter 10
Phrases

. Introduction

Strictly speaking, in grammar, a phrase may consists of one word or a
group of words. However, the word phrase means to most people a group of
words. Let's consider the following statements:

    (1) . I like her <u>smiling face</u>.
    (2) . She is <u>a religious person.</u>
    (3) . You see that girl wearing <u>a green dress</u>.
    (4) . This offer is <u>most acceptable.</u>
    (5) . He spoke <u>very abruptly</u>.
    (6) . She answered <u>rather quickly</u>.
    (7) . They <u>talked</u> to me.
    (8) . They <u>might have thought about it</u>.
    (9) . We met <u>at the airport</u>.
    (10) . I have discussed your proposal <u>with my parents</u>.

In each of the above statements, the underlined group of words is a phrase. In
fact, they are five kinds of phrases. Each type of phrase is recognised by analysing its internal structure which is discussed below.

. Types of phrases

A phrase has an internal structure. This is illustrated below:

    (11) . my ***book***
          ⇑

key word in this phrase is *book* - ***noun*** known as **headword**
      (12) . very ***old***

        headword ↵ - *old* ⟹ adjective
      (13) . may have ***gone***

          headword ↵ - *gone* ⟹ verb
     (14) . very ***slowly***

        headword↵ - *slowly* ⟹ adverb
     (15) . ***in*** the house

    headword↵ - *in* ⟹ preposition

These examples illustrate five different types of internal phrase structures. The internal structure is analysed in terms of its <u>headword</u> and its <u>modifier.</u> Let's consider another example:

(16) . <u>certainly</u> <u>nobody</u>

⇑   ⇑

1   2

$\left[1+2 = \text{phrase}\right]$

Here:

1 = adverb used to modify the pronoun nobody

2 = The headword ⇒ nobody ⇒ pronoun

In examples (1) to (10) above, we can identify each headword as follows:

Example	Phrase	Headword	word class	Modifier
(1)	smiling face	face	noun	smiling ⇒ adjective
(2)	a religious person	person	noun	religious ⇒ adjective
(3)	a green dress	dress	noun	green ⇒ adjective
(4)	most acceptable	acceptable	adjective	most ⇒ adverb
(5)	very abruptly	abruptly	adverb	very ⇒ adverb
(6)	rather quickly	quickly	adverb	rather ⇒ adverb
(7)	talked	talked	verb	
(8)	might have thought	thought	verb	
(9)	at the airport	at	preposition	
(10)	with my parents	with	preposition	

• In a phrase the headword/keyword is at its heart. If you remove the headword in a phrase, you will change its structure. Furthermore, the phrase will not contribute towards the intended sense of the statement.

• The structure of a phrase does not always end with the headword, i.e. headword at the end of the phrase. It is illustrated by the above examples. The headword can also occur at the beginning of the phrase.

• **How can you identify the type of phrase?**

As shown above, the headword is a key word, which enables us recognise the phrase type. If you know the class of the headword, you can identify any of the above types of phrases. Indeed, there are some exceptions to this rule. One exception to this rule is that a noun phrase does not always have a noun as a headword. This exception is exemplified by example (16) above. The other exceptions are discussed with examples at the appropriate place in this chapter. The following examples show each type of phrase first.

. There are five main types of phrases as follows:

        (1) . **Noun phrase**
        (2) . **Verb phrase**
        (3) . **Adverb phrase**
        (4) . **Adjective phrase**
        (5) . **Prepositional phrase**

You can identify a phrase in a sentence. A sentence may have more than one phrase. Furthermore, a phrase may contain one or more phrases within itself. Before we discuss these features, examine the following five statements, which contain five different types of phrases:

(1) . Joan likes *James as a doctor*.

        noun phrase ↵ - noun ⇒ James/doctor

(2) . Our journey *has finished*.

        verb phrase↵ - verb ⇒ has finished

(3) . He returned *quickly from the office*.

        adverb phrase ↵- adverb ⇒ quickly

(4) . I am *very pleased to see you*.

        adjective phrase↵ - adjective ⇒ very

(5) . I have been thinking *of you all day*.

        prepositional phrase ↵ - preposition ⇒ of

. <u>Noun Phrases</u>

A noun phrase has a noun or pronoun as its headword. Noun phrases occur more often than other types of phrases. They also tend to be longer and more complex. In example 1 above, the <u>modifier</u> *as a doctor* is added after the main noun *James* in order to modify/qualify it. The phrase is a noun phrase because the <u>headword </u>is a noun. In addition to this headword (noun or pronoun), a noun phrase may include:

    . <u>a determiner</u> before the headword, e.g., <u>a </u>book, <u>the</u> map,
    <u>an</u> apple, <u>this</u> computer, <u>that </u>hat, <u>these</u> chairs, <u>those</u> ladies, <u>my</u> coat.
    Determiners occur at the beginning of a noun phrase <u>only</u>.
    . <u>a modifier</u> before the headword is used to modify the noun. A
    modifier may be another noun, an adjective, a verb used adjectivally
    (in 'kitchen knife' the word kitchen is used adjectivally) or a
    participle(a word formed from a verb, ending in 'ing' e.g., seeing .
    Here are some examples:

        (6) . the <u>beautiful</u> women

adjective used as pre-modifier ↵

. When a modifier comes before the headword, it is called a *pre-modifier*.
  It is possible to have more than one modifier as illustrated below:

(7) . a <u>delicious</u> *hot* meal

pre-modifier adjective 1 ↵   ⇑

pre-modifier adjective 2

In this example, the headword ***meal*** is pre-modified by both adjectives.

(8) . a <u>British</u> <u>insurance</u> company

pre-modifier adjective ↵   ⇑

pre-modifier noun

The headword ***company*** is pre-modified by both adjectives.

. It is important to note that when the headword is pre-modified by more than one type of modifier, the pre-modifying noun comes near to the headword/noun. Therefore, 'an insurance British company' would be <u>incorrect</u>.

(9) . a <u>really</u> <u>workable</u> plan

pre-modifier adverb↵   ⇑

pre-modifier adjective

In this case, there are two pre-modifiers before the headword ***plan***. Here the noun is pre-modified by the <u>adverb </u>and the <u>adjective</u>.

. Examples 7, 8 and 9 demonstrate that you can have more than one adjective to pre-modify the headword/noun. It is also possible to have an adverb and a noun to pre-modify the headword. For instance:

(10) . <u>Indeed</u> a <u>police</u> station

pre-modifier adverb ↵   ⇑

pre-modifier noun

. **How many adjectives are permissible before the headword?**

There is no restriction on the number of adjectives which can come before the headword. However, if you use too many adjectives, their meanings may become blurred due to adjectives contrasting with each other. It is best to avoid using more than three adjectives before the headword.
For instance:

(11) . a <u>brave, dangerous, ruthless</u> **incursion**

adjective↵ adjective↵adjective↵ headword↵
headword/noun

In this case, the headword/ noun is pre-modified by three adjectives.
. A participle can pre-modify the headword:

(12) . a <u>running*</u> total

pre-modifier ↵

---

* Running is also an adjective and a noun. Running total means a total of expenses or whatever which includes each item as it occurs.

. The headword may be ***post-modified***. Post-modifiers come after the
  headword. These may prove to be more complex than pre-modifiers are.
  The reason for this complexity is that a variety of elements can function
  as a post-modifier. This is illustrated below:

(13) . a new bookshop in our shopping precinct

         1◡ 2◡   3◡   4◡

In this example: 1 = determiner   2 = pre-modifier - adjective
3 = headword/noun   4= post-modifier
The post-modifier is a prepositional phrase because in is a preposition
of place. After the headword/noun, a prepositional phrase is added to qualify
or pre-modify the headword. There can be more than one
pre-modifier:

(14) . a new bookshop in our shopping precinct which is a good idea.

  headword/noun ◡ prepositional phrase ◡   relative clause◡

Example (14) is expanded by adding a relative clause. Thus, the headword is
pre-modified by a prepositional phrase and by a relative clause.

(15) . the small shop on the corner from where I buy newspapers.

      1◡ 2◡ 3◡   4◡   5◡   6◡

1 = definite article
2 = adjective modifying the noun - shop
3 = headword – shop
4 = adverb phrase modifying the noun - shop
5 = prepositional phrase of place modifying the noun - shop
6 = clause modifying the noun - shop
. This example shows that the headword/noun can be post-modified by
  both phrases and clauses. In addition, it illustrates that several phrases
  can be joined together. This example has three phrases put together to
  make one long phrase: '*the small shop on the corner from where*'

. How big can a phrase be?

The size of a phrase is not restricted. The idea is not to make it too long. If
you do so, your reader or listener may not receive it well. As highlighted by
the diagram on page 146, the largest unit of construction is a sentence. The
second largest unit of construction is a clause. As a unit of construction, then,
the smallest unit of construction is the phrase. The fact is that phrases are
formed from words and clauses are formed from phrases. Therefore, the
clause as a unit of construction is larger than the phrase. Phrases constitute
clauses. All three constructions are units of **syntactic** -connected with grammatical rules and construction of structures.

. Possessive pronouns both proper and common can also be used as
  determiners:

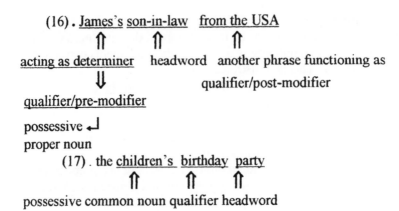

(16) . <u>James's</u> <u>son-in-law</u>   <u>from the USA</u>

acting as determiner   headword   another phrase functioning as
<u>qualifier/pre-modifier</u>   qualifier/post-modifier

possessive ↵
proper noun

(17) . the <u>children's</u> <u>birthday</u> <u>party</u>

possessive common noun qualifier headword

---

* Here the correct form is children's **not** childrens

. <u>Noun phrases can function as the **subject** of a sentence, e.g.</u>
     (18) . <u>The policeman</u> arrested the suspect.

     Noun phrase functioning as the *subject* of this sentence.
. A <u>complement</u> is an adjective or a noun which comes after a
linking/copula/copular verb. A linking/copula/copular verb all mean the
same. See ⟹ copular verbs
. <u>The noun phrase can function as a complement that is as an **object or**
object element*, e.g.</u>

     (19) . I asked <u>the traffic warden</u>.

     Noun phrase functioning as the *object* (element) of a sentence.
         (20) . He seemed <u>**to be**</u> <u>an expert in mathematics</u>.

         copula verb ↵   ⇑
         noun phrase functioning as the *object (element)* - describing
         the subject
. When the complement is a noun phrase, and the copula is 'seem' or
'look', use '*to be* 'with them in order to describe or identify the subject:
         (21) . He looks to be** <u>a perpetrator</u>.

noun phrase functioning as an *object* ↵

---

*An object or an object-word is one word, the object element has more
 than one word acting as an object.
** One can leave out '*to be*', if the noun phrase gives some other kinds
   of information instead of identifying the subject.

. A noun phrase may be followed by another noun phrase. In such cases, the purpose of a second noun phrase is to give explanatory information about the headword/noun. The second phrase is termed as 'an apposition' to the first phrase. Here are two examples:

(22) . The City of York , in north-east England, is visited by 3 million
               first phrase ↵   tourists a year.

                              second phrase↵
(23) . Gamal Abdel Nasser, once president of Egypt, nationalised the
      first phrase ↵   second phrase↵   Suez Canal.

. Verb phrases

The headword of a verb phrase is a verb. A verb phrase may have only one base verb. Here are two verb phrases. Each has only one word, which is the base/basic form of the verb given in a dictionary:

                         (1) . Go
      headword - the base form of the verb go↵
                         (2) . Run
headword - the base form of the verb run ↵

Yes, indeed, grammatically speaking one word is also a phrase.

. The headword (main verb) of a verb phrase may be one of the following forms:
        . **the base form** – arise, catch, know, show, e.g.
                (3) . I *arise* at 6 am.
                (4) . They *know* me well.
        . **the present 's' form** – writes, talks, sees, goes, loves, washes, e.g.
                (5) . Anna *writes* to me regularly.
                (6) . She *loves* both her children.
        . **present participle –ing form** - dancing, running, singing, talking, writing walking:
                (7) . We *are talking* about your success.
                (8) . She *is singing* her own song.
        . **Past participle -ed form** (both regular and irregular verbs) – driven, felt, ran, sang, striven, talked, torn, understood, written:
                (9) . I *have written* to her today.
                (10) . She *has understood* you.

. Verb tense

A verb phrase always has a verb as its head. A verb always has a tense. Therefore, it is important to understand the inter-related relationship between tenses and phrases. First, consider the following examples:

(1). Janet <u>laughs</u> a lot.

present tense ↵ - laughs –*s* form of the regular verb *laugh*

(2) . I <u>work</u> here.

present tense ↵ - work – *base* form of the regular verb *work*

(3) . I <u>proved</u> that he was wrong.

past tense ↵ - proved - *-ed form* for the irregular verb *prove*

(4). Jane <u>left</u> the office a few minutes ago.

past tense ↵ - *left* - *-ed form* for the irregular verb *leave*

These examples illustrate that verbs are used to express the time when the action of a verb takes place. Verb phrases give information not only about tenses, but also about other aspects of grammar such as voices. Verb phrases contain lexical verbs and modal verbs.

See also ⟹ Chapter 2 for Verb Related Topics

. Adverb phrases

An adverb phrase can have only a headword, which is an adverb. It may be a group of words, in which the headword is an adverb. It does not contain a finite verb. It can modify an adjective or adverb. Let's examine some examples:

(1). She walks *<u>slowly</u>*.

adverb phrase of manner *headword* ⟹ *slowly* (describes how she walks)

Here, the adverb phrase consists of only the headword. *<u>The headword or the main word is an adverb</u>*.

(2). You can enter the main library <u>through this doorway</u>.

adverb phrase of time consists of two adverbs ↵ - *through* ⟹ *adverb*

(3). He left our home <u>fairly quickly</u>.

both are adverbs↵

The adverb **fairly** is pre-modifying the other adverb **quickly** by intensifying the meaning of the adverb quickly.

See ⟹ Intensifiers

(4). We found travelling by buses in that country <u>incredibly slow</u>.

adverb phrase of time ↵

The adverb **incredibly** is pre-modifying the <u>adjective slow</u>. Thus, the pre-modifier incredibly intensifies the meaning of the adjective slow. Thus, it is functioning as an intensifier.

      (5) . This reason is not <u>really</u> <u>sufficient</u> to secure a loan.

                      ⇑   ⇑

               adverb   adjective

adverb is modifying the adjective ↵

This is an example of an adverb phrase of *degree*. An adverb of degree can be used before some adverbs and adjectives. By degree, we mean an extent, or a measure of something. In this case, the adverb *really* is used to express the actual fact or truth about something. Here, it is about the reason to secure a loan. The adverb *really* is pre-modifying the adjective *sufficient*.

      (6) . The cake is <u>quite tasty</u>.

adverb phrase of degree ↵

In this context, the adverb *quite* means somewhat, <u>to some extent</u>, not very or fairly. The adjective *tasty* is pre-modified by the adverb *quite*. In fact, *quite* is intensifying the meaning of the adjective *tasty*. It attaches to this cake's quality, a medium degree(a measure of taste). The word *delicious* is another adjective. When *quite* is used with delicious, it expresses a different meaning. For instance:

      (7) . The cake is <u>quite delicious</u>.

adverb phrase of degree ↵

In this example, the adverb *quite* is pre-modifying the adjective *delicious*. Depending on the meaning of the adjective *delicious*, the adverb quite means <u>completely to the full extent</u>.

      (8) . My son speaks German <u>fluently</u>.

              adverb of manner ↵

      (9) . You must take action <u>quickly</u>.

             adverb of manner ↵

. **<u>An adverb of manner modifies a verb.</u>**

In examples 8-9, the adverbs *fluently and quickly* are modifying the verbs *speaks* and *must take* respectively. Most adverbs of manner are formed from adjectives. Often they end with *-ly*. Of course, there are a few adverbs of manner without *-ly* endings (e.g. fast, loud). The following two examples show the use of adverbs of manner <u>without</u> *-ly* endings:

See ⇒Adverbs

      (10) . You should do your best to do it <u>right</u> next time.

               adverb of manner ↵

answering the question *how?* ↵

(11) . She often arrives *late* by train.

       adverb of manner ↵ - it answers the question *when* ?

                             - **late** or *how?* - **by train**

. It is unusual to post-modify the head adverb with an another adverb.
  For instance:

               (12) . Indeed I visit them ***sometimes***.

                   adverb of time ↵

The pre-modifier adverb **indeed** intensifies the meaning of the adverb **some-times**. This is rather formal.

. Adjective phrases

An adjective phrase may consist of only a headword, which is an adjective. It
 may be a group of words in which the headword is an adjective. An adjective phrase does not contain a finite verb. It has an adjective. These phrases
are similar to adverb phrases. Like adverb phrases, adjective phrases can also
be modified. Like an adverb phrase, sometimes, it has an adverb of degree.
Here are some examples:

         (1) . He is **brave**.

        adjective phrase

headword ⟹ adjective ⟹ *brave* - just a single word

        (2) . It is **easy to carry it**.

       adjective phrase headword ⟹ adjective ⟹ *easy*

    (3) . He is ***very intelligent***.

adjective phrase ↵ - *very* ⟹ adverb of degree before an adjective

This adjective phrase consists of one adjective and one adverb.

headword ⟹ adjective ⟹ *intelligent* is pre-modified by *very* ⟹ adverb

. When *very* is used before an adjective, it is an adverb.

       (4) . This is **good enough** for me.

       adjective phrase ↵

headword ⟹ adverb ⟹ **enough** is pre-modified by *good* ⟹ adjective

    (5) . We went to see a film, but the cinema was ***almost empty***.

                adjective phrase ↵

headword ⟹ adjective ⟹ **empty** is pre-modified by *almost* ⟹ adverb

. *Almost,* *nearly* and *practically* are adverbs of degree with similar
  meanings. For instance:

(6). The hall is **practically/nearly/almost full** with the audience.

adjective phrase ↵

headword ⟹adjective⟹ **full** is pre-modified by one of the

adverbs ⟹ *practically/nearly /almost*

(7). His financial hardship was **so unbearable** that he sold his car.

adjective phrase ↵

headword ⟹ adjective ⟹ **unbearable** is pre-modified by *so* ⟹ adverb

(8). It was ***extremely noisy*** when the police arrived at the party

adjective phrase ↵

headword⟹adjective⟹**noisy** is pre-modified by

extremely⟹ adverb of degree

. Prepositional phrases

What you have seen so far is that all four types of phrases have one thing in
common, which is a headword. Indeed, in these types of phrases the headword can stand alone. In prepositional phrases, the headword cannot stand
alone. *Why is it so?*

The headword, in a prepositional phrase, is a preposition. The headword and
the prepositional complement, together form the prepositional phrase. Without the prepositional complement, the prepositional phrase is incomplete.
Thus, the headword in a prepositional phrase cannot stand alone. Usually, the
prepositional complement is a noun phrase. The typical structure of a prepositional phrase may be represented as:

Prepositional phrase = headword + prepositional complement

preposition ↵   noun phrase↵

. A prepositional phrase may be complemented by certain types of

clauses. See ⟹ Clauses

. A preposition can be a single word or a group of words.

See ⟹ Prepositions

Here are some examples of prepositional phrases:

(1). Sarah sat next to* her husband John.

⇑   ⇑

headword/group preposition(two words) prepositional component

noun phrase ↵

---

* **next to** - meaning in a position right beside her husband John

In fact, the preposition *next to* is complemented by the noun phrase
her husband John. The prepositional phrase is 'next to her husband John'

(2) . You can walk <u>along the footpath</u>.

⇑   ⇑

Preposition + noun phrase = prepositional phrase

The preposition **along** is complemented by the noun phrase the footpath.

(3) . Rachel was walking <u>towards Tesco supermarket</u>.

⇑   ⇑

Preposition + noun phrase = prepositional phrase

(4) . Everything must be ready <u>before   this evening's seminar</u>.

Preposition↵   +   noun phrase ↵

Prepositional phrase: towards Tesco supermarket

In the following examples, prepositional phrases are shown in *italics*:

(5) . She looks nothing *like her sister*.

like(means similar) ⟹ preposition

(6) . Our house is situated *behind the church*.

(7) . He has been my best friend <u>*since* my childhood</u>.

also a conjunction and an adverb↵

(8) . I want to go out *for ten minutes*.

. A prepositional phrase can function as the complement of a verb or
adjective: For instance:

(9) . She is <u>in a rush.</u>

Prepositional phrase ↵ - complement of verb ⟹ *is*

(10) . It is big <u>*for my family.*</u>

Prepositional phrase ↵ - complement of adjective ⟹ *big*

Here are some more examples, indicating prepositional phrases in *italics*:

(11) . You do not have to be sorry *for us*.

(12) . We have spent a lot *of money*.

(13) . He was singing *on the stage*.

(14) . They were running *towards a bus stop*.

. A prepositional phrase can function as a post-modifier:

(15) . He is a <u>*heavyweight boxer*</u> <u>*of great achievements.*</u>

noun phrase↵   preposition phrase ↵

In this case, the headword *boxer* of the noun phrase *is* <u>pre-modified</u> by the
adjective **heavyweight** and <u>post-modified</u> by the prepositional phrase *of great
achievements*. In this sentence, '*of great achievements*' cannot be placed in a
different position.

(16) . There is *a nice girl* in a red uniform.

noun phrase↲ preposition phrase ↲

The headword **girl** of the noun phrase is pre-modified by the adjective *nice* and post-modified by the prepositional phrase *in a red uniform*.

. Prepositional phrases can occur in clusters in extended sentences, e.g.

(17) . There is **a girl** *in a red uniform* **with her mother**.

noun phrase↲   ⇑   ⇑

prepositional phrase   prepositional phrase

(18) . She lives in *a cottage* *with her mother in a village near Stuttgart in south Germany*.

In this example:

. a cottage ⇒ noun phrase . with her mother⇒prepositional phrase

. in a village⇒prepositional phrase

. near Stuttgart⇒ prepositional phrase

. in south Germany⇒ prepositional phrase

(19) . I saw a herd of reindeer with long antlers on a country road in Finland.

We can analyse the above sentence as follows:

Noun phrase	**verb phrase**	**prepositional phrase**
I	saw	
a herd		of reindeer
		with long antlers
		on a country road
		in Finland

In the noun phrase **a herd** , the following prepositional phrases occur:

of reindeer = *preposition + noun phrase ⇒ Prepositional phrase*

with long antlers = *preposition + noun phrase⇒ Prepositional phrase*

on a country road = *preposition + noun phrase ⇒ Prepositional phrase*

in Finland = *preposition + noun phrase⇒ Prepositional phrase*

In these prepositional phrases, you cannot change the position of any of these prepositions in their respective phrases because each preposition is the integral part of the prepositional phrase. It demonstrates that phrases can occur within a phrase.

. Sometimes, you can change the position of phrases or a phrase within the sentence without altering the meaning. For instance, we can re-write example (19)as:

.On a country road, in Finland, I saw a herd of reindeer with long antlers.
Or:

. In Finland, on a country road, I saw a herd of reindeer with long antlers

. In the phrase 'with long antlers' long antlers is described as a noun
phrase. Can it be labelled as an adjective phrase?
If you isolate the long antlers from the rest of the sentence, you can see
that the adjective 'long' is pre-modifying the noun antlers and thus it is
a noun phrase.

. **A prepositional phrase can be embedded in another:**
For instance:
  (20) . I was waiting *in* a bus shelter *opposite* a bakery *for* my wife.
                              ⇑   ⇑   ⇑
                      Prepositional   Prepositional   Prepositional
                         phrase   phrase   phrase

The following phrasal analysis in detail shows how these prepositional
phrases are embedded in one another. The headword in each phrase is highlighted.

[*in* a bus shelter *opposite* a bakery *for* my wife]⇒*prepositional phrase*

[a bus **shelter** *opposite* a bakery *for* my wife] ⇒ *noun phrase*

[*opposite* a bakery *for* my wife] ⇒ *prepositional phrase*

[a **bakery** *for* my wife]] ⇒ *noun phrase*

[*for* my wife] ⇒ *prepositional phrase*

[*my* **wife**] ⇒ *noun phrase*

(21) . You must telephone **John** *after* lunch *about* the meeting *with*
           Simon *in* my office.
In this sentence, prepositional phrases are also embedded in one another as
shown below.
The headword in each phrase is highlighted.

[**John** *after* lunch *about* the meeting *with* Simon *in* my office] ⇒*noun
phrase*

[*after* lunch *about* the meeting *with* Simon *in* my office] ⇒*prepositional
phrase*

[**lunch** *about* the meeting *with* Simon *in* my office] ⇒ *noun phrase*

[*about* the meeting *with* **Simon** *in* my office] ⇒ *prepositional phrase*

[the **meeting** *with* Simon *in* my office] ⇒ *noun phrase*

[*with* Simon *in* my office] ⇒ *prepositional phrase*

[**Simon** *in* my office] ⇒ *noun phrase*

[*in* my office] ⇒ *prepositional phrase*

[my **office**] ⇒ *noun phrase*

. **Phrases in apposition**

When in a sentence or clause, two *noun phrases* come one after the other and both refer to the same thing, then phrases are in apposition. In the following examples, phrases in apposition are shown in *bold*.

(1) . Most tourists in London visit *Buckingham Palace, the London Office of the Queen*.

(2) . She has shown me a letter from her *English tutor, a university lecturer*.

. **Sometimes, the second phrase is used to place emphasis on the adjacent noun phrase**. For instance:

(3) . You must visit *Windsor Castle, The Queen's residence near London*.

  placing an emphasis on the adjacent noun phrase   ↵

(4) . *Nelson Mandela, the most famous African leader*, was imprisoned

emphasizing the meaning of the first phrase ↵   for 27 years.

In examples 3-4 each second phrase is giving additional information about its adjacent noun phrase. In these cases, a comma is needed to separate adjacent phrases.

. **When the purpose of the second noun phrase is to identify the first one, there is no need for a comma to separate them**. Here are two examples:

(5) . *Prince Charles the Prince of Wales* is heir-apparent to the throne.
  ⇑   ⇑
first noun phrase   second noun phrase

(6) . What today's newspapers have revealed about *Mr John Major a famous politician* is disgusting. (identifying phrase is underlined)

. **Coordination of phrases**

Coordinating and subordinating conjunctions are discussed under conjunctions. In grammar, coordination means joining together two elements of the same status. These two elements can be phrases or clauses. The coordination is achieved by using coordinating conjunctions. Let us examine the following sentences:

(1) . We visited Frankfurt city *and* Stuttgart city on the same day.
      noun phrase↵   ⇑   noun phrase↵
            coordinating conjunction

(2) . She likes to eat soup made from *fresh cauliflower* **and** *fresh cabbage*.

(3) . Anne can write *in German or in English.*

    (4) . He *cleaned and polished* his shoes.

verb phrases coordinated ↵ - coordinating conjunction ⇒*and*

. <u>You can join other types of phrases as well.</u>
  Here are some examples:

      (5) . We drove in heavy snowfall *slowly and safely.*

        adverb phrases coordinated ↵

      (6) . He was *successful and happy.*

     adjective phrases coordinated ↵

(7) . He was sitting *in the waiting room in Thomas Hospital.*

      prepositional phrases coordinated ↵

Both coordination and apposition help us in explaining the meaning by merging words, that is using fewer words. For instance: the above example without the apposition might have been written or uttered as:

    He was sitting in the waiting room and he was in Thomas Hospital.

In summary, in the grammatical structures, phrases are the smallest structures. We can analyse a phrase in terms of the headword and its modifier(s).

Chapter 11
Clauses

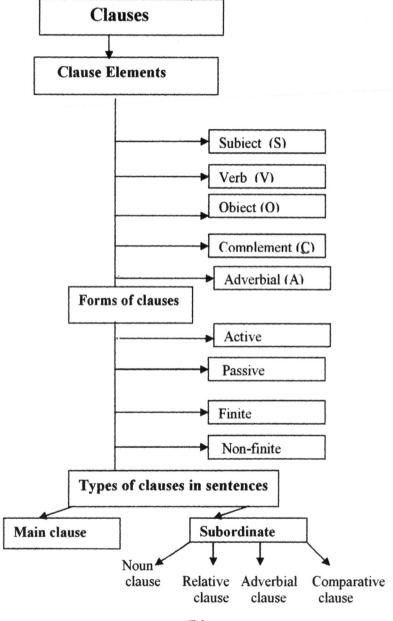

Clauses

↓

Clause Elements

- Subject (S)
- Verb (V)
- Object (O)
- Complement (C)
- Adverbial (A)

Forms of clauses

- Active
- Passive
- Finite
- Non-finite

Types of clauses in sentences

- Main clause
- Subordinate
  - Noun clause
  - Relative clause
  - Adverbial clause
  - Comparative clause

Diagram 1

. Introduction

A **clause** consists of some words that include a subject and a verb. It is in its own right a sentence. It can also be a part of a sentence. A **sentence** may consist of just one clause, or it may have two or more clauses. It may be a simple, compound or complex sentence. A **simple sentence** has at least one clause. **Compound** and **complex sentences** consist of a number of clauses. Both clauses and sentences have their own particular internal structures. Diagram1 gives a summary of the topics which are discussed in this chapter in order to understand the structures, types and functions of clauses and sentences. Sentences are discussed in the next chapter.

. A clause or a sentence

Let's examine first some clauses:

(1) . Wolfgang went home.

subject ↵   ⇑   ⇑

finite verb object ⇒noun

(2) . Annemarie has written a letter.

subject ↵   ⇑   ⇑

verb group   object ⇒noun phrase

Both examples make sense without any further information added. Each example includes a *subject* and a *verb.* In fact, these are two clauses as well as two sentences. If the structure of a sentence can not be broken down into smaller sentences, than the sentence is a *simple sentence*. A simple sentence has only one verb or verb group. The above sentences can not be broken down into smaller sentences because they are simple sentences.

Both verbs in these examples are finite and active. The meaning or action (something changing or happening) of each verb is indicated by the non phrase. These clauses do not require any further information to be grammatically complete. These clauses can stand alone. Any clause which can stand alone is *a main clause.* Since a main clause makes sense without the aid of any further information or clause, and is grammatically complete, it is also known as an *independent clause*. In terms of grammar, it makes syntactical sense on its own. Here are some more examples of main clauses. *The verb is shown in italics in each clause*:

(3) . Karen *telephoned.*
(4) . Mr. Taylor *will come.*
(5) . The Prime Minister *has arrived.*
(6) . Our guests *have left.*

. A simple sentence must have one subject element and one verb element. The structure of the following examples is based on the subject (abbreviated as **S**) followed by the verb (abbreviated as **V**). *SV is the minimum clause structure*. Clause structures and elements are discussed later.

(7) . I opened the door *and* Anne entered the room.

main clause 1⏎   conjunction⏎   main clause 2⏎

⇑   ⇑

the door is a noun phrase   **the room** is a noun phrase

. Example 7 consists of two main clauses joined together by a conjunction *and* to form one sentence. We use '*and*', '*or*', or '*but*' as *coordinating conjunctions* to join main clauses, which have the same status in a sentence, i.e. SV = SV.

. This is, in fact, a *compound sentence*. Unlike a simple sentence, a compound sentence can be broken down into smaller sentences or clauses. Example 7 meets this criterion.

. In this sentence, both clauses can stand alone. It implies that the meaning of the verb in each clause is completed by its respective noun phrase. Thus, both clauses are main clauses.

. If we change Example 7 to read as in Example 8:

(8) . *When I opened the door,* Anne entered the room.

clause 1⏎   clause 2⏎

This sentence still has two clauses. Clause 1 begins with a *subordinating conjunction*, '*when*'. This clause is now dependent on clause 2 (⇒ main clause) in order to make syntactical (grammatical) sense. Therefore, any such clause is a *dependent clause.* The function of a dependent clause is to support the main clause as its subordinate. This is why it is also known as a *subordinate or sub clause*. A *complex sentence* can have a number of clauses. One clause must be a subordinate clause. Example 8 shows a complex sentence, as it has both main and subordinate clauses. See ⇒Sentences.   See ⇒subordinate clauses.

. Typical clause structure

Now examine the structure of the following declarative statement:

(9) . Robin Taylor *has made* a big profit.

noun phrase⏎ verb phrase ⏎ noun phrase⏎

⇑   ⇑   ⇑

subject   finite and active verb   *object* = verb complement

We can also analyse this structure as:

. verb is preceded by the subject ⇒Robin Taylor
. the essence or the action of the verb is given by the verb

complement - noun phrase ⇒ a big profit
. this statement makes a declaration about the subject's action, that is giving information about the subject
. all three structural elements (subject phrase, verb phrase and verb complementation) are core or *obligatory elements*
. the removal of any of these obligatory elements would make this clause syntactically incomplete.

This example typifies the structure of clauses. Since this structure relates to a declarative statement, it is known as a *__declarative structure__*. In this example, the verb complement is an object (abbreviated as **O**), *a big profit* The object follows the verb element. The clause structure displayed by this example is an **SVO**. It is widely used in English.

. Indeed, you can add information to the SVO structure by adding some non-obligatory items. For instance, we can re-write the above example as:

(10) . *Most certainly*, Robin Taylor has made a big profit *by selling shire horses*.

Here, the information in *italics* is adverbial. The adverbial elements usually provide detailed information. This is not essential as, without it, the clause is syntactically complete.

.Clause elements

Clauses are constructed by combining certain clause elements. There are five clause elements, each of which has a particular function and renders a specific meaning. These clause elements are listed below with their abbreviations in brackets:

. Subject   (S)
. Verb   (V)
. Object   (O)
. Complement (C)
. Adverbial   (A)

A clause may have some or all of these elements. All clauses contain subject and verb elements. Furthermore, the meaning of the verb has to be complete. For this reason, the verb element is followed by an object or complement. Usually, the object and complement elements follow the SV in a clause. There may be some adverbial elements.

. Subject element

The subject usually comes in the *subject position* which is usually before the verb element. The following examples illustrate the position of the subject and other elements in clauses:

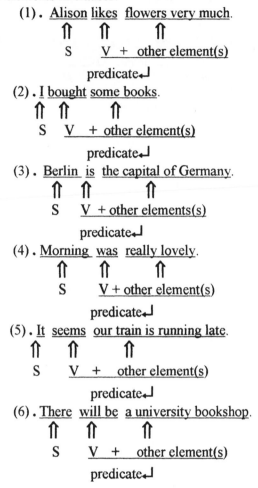

(1). Alison likes flowers very much.

⇑   ⇑   ⇑

S   V + other element(s)

predicate⌐

(2). I bought some books.

⇑ ⇑   ⇑

S   V + other element(s)

predicate⌐

(3). Berlin is the capital of Germany.

⇑ ⇑   ⇑

S   V + other elements(s)

predicate⌐

(4). Morning was really lovely.

⇑   ⇑   ⇑

S   V + other element(s)

predicate⌐

(5). It seems our train is running late.

⇑   ⇑   ⇑

S   V +   other element(s)

predicate⌐

(6). There will be a university bookshop.

⇑   ⇑   ⇑

S   V +   other element(s)

predicate⌐

. All the above examples show that the subject controls the verb in terms of singular or plural form.

. Examples (1) - (4) illustrate that normally the subject element is a *noun phrase*.

. Examples (5) and (6) indicate that in the subject position, sometimes, there can be *it* or ***there***. In fact, these words do not relate to any specific thing. When *it* or ***there*** is used in the subject position, it is called an *empty subject* or a ***dummy subject***. Let's re-write example (6) as:

A university bookshop will be there.

No doubt, this is a possible construction. Therefore:

. There will be a university bookshop = *A university bookshop will be there.*

Usually, a phrase that contains some new information begins with *a* or *an* as in this case. Normally, such a phrase does not start a sentence. It is the dummy or the empty subject, which starts the sentence.

. When the verb *be* is followed by *some* , *a*, or *an*, it is not preceded by a real subject. In such a case, an empty subject *"there"* is placed in the subject position. This is the reason for starting the phrase with an empty subject *there*. Similarly, we can re-write example (5) as:

Our train seems to be running late.

Thus:

It seems our train is running late. = *Our train seems to be running late.*

The re-written clause is not so usual. It is preferable to begin the phrase with an empty subject *it*. The following examples also demonstrate the use of an empty subject:

(7) . *It* was a cold night.

('a cold night it was' - unusual construction)

(8) . *There* is a bank round the corner.

('a bank is round the corner'- unusual)

. The verb is controlled by the subject. The following examples illustrate this rule:

(9) . She is a cook.

3rd person singular⏎ ⇑

    subject   singular verb

(10) . We are listening.

1st person plural subject ⏎ ⇑

           plural verb

(11) . They are at home.

3rd person plural⏎   ⇑

    subject   plural verb

(12) . I am going to Austria.

1st person singular subject ⏎ ⇑

  subject   singular verb (group verb – two words)

(13) . You are working very hard.

2nd person singular⏎   ⇑

  subject   plural verb (group verb – two words)

(14) . You were wrong at that time.

2nd person plural ⏎   ⇑

   subject   plural verb

Both second person singular and second person plural take the plural form of the verb.

. The subject of a clause is an important element. Indeed, it can be said that it is the subject which gives the clause its theme or topic.

. In examples (1) to (6), you can see that *V+ other element(s)* are marked as *predicate*.

The predicate is a traditional grammatical term for verb and any other element(s) that follow the verb. Traditionally, the clause was divided into two parts, namely the subject and the predicate. Here is another example:

(15) . Denmark *is a small country*.

theme of this clause subject ↵   ⇑

              information about the theme or the subject ⇒ *predicate*

. In summary, the predicate includes all other elements except the subject element of a clause.

.Verb element

The verb element is considered as the focal point of the clause. Let's first examine the following examples:

(1) . A guest *has written* to the hotel manager.

subject ↵   ⇑

          verb element⇒*verb phrase* (auxiliary verb + transitive verb)

. A guest is the topic

. *has written* to the hotel manager - this is the information about the

subject which the writer/speaker wants to say ⇒*predicate*

(2) . She *walks*.

      verb element ↵ - *verb phrase*

Here the verb *walks* is intransitive, the predicate ends at walks.

walks ⇒*predicate*

(3) . Romania *is* a country in Europe.

      verb element↵ - *verb phrase* (copular/linking verb)

Here *is* a country in Europe ⇒*predicate* what the writer/speaker wants to say about Romania

If you remove the verb phrase, the clause will not make any sense. Furthermore, it will be grammatically incomplete. As the subject sets the theme, there must be something about it. It is the verb in the form of a verb phrase which tells us about the action or the state relating to the subject. It is suggested that you browse the chapters on verbs and phrases, where you can see more relevant information on the verb element.

. Object element

The object element comes after the verb in a clause. Here are some examples:

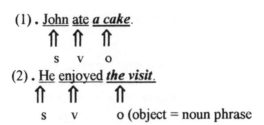

(1) . John ate *a cake*.

⇑ ⇑ ⇑

S   V   O

(2) . He enjoyed *the visit*.

⇑ ⇑   ⇑

S   V   O (object = noun phrase

. In these examples verbs are transitive. The transitive verb takes an objective. Here are some more examples in which the verbs are also transitive:

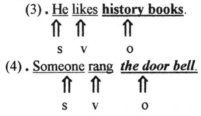

(3) . He likes **history books**.

⇑ ⇑   ⇑

S   V   O

(4) . Someone rang *the door bell*.

⇑ ⇑   ⇑

S   V   O

. **A clause can have two objects with some verbs as illustrated below:**

(5) . Mary gave *[to]*Margaret some seeds.

object 1 - indirect object ↵   ⇑

object 2 - direct object

In this case, the action of the verb *gave [to]* directly affects *some seeds (primary effect)* as these were given to Margaret. Margaret is also indirectly affected *(secondary effect)* by the action of the verb as she received *some seeds*. Also note:

Margaret ⇒noun   *some seeds* ⇒ noun phrase

(6) . Alex has written a letter to his mother-in-law.

object 1 – *direct object* ↵   ⇑

object 2 – *indirect object*

. It should be noted that both objects are noun phrases but 'to his mother-in-law' is *a* **Prepositional phrase**. (Remember that a phrase can be just one word.)

(7) . I bought some perfume for my wife.

object 1 - *direct object* ↵   ⇑

object 2 – *indirect object* -
'*for my wife*' is a *Prepositional phrase*

Both objects are noun phrases. The primary effect of the verb *bought* is on perfume. For this reason it is the first object. Of course, the second object is also affected to the extent that the perfume is for my wife. Thus, the secondary effect of the verb *bought* is on the second object.

. **As shown above, the object is usually a noun phrase. Sometimes a clause functions as an object.**

        (8) . No one believed that *he was alive*.

    finite clause functioning as an object ↲

        (9) . We look forward *to our weekend in Prague*.

      finite clause functioning as an object ↲

. **In a clause, an object can be either *direct* or *indirect*. The difference between the direct and indirect object is that:**

      . the primary effect of the verb is on the direct object

      . the secondary effect of the verb is on the indirect object

      . the indirect object can be preceded by *to* or *for*

      (by converting a noun phrase into a prepositional phrase as in examples 6-7)

. Complement element

A complement is a word or a group of words in a clause or a sentence. It is used after

    . linking (copular) verbs and

    . some transitive verbs, which take *an object* and *object complement*.

Often in constructing a clause or a sentence, a complement is an essential grammatical requirement. A complement which follows a linking verb is known as ***subject complement***. A complement which comes after a transitive verb and an object is called ***object complement***. For instance:

      (1) . It <u>looks</u> <u>very pretty</u>.

  copular verb↲   ⇑

         subject complement – tells us more about the subject - *it*

      (2) . The head teacher <u>presented</u> <u>Jane</u> <u>with a medal</u>.

       transitive verb ↲   ⇑   ⇑

              object   object complement

. **A complement may be an adjective, noun or adverbial.**

Here are some examples:

      (3) . Adam seemed to be *a very good person*.

    noun phrase type complement↲

        (4) . Morris was *angry*.

    adjective type complement ↲

          (5) . He is *in a real mess*.

    prepositional phrase - complement ↲

      (6) . Sara appears *very patient*.

complement - adjective phrase↲

In examples (3) to (6), the complement refers to the subject of the clause (Adam, Morris, he and Sara). <u>Without the complement, the linking or copular verb cannot function in a clause.</u>

When the complement relates to the subject of the clause, it is also known as the *subject predicative*, which is the <u>***subject complement***</u> . The linking or copular verbs are useful for describing the subject's attributes such as *patient (attribute)* or *state* in which one finds oneself, i.e. *in a real mess*.

The weakness of linking verbs is that they cannot take an object and object complement. Furthermore, a clause containing a linking verb cannot be turned into a <u>passive clause</u>. However, the most used copula/copular verb *be* can be utilised to denote the association between the object and <u>***the object complement***</u>. The object complement is also known as <u>***the object predicative.***</u> This is exemplified below:

(7) . <u>Our guests</u> <u>made</u> <u>my mother</u> <u>very happy</u>.

    subject↵   ⇑   ⇑   ⇑

              verb   object   <u>object complement</u>
                                   <u>or object predicative</u>

                  adjective phrase type↵

Since *very happy* is an adjective phrase, the object complement is considered as the adjective phrase type. In this case, the complement is <u>related to the object</u> instead of the subject. For this reason it is the <u>***object complement***</u> or <u>***object predicative***</u>. Here are some examples of object complement (object is in **bold**):

    (8) . Students Union elected **her** *treasurer.*
             object complement - noun ↵
    (9) . The chairman has declared **the meeting** <u>open</u>.
                object complement – object ↵
    (10) . They consider **their captain** <u>as</u> *the best team leader.*
         object complement = as + noun phrase ↵
    (11) . The Lottery money helped **me** *to retire from work*.
                 object complement ↵ – noun-finite clause with
                           to-infinitive
    (12) . Our trainer kept **us** *practising for another hour*.
              object complement ↵ – noun-finite clause with
                      -ing participle
    (13) . John helped **Dolly** <u>solve this puzzle</u>.
            object complement ↵ - non- infinitive clause with
                     bare infinitive

. Adverbial element

The adverbial element is often an adverb phrase or prepositional phrase. It functions as an adverb. A clause can also function as adverbial. An adverbial element can occur anywhere in a clause. The following examples illustrate the adverbial element in clauses:

     (1) . Anne works *very hard.*

         adverbial ↲ - an adverb phrase functioning as adverbial
    (2) . *Currently,* my boss is away in London.

   adverbial ↲ - an adverb phrase functioning as adverbial
    (3) . At present, he is having a shower.

   adverbial ↲ - prepositional phrase acting as adverbial
    (4) . My wife will not return from Russia *until* tomorrow.

         prepositional phrase acting as adverbial
    (5) . I am not *against* his brilliant idea.

     adverbial ↲ - prepositional phrase acting as adverbial
   (6) . He talked slowly *because of* his recent illness.

   prepositional phrase functioning as adverbial

. Adverbial elements are often optional. For instance, examples (2) and
  (3) can still make sense without any adverbial element. These examples
  will also be grammatically complete without adverbs.

. An adverbial element may not contain an adverb, but it still functions
  like an adverb. For instance:

     (7) . Adam is in London *to visit his sister.*

       non-finite verb phrase ↲ ⟹ *to-infinitive*
Example (7) answers the following adverbial questions:

     (8) . *Where* is Adam ? - Adam is in London.

     adverb↲
     (9) . *Why* is Adam in London? - to visit his sister

     adverb↲
Example (7) does not have any adverb. Since it answers adverbial questions, it contains an adverbial element. This is the reason for calling the adverbial element by this name.

. Forms of clauses

There are four different forms of clauses based on the verb used in each form of clause. Their specific features are listed below in Table 1, so that they can be compared at a glance.

Forms of Clauses

Finite

. It has a finite verb, which is marked for tense.

. The subject precedes the verb.

. The subject may be left out in order to avoid repetition.

Non -Finite

. It has a non-finite verb.

. The verb is to-infinitive or bare infinitive, present participle –**ing** form, and past participle –**ed** form.

. Usually, it is a part of the finite clause.

. By itself it does not seem grammatically correct.

. It may not include a subject

. All verbs except modal auxiliaries have non- finite forms.

Active

. It has an active verb form which shows the agent's activity, i.e. doing something/something happening.

. Agent is the subject

. It is extensively used as it is the typical voice in both spoken and written English

----

Passive

. It has a passive verb form indicating something is done to the agent/ subject.

. A statement with a transitive verb can be converted to a passive clause.

. It sounds rather formal.

Table1

. Here are some examples of **finite clauses**:

(1) . Daniel ***works*** for our company.

finite verb ↵ – present tense

(2) . Adam ***is walking*** towards Hyde Park.

finite verb↵ – present continuous tense

(3) **.** He is very pleased *that everything has worked well*.

main clause↵   subordinate clause with a finite verb↵
with a finite verb

. You can see that all three above examples contain subjects . In fact,
  often a finite clause has no subject as illustrated below:

(4) **.** Sylvia corresponds with us and **_(she)_** visits us regularly.

finite clause ↵   you can leave it out ↵   finite clause ↵
also main clause   also subordinate clause

This sentence has two clauses: namely main and subordinate. These are discussed later. Both clauses have finite verbs. Here are two more examples of
finite clauses *(in italic bold style)* without subjects:

(5) **.** She is very busy at work and *cannot go out with you*.

(6) **.** The weather was terrible and *caused some train cancellations*.

. <u>Non-finite clauses</u>:

(1). **We went to Agra** *to see* *the Taj Mahal*.

to-infinitive verb form↵

object

In the structure of this sentence, the main clause is shown in **bold style**. The
subordinate clause has a "*to-infinitive verb*", which is not marked for tense.
Thus, it is a non-finite clause. It is without the subject.

. In this sentence, when you read the non-finite clause only, you can see
  that by itself it does not seem grammatically correct. For this reason, the
  non-finite clause is usually a part of a sentence which also has a finite
  clause. In this sentence, "we went to Agra" is a finite clause, because it
  has a finite verb *went* – past tense form of the verb *go*.

(2). **The plan was** *to take* *a night train*.

to-infinitive verb form↵

object

The non-finite clause *(in italics)* is without the subject.

(3) **.** He eats *a variety of vegetables* *to reduce* *his weight*.

subject of the non-finite clause↵ non-finite verb ↵   ⇑

object of the non-finite clause

In this example, the non-finite clause *(in italics)* has a subject.

(4) **.** Antonia wanted *Ivan* *to marry her.*

subject of non-finite clause ↵   ⇑   ⇑

non-finite verb object of the non-finite clause

In Examples 3 and 4, each non-finite clause *(in italics)* has its subject.

(5) . Jane assisted _John_ _to develop_ _a CV_.

subject of non-finite clause ⤶to- infinitive⤶ ⇑
                      verb   object of the
                                     non-finite clause

(6) . We wanted _to eat_ _the Indian food_.

to- infinitive verb ⤶   ⇑
              object of the non-finite clause

In Example 6, the non-finite clause _(in italics)_ is without the subject.

. Active and passive clauses

Here are some examples of **active clauses**:

(1) . Frank _is driving_ the car.

agent ⤶   ⇑
         active verb - agent doing something / activity

Therefore, it is an _active clause_ with present continuous tense. The active clause structure is considered as the primary structure. From it, the structure of the passive clause is derived as:

(2) . The car _is being driven_ * by Frank.

agent ⤶   ⇑   ⇑
         something is   adverbial element (optional information)
         done to the agent

---

*   (2 A) . The car _is being driven_.

passive clause grammatically complete ⤶

. A comparison between examples (1) and (2) reveals that the object in example (1) is now in the subject position in example (2) - the passive clause.

. The verb phrase, "_is driving_" in example (1) has been modified to be come, "_is being driven_" in example (2).

The reason for doing so is that the verb phrase in the active clause indicates the present continuous tense. The passive clause must also express the present continuous tense by using the passive verb form:

is being _driven_

present continuous form of the verb _be_⤶   ⇑
                                  passive participle

. In example 2, the agent, _Frank_ is preceded by the adverb _by_. Thus, _by Frank_ is the adverbial element added to the passive clause. It is an optional piece of information.

. The adverbial element is not necessary as without it, the passive clause "The car _is being driven_." is grammatically complete, as in example (2A).

. In Examples 2 and 2A, since the agent *(= the car)* is receiving the action *(=affected)*, it is the same passive clause expressing present continuous tense. Here are some examples of both active and corresponding passive clauses:

(3) . She loved her children. ⇐ *active clause*

(4) . Her children were loved (by her). ⇐ *passive clause*

(5) . They ***should count*** the money. ⇐ *active clause*
⇑
        modal + infinitive = active verb

(6) . The money ***should be counted***. ⇐ *passive clause*
⇑
        modal+ infinitive = active verb

(7) . We admire your sincere desire ***to help*** the aged. ⇐ *active clause*
        active/ to-infinitive verb↵

(8) . Your sincere desire ***to help*** the aged is admired (by us).
⇑
    active to-infinitive converted to passive to- infinitive

(9) . There is something ***to do*** this afternoon. ⇐ *active clause*
    active to-infinitive↵

(10) . There is something ***to be done*** this afternoon. ⇐ *passive clause*
⇑
    active to-infinitive changed to passive infinitive

(11) . They left without ***eating*** their lunch. ⇐ *active clause*
    active gerund↵

(12) . They left without the lunch ***being eaten***. ⇐ *passive clause*
⇑
    active gerund converted to passive gerund

. Types of subordinate clauses
A subordinate clause supports the main clause. Subordinate clauses are categorized as:

      . Noun or Nominal Clauses
      . Relative Clauses
      . Adverbial Clauses
      . Comparative Clauses

This categorization is based on the function of clauses in relation to the main clause. When a subordinate clause is linked to the rest of the sentence, it performs its specific function as discussed here.

. Noun or nominal clauses

A noun clause can act as an object, subject or complement of the main clause. You will see that a noun clause functions in the same manner as a noun phrase does. Usually, a noun phrase commences with *that*, *if* or with a *wh-question* word such as *what*. It can also come after a <u>preposition, adjective</u> or a <u>noun</u>. The following examples illustrate their characteristics:

(1). <u>We believe</u> *that the business will grow*.
⇑   ⇑

main clause   noun clause acting as an object

(2). <u>The teacher didn't think</u> *that she was an able girl.*
⇑   ⇑

main clause   noun clause acting as an object

. Without *that* the above clauses will still convey the same meaning and are grammatically correct.

Examples(1) and(2)

The following comparison illustrates the similarities between noun phrases and noun clauses:

. the business ⇒ noun phrase   . the business will grow ⇒ noun clause

. she ⇒ noun phrase (grammatically: just one word can be a phrase)

. She was an able girl ⇒ noun clause

Here are some more examples of a noun clause acting as an object:

(3). We were thinking *whether you would come.*

noun clause acting as an object ↵

(4). I wonder *if you would stay with us*.

noun clause acting as an object ↵

(5). We told <u>the police</u> *that we were strangers in London*.
⇑   ⇑

direct object – noun phrase   indirect object – noun clause

It demonstrates that a noun clause can be an indirect object.

. <u>The following examples demonstrate that a clause can function as a subject:</u>

(6). ***Whether* I'll be able to attend a meeting*** depends on the transport.

noun clause acting as subject ↵

---

*When a noun clause is the subject, it does not start with *if*.

(7) . _That my son returned from the war_ was the most memorable day.

noun clause acting as subject ↵

(8) . _What you say_ is nonsense.

noun clause - subject ↵

• A _wh- question_ word begins a question with any of the nine question words: _what, when, where, which, who, whom, whose, how_ and _why_.

(9) . _Who_ can come with me?

noun clause begin with _wh-question*_ word

**Possible answer** ⇒ _Someone can come with me._

declarative sentence/statement*↵

---

*If the word order in an interrogative sentence is the same as in a declarative sentence/statement as shown above then there is _no inversion_ (change) of the normal word order in the wh-question.

• Here are some examples of noun clauses when a noun clause can function as a complement of the main clause.

(10) . Our problem is _how we are going to reach the airport on time by public transport._

noun clause acting as the complement of the main clause

(11) . The fact is _that they are happily married._

complement of the main clause _the fact is_ ↵

• The following examples illustrate that noun clauses can come after some adjectives and nouns.

(12) . I am _afraid_ that I shan't see you tonight.

adjective ↵   noun clause ↵

(13) . I am _confident_ that she will soon recover from her illness.

adjective↵   noun clause↵

(14) . I am _glad_ _that Joan has returned home safely._

adjective↵   noun clause↵

• You can leave out _**that**_ in the above examples and similar cases, but after some nouns such as shown below '**that**' usually begins a noun clause:

(15) . Your _belief_ that she is rich is only imagination.

noun ↵   noun clause ↵ - **do not leave out** ⇒ _that_

(16) . What gave you the _idea_ that Rachel is abroad?

noun ↵ noun clause ↵ -**do not leave out** ⇒ _that_

(17) . The <u>news</u> <u>that he is already married has shocked Monica</u>.

noun ↵   noun clause ↵ - **do not leave out** ⟹ *that*

In examples (15) – (17) *that –clause* comes after a noun which relates to
a thought or speech. In such cases, 'that' begins *'that-clause'*.
. <u>A noun clause can occur after a preposition as illustrated by the
following examples.</u>

(18) . Our jobs depend <u>*on*</u> <u>what management decide(s)* today</u>.

preposition ↵   noun clause ↵

---

* The word management is a countable group noun. It can be singular
   or plural.

---

(19) . We were amazed <u>(*at**)</u> <u>how colourful and bright the</u>

preposition↵   <u>Christmas lights were.</u>

noun clause ↵

---

* You can also say *by* instead of *at* or no preposition at all.

. <u>Relative clauses</u>

A clause introduced by any of the relative pronouns or a relative phrase,
which refers to an earlier noun or a noun phrase, is a relative clause. It acts as
a post-modifier of the noun or the noun phrase. For instance:

(1) .   The lady **who** *bought some tea bags* is my aunt.

relative clause↵ - post-modifying the noun phrase - *the lady*

. The word *who* is **a relative pronoun** which joins the relative clause to
the **main clause** *the lady is my aunt*. The noun or the noun phrase
which is post-modified (or refers back) is called the *<u>antecedent of the
relative clause</u>*. Here, *the lady* is the **antecedent**.

(2) . The cricket team* *<u>who were in red outfits</u>* won the game.

relative clause ↵

The relative pronoun *<u>who</u>* links the relative clause to the main clause - *the
cricket team won the game*.

---

* You may think that the word team is not a person. On the contrary, it
   consists of persons. It is a countable group noun, which can agree with
   a singular or plural verb.

. In examples (1) and (2), there is no need to place a comma before and
after the relative clause. The reason for omitting commas is that both
relative clauses are acting as **identifying clauses**– identifying nouns

in each clause. The purpose of the information given by an identifying clause is to identify the earlier noun in the main clause. The following examples illustrate this rule as well:

(3) . The footballer *who had short blonde hair* was not from Denmark.

relative clause ↵ - *who* ⟹ *relative pronoun (linkage)*

Here, the head word *footballer* in the main clause is post-modified by the relative clause. The relative clause is telling us which footballer we mean.

(4) . The lady *who is wearing a white dress* is married to our mayor.

relative clause ↵ - *who* ⟹ *relative pronoun*

. The pronoun *whose* denotes possessive meaning. In the following examples, it begins relative clauses, which are functioning as identifying clauses:

(5) . Our neighbours *whose daughter lives in Spain* have gone to Spain

⇑   for a week.

relative clause - functioning as identifying clause

(6) . Some motorists *whose vehicles were damaged by the crowd*

complained to the police.   ⇑

relative clause - identifying which motorists (some)

(7) . Wolfgang *whose car is a black BMW with an open roof*

is a German insurance expert.   relative clause ↵

It informs us which Wolfgang is being talked about.

. When a relative clause functions as an identifying clause, the determiner 'the' is usually placed before the noun instead of a possessive pronoun, i.e. 'my', 'your', 'her', etc. For instance:

(8) . James is driving **the** car **that he bought from me**.

determiner preferred ↵   relative clause ↵

that relative pronoun refers to **car**↵

Here, the head word *car* in the main clause is post-modified by the relative clause.

(9) . She liked ***the*** car *that she bought last year*.

determiner preferred ↵

⇑

relative clause functioning as identifying clause

(10) . I went to ***the*** cottage *that I inherited last year*.

determiner preferred ↵   ⇑

relative clause used as identifying clause

(11) . I went to ***my**** cottage *that I inherited last year*.

> * In this context, it implies which cottage. Replace it with **the**.

. The relative pronouns *who* and *that* are used for both things and people
as shown above. On the other hand, the relative pronouns *which* and
that are usually used for things and ideas. Here are some examples:

(12) . Flats *which/that* overlook the sea cost a great deal more.

relative clause ↵ - you can use *which* or *that*

(13) . She doesn't know much about the job *which/that has been
                                                      offered to her*.

(14) . It was a dream *which/ that never came true*.

You can see that the pronoun *that* can be used with any noun.

. A relative clause also functions as *a classifying clause*. The idea of
classifying is to describe the head noun in the main clause by its nature,
types or class. Classifying clauses *do not* have commas around them.
The following examples illustrate this rule:

(15) . Anne does not want **customers** *who waste her business time*.

head word/noun ↵   relative clause ↵

Here, the purpose of the relative clause is to say what type of customers.

(16) . They were asking for the **shopping centre** *that has a car park in*

head noun ↵   *front of it.*

relative clause classifying the head noun ↵

(17) . We need some young persons **who** *can do some community work
                                                      once a week*.

relative/ classifying clause ↵

(18) . Motorists **who** *have caused fatal accidents* should be banned from

relative/ classifying clause ↵   driving.

. A relative clause can function as *an adding (or identifying/
non-restrictive)clause*. An adding clause provides some additional
information about the head word in the main clause. The relative clause
is separated from the main clause by a commas(s)*.

> * The punctuation rules regarding the use of comma with subordinate
>   clauses are not universally the same rules.

The following examples of relative clauses exemplify how they can function
as adding clauses:

(19) . **Buda,** **which** *is a part of Budapest in Hungary*, has many
            historical buildings.

The relative clause which is within ' ' is giving additional information about
the noun **Buda**.

If you remove it, the main clause will still make sense. In the following examples, adding clauses are *in italics*.

(20) .The gentleman, **who** *asked so many questions during the meeting*, is my boss.

(21) . All football hooligans, **who** *have caused so much disturbance in London tonight,* should be expelled by their clubs.

(22) . Nobel, **who** *was the captain of the Test Cricket Team in 2001*, made 200 runs against Australia.

(23) . Some boxes, **which** *had been missing for two months*, were found hidden under the staircase.

(24) . Margaret Thatcher, **who** *was the first female British prime minister*, was replaced by John Major in 1990.

. In examples (19) to (24) you can leave out adding clauses and these sentences still make sense. The information between the commas is not restricted. This is the reason for calling these types of clauses non-restrictive/adding clauses.

Usually, **whose** relates to people as shown by examples 6 and 7. Here are some more examples.

(25) . Anne, *whose husband Wolfgang drives a Rolls-Royce*, is a

relative/adding clause ↵   businesswoman.

(26) . We wish to interview some students *whose overall performance is above B grade*.

relative/classifying clause ↵ - no comma needed

(27) . Our neighbours **whose** *house was burgled last night* called the

relative/ identifying clause ↵   police.

(28) . Mahatma Gandhi, **whose** *courage I admire greatly*, was a pioneer and campaigner of a non-violent movement for freedom and justice. In

this example, **whose** *courage I admire greatly* ⇒ relative clause - functioning as an adding clause

. Whose can also refer to an organisation or a country. This is illustrated below.

(29) . Switzerland, **whose** *inhabitants speak four official languages*,

is in West Europe.   ⇑

relative/adding clause - giving extra information about the head noun

(30) . IBM, **whose** *ideas have been copied by many PC manufacturers*, is

a large company.   ⇑

relative/adding clause - giving extra information about the head noun

Organisation ⇒ *group/collective noun* -considered as singular noun but it renders plural meaning.

The relative pronoun *whose* indicates that something belongs to something (possessiveness). When it relates to things (entities), it is a group noun as in examples (29) and (30). It can refer to people as shown above.

. We can use relative pronouns *which* and *that* for constructing identifying and classifying clauses. This is exemplified below.
>   (31). The city **which *I have marked on this map*** is a large place in England.
>   (32). This schedule **which *our supervisor submitted to the manager*** has been rejected.
>   (33). These are imported garments **which *can not be exhibited as made in England.***
>   (34). A passage to India was her big ambition **that *was fulfilled.***
>   (35). It is a home-made cake **that *is delicious.***

relative clause ↵

. When should you use *which* or *that* as a relative pronoun?

In examples (31) to (35) both *which* and *that* are possible relative pronouns in order begin a relative clause. In these examples, you can replace *that* with *which* or *vice versa* without altering the meaning rendered in each case. The use of *that* is generally recommended with any noun, but *which* with ideas and things. For instance:
>   (36). Your silly plan **which/that** *has ruined our trip should not have been accepted.*
>   (37). I have developed a database system **that/which** *generates my mail shot.*

. Some people consider the use of *which* as somewhat formal when it relates to only head noun. On the other hand, when *which* relative pronoun refers to the whole clause instead of head noun, *which* relative pronoun is used. This is illustrated below:

>   (38) .The Indian touring cricket team drew the final test mach, **which** *ended the current test series in a draw.*
>   (39). Our coach driver suddenly felt a sharp pain in his chest, **which** *caused this terrible accident.*

. In informal English, often the relative pronoun is omitted when it is not the subject of the relative clause **(in italics)**, i.e.:
>   (40). The book *I am reading* is really useful for my work.
>   (41). The big man *my brother is talking to* is a well-known boxer.
>   (42). The urgent letter *I posted to Anne last Friday* still hasn't reached her.

. When a relative pronoun is the subject of the relative clause, the relative pronoun cannot be discarded. This rule is illustrated below:

(43). The lady **who** *was wearing a flowery hat* was his grandmother.

relative clause ↵ - *who* ⟹ subject

(44). A student **who** *gave a talk on morality* lives in our area.

relative clause ↵ - *who* ⟹ subject

(45). I have a number of software packages **that /which** *are used for*
                                                            administrative work.

relative clause - subject that/which↵

. A relative clause can have either an active or a passive participle
  without a relative pronoun. Here are some examples:

(46). Some overseas students *taking* part in the debate tonight*

are Asians.   relative clause ↵

who are(= relative pronoun + auxiliary) omitted ↵

---
* taking is active participle here as it relates to some overseas students
  and their on-going activity.

---

(47). Sarah spotted the car *coming fast from the opposite side of the*
                                                                road.

relative clause ↵

which was (= relative pronoun + auxiliary) omitted ↵

  coming ⟹ *active participle*

(48). Projects **submitted*** *today* will be assessed and returned to you by

relative clause ↵   30th June.

⇑

which were (= relative pronoun + auxiliary) omitted

---
* submitted is a passive participle here as it relates to projects
  handed in – the activity performed by other persons.

---

(49). Some sweets made in Bridlington *presented to the Ramsey family*

were eaten up fast by us.   relative clause ↵

⇑

which were (= relative pronoun + auxiliary) omitted

presented ⟹ *passive participle* – sweets were given...

. **Use of *whom* and *which* pronouns with prepositions**

. The relative pronoun **whom** is not used very often in spoken English.
  Its use in the relative clause after a **preposition** is rather formal.
  For instance:

(50) . The Plew family **with whom** *I stayed in Germany* is visiting us.

   relative clause ↵ - preposition *with* comes before the pronoun

(51) . We will telephone John Russell *to whom we supplied a red car*.
                                              ⇑

   relative clause - preposition *to* placed before the pronoun

. In identifying and classifying relative clauses the relative pronoun *whom* can be the **object** **pronoun**. It is usually not used as an object pronoun. Instead of whom you can use *that* or *who*. Often, the relative pronoun is omitted altogether in identifying and classifying relative clauses. For instance:

(52) . John Smith *who/that I interviewed yesterday* has been appointed.

(53) . Robin Taylor **who/that** I telephoned today was pleased to accept our invitation.

(54) . Yvonne **[who/that/whom]** *I met in France* will visit us soon.

   relative clause ↵ – [the relative pronoun can be omitted]

. In spoken English the use of *whom* is not common. It is preferred to use who and place the preposition at the end of the sentence. For instance:

(55) . You are not telling me *who you went out last night with*.
                                        ⇑

   relative clause - preposition *with* at the end of the sentence

(56) . Please let me know **who** *you address the letter* **to**.
                                     ⇑

   relative clause - preposition *to* at the end of the sentence

. In adding clauses the relative pronoun *who* is often used instead of *whom. In such cases,* you cannot leave out the relative pronoun as exemplified below.

(57) . James Berg, **who*** *we liked as a tutor*, is a science journalist for
                                                           "The Times."

(58) . Our Russian colleague, **who*** *we bought a wedding present for*, is a father now.

---

* In examples 57 and 58 the use of '**that**' instead of '**who**' or '**whom**' is inappropriate.

. Like *whom* we can also put the preposition before the relative pronoun *which*.

(59) . My long overseas trip **for which** *I saved for so many years* was

   memorable.   ⇑

                              relative clause - identifying trip

(60) . The current upheaval **for which** *we are not prepared* is very

   harmful.   relative clause ↵ - identifying upheaval

. Adverbial clauses

An adverbial clause in a complex sentence functions in the same way as an adverb in a simple sentence. It modifies the main clause by adding information about time, place, manner, cause, etc. An adverbial clause may be in the first position, in the middle position or in the end position in a sentence. So, it can occur anywhere in the sentence. The adverbial clause is joined to the main clause by a conjunction.

. <u>A comma is inserted between the adverbial clause and the main clause when the adverbial clause is in the first position in a sentence.</u> The following examples demonstrate adverbial clauses.

(1) . They can visit us *if they wish*.

adverbial clause — pointing to a wish /desire   *if* ⟹ *conjunction*
Here, the adverbial clause modifies the main clause, "***They can visit us***" by giving additional information.

(2) . *If she likes it*, she can have it as a present.

adverbial clause ↵ - *if* ⟹*conjunction*

(3) . We'll go out for a walk by the sea *as soon as I finish my gardening.*

adverbial clause of time   - *as soon as* ⟹*conjunction*

(4) . *Since you are not coming with me*, I don't want to travel

                                                  alone.

adverbial clause of reason - *since* ⟹ *conjunction*

(5) . *Where an Indian restaurant is*, there is a Chinese take-way

                                   at the corner.

adverbial clause of place - *where* ⟹*conjunction*

(6) . I went to Germany *in order to attend an international book*

                                              fair.

adverbial clause of purpose - *in order to* ⟹*conjunction*

(7) . *If we meet at Heathrow*, we can discuss the final draft.

adverbial clause of time - here **if + present simple = future time**

(8) . *As far as I can remember*, she was with her husband at that

                                                  time.

adverbial clause - expressing truth - *as far as* ⟹*conjunction*

(9). How can she be happy *as though nothing had happened in*
⇑   *her family?*

adverbial clause of manner - *as though* ⇒*conjunction*

You can also say *as if* instead of *as though**.

```
* instead  ⇒adverb  but  instead of ⇒ preposition
```

(10). You should rest tomorrow *so that you can recover after your*
                                                          long journey.
                                                              ⇑

adverbial clause of purpose - *so that* ⇒*conjunction*

. **There may be several adverbials in a clause.**

(11). We arrived *happily* *at* the airport *to* fly home   *for* a wedding
⇑   ⇑   ⇑   ⇑   ⇑   ceremony.
1   2   3   4   5   ⇑
                                                               6

We can analyse the above sentence as follows:
1 = noun phrase*
2 = verb phrase*
3 = adverbial = adverbial phrase
4 = adverbial = prepositional phrase
5 = adverbial = non-finite phrase
6 = adverbial = prepositional phrase

```
* Repeat:  A phrase can be just one word .
```
Now consider the following questions and answers in relation to
the above analysis:

  . How did they arrive ?   ⇒ *happily*
  . Where did they arrive ?   ⇒ *at the airport*
  . Why did they arrive at the airport?   ⇒ *to fly home*
  . What was the purpose of flying home? ⇒ *for a wedding ceremony*

The above analysis shows that a clause can have a number of adverbials. Furthermore, it demonstrates that not all adverbials consist of adverbs, but adverbial phrases. Adverbial phrases do not always contain an adverb as illustrated by this example.

. Comparative clauses

These clauses express comparison. Some comparative clauses involve the use of the subordinating conjunction *than*. On the other hand, some comparative clauses introduce the second part of the comparison by means of correlative subordinators *as .... as*. The following examples illustrate the use of comparative clauses relating to different situations:

(1). <u>She is less interested in this job</u> ***than I thought***.

　　　　　main clause ↵　　　　　　　　⇑

comparative clause - subordinating conjunction/subordinator ⇒***than***

(2). <u>The corner house looked more impressive</u> ***than I had expected***.

　　　　main clause ↵　　　　　　　comparative clause ↵

(3). **He doesn't earn** <u>as</u>　much*　<u>money</u>　<u>as James does</u>.

first correlative subordinator ↵　　　⇑　　　　⇑

　　　　　　　　　　　head word　　comparative clause

　　　　　　　　　　　noun　　　introduced by the second

　　　　　　　　correlative subordinator ⇒*as*

---

* as much – it is also used as an idiomatic expression meaning ***the same***, e.g.

. Joanna refused to accept John's financial offer for their divorce settlement. I thought as much.

. He did help me when I was in trouble. Now I should do as much for him.

---

(4). You are <u>as</u>　<u>handsome</u>　<u>as your father was some years ago</u>.

　　　⇑　　　⇑　　　　　　　　　⇑

correlative subordinator head word　comparative clause introduced by

　　　　　　　　　　the second correlative subordinator - **as**

(5). She danced *as* <u>*elegantly*</u> as <u>*other winners did*</u>.

　　head word - adverb ↵　　　⇑

　　　　　　　　comparative clause introduced by the

　　　　　second correlative subordinator ⇒*as*

(6). Wolfgang replied <u>*as quickly*</u> <u>*as Sylvia replied*</u>.

　　head word - adverb ↵　　⇑

　　　　　　　comparative clause

These examples illustrate that comparative clauses pre-modify the head word. The head word may be a noun, pronoun, adverb or adjective.

This chapter begins with an introduction to clauses and sentences. Since a sentence consists of at least one clause, the idea of clauses is explained and exemplified in some depth. A sentence is the biggest unit of syntactic structure. For this reason, the next chapter is devoted to sentences. A classification of sentences is drawn for the purpose of understanding the meaning, types and structures of sentences.

Chapter 12
Sentences

. Introduction

In the last chapter, the idea of sentences is introduced and discussed in relation to clauses. For the sake of understanding the structures, types and intended meaning conveyed by sentences, a classification of sentences is shown in Table 1. This forms the basis of our discussion in this chapter.

A classification of sentences

Meaning	Types	Structure
Positive	Declarative	Simple
Negative	Interrogative	Compound
Active	Imperative	Complex
Passive	Exclamative	

Table 1

. Positive and negative sentences

A positive sentence expresses positive meaning. A negative sentence communicates a negative idea. A positive sentence can be converted to a negative sentence and vice versa. These are discussed below:

. Often a negative sentence is formed by using the word *not* or its short version *n't* after the auxiliary. If there is no auxiliary, the *dummy do* or *does* auxiliary is inserted. For instance:

(1) . She *has* spoken to me about this matter. ⇐ *positive sentence*

(2) . She *has not* spoken to me about this matter. ⇐*negative/sentence*

(3) . Angelica *will* call you tomorrow evening. ⇐ *positive sentence*

(4) . Angelica *won't* call you tomorrow evening. ⇐*negative sentence*
         ⇑

the auxiliary *will* and *n't* (not) are written as one word - *won't*

(5) . Frank likes a hot drink in bed. ⇐ *positive statement/sentence*

(6) . Frank *does not/ doesn't* like a hot drink in bed.

         dummy auxiliary ↵ - because example(5) is without the auxiliary

Sentences   **Analysis, Transformation & Synthesis**   **191**

****

(7) . They were running in that direction. ⇐ *positive statement/sentence*

       (8) . They **_were not/ weren't_** running in that direction.

negative statement/sentence ↵

(9) . You **_should have_** done this work.⇐ *positive statement/sentence*

         (10) . You **_should not/shouldn't_** have done this work.

not/n't placed after the auxiliary ↵ - negative sentence

(11) . The gold medal **_had been_** stolen. ⇐ *positive sentence*

(12) . The gold medal **_had not/hadn't been_** stolen. ⇐ *negative sentence*

(13) . Andrea **_might have_** told you about it. ⇐ *positive sentence*

(14) . Andrea **_might not/ mightn't_** have told you about it.

negative statement/sentence ↵

(15) . Colin knew that I was visiting him. ⇐ *positive statement/sentence*

       (16) . Colin **_did not/didn't_** know that I was visiting him.

negative statement/sentence ↵

. You can include an appropriate **_negative word_** in a positive sentence to
turn it into a negative sentence. There are many such words. A few such
negative words are used in the following examples:

       (17) . The teacher says **_never_** to do it again.

           negative word ↵ - means not ever

       (18) . My parents allow **_no_** one to visit me after 20.00 hours.

           negative word ↵ - means not any person

       (19) . She says **_nothing_** about her long holiday in Australia.

           negative word ↵ - meaning not any thing

       (20) . We tried hard but **_nowhere_** could we find him.

           negative word ↵ - means not anywhere

       (21) . Our old house **_no longer_** exists.

           negative words ↵ - not any more/ not any longer

. An adverbial phrase with a **_negative word_** creates a negative sentence.
The adverbial starts the sentence in order to emphasize the negative
meaning. It also requires inversion of 'subject' and 'verb'. For instance:
positive sentence:

       (22) . Before in my life, I have experienced such a terrifying
         road accident.

negative sentence

       (23) . **_Never before in my life_** **have I** experienced such a

adverbial with a negative word ↵   ⇑   terrifying road accident.

           inversion of subject and verb

**positive sentence**

    (24) . You should telephone her today.

**negative sentence**

    (25) . _**Under no circumstances**_   **should you** telephone her today.

negative adverbial phrase ↵   ⇑

                         inversion of subject and verb

- An adverbial phrase with a _**negative word**_ in a place other than the beginning of the sentence **does not** cause any subject and verb inversion. For instance:

    (26) . Rachel _**calls**_ us.   ⇐ _positive sentence_

    (27) . Rachel _**hardly ever**_ calls us. ⇐ _negative sentence_

negative adverbial phrase ↵ - here it means _**almost not**_

    (28) . We always **agree** where to lunch. ⇐ _positive sentence_

    (29) . We _**rarely agree**_ where to lunch.   ⇐ _negative sentence_

negative adverbial phrase ↵ - it means _**not very often**_

    (30) . You can pay _**either**_ today _**or**_ tomorrow.

         positive sentence / alternative offers

    (31) . Their car is _**neither**_   big _**nor**_ small   ⇐ _negative sentence_

                  1   2

In Example (31), 1 and 2 together show that two attributes (big and small) of a car are compared. It is true that the car is not small and not big. The negative statement is true for both attributes.

- An adverbial phrase can be used with a negative word for the emphatic negative.

    (32) . We _**do not**_ see your point of view _**at all**_.

     negative↵   ⇑

              it means _**in any way**_ - emphasizing negative meaning

    (33) . We haven't yet finished our journey, _**not by any means / by no**_

     negative ↵   _**means**_.

                             ⇑

         meaning _**not at all**_ ↵ - emphasizing negative meaning

    (34) . There is _**absolutely**_   _**nothing**_ more we can do to help you.

     emphasizing ↵   ⇑

     negative meaning   negative word means _**not a single thing**_

The word _**absolutely**_ means something is completely true. In this example, it stresses that it is true that there is not a single thing we can do to help you.

(35). We are **_not_** **_in the least_** hungry.

negative word ↵   ⇑

to underline negative meaning - it means **_not at all_**

. Active and passive sentences

In the last chapter, under active and passive clauses, a number of examples were given to explain the meaning of active and passive and their differences. Here are some more examples:

"The Principal chaired the emergency staff meeting. At this meeting, the staff were addressed by the principal, who outlined current financial circumstances facing the college. The staff were also informed by the principal about the circular the college received from the Government concerning lower grants during the new financial year, which was to commence next month. The staff were told about the current unfilled vacancies and a cash shortage to pay wages. The staff, who were already under the stress of their workload, feared job threats, and greeted the announcement with dismay and anger ."

The above paragraph contains five reported sentences. We can identify each sentence in terms of active and passive:

The Principal .... meeting. ⇐ *active sentence*

Because the principal **(subject)** which is the agent did something, that is chaired **(active verb)** the meeting. For this reason, it is an active sentence. As the verb element in this sentence is active, you can say it is *active voice*.

. *At the meeting..........facing the college.* ⇐ *passive sentence*

The action **(were addressed)** is a **passive verb** directed at the subject **(the staff)**. We can say something was done to the staff. As the verb element in this sentence is passive, you can consider it as *passive voice*. By applying the same rules:

. *The staff ----------next month.* ⇐ *passive sentence*

. *The staff --------- pay wages.* ⇐ *passive sentence*

. *The staff -------- and anger.* ⇐ *active sentence*

. An active sentence has a topic and some new information which is of some interest. The topic of the sentence is the *agent*, which is at the front of the sentence. When a sentence contains a transitive verb, you can convert it into a passive sentence. For instance:

(1) . <u>A young neighbour</u> has ridden <u>our motorcycle.</u> ⇐ *Active sentence*

⇑   ⇑

agent – the **topic** of the sentence   point of interest –

new information in the sentence

. **What has the agent done?** - has ridden our motorcycle. Thus, the active sentence contains some new information in relation to the topic of the sentence. You can convert this sentence into a passive sentence with an agent as shown below:

(2) . <u>Our motorcycle</u> has been ridden <u>by *a young neighbour*</u>.

       ⇑   ⇑

topic of the sentence-   new information in the sentence
agent   of some interest

In example (2), the topic is 'what is the new information' in Example (1). It is also at the front of the sentence. The *topic* in example (1) became **new information** in example (2). It is now a part of the phrase which is at the end of the sentence.

. <u>You can have a passive sentence *without an agent*. The presence of an agent in a passive sentence is relevant only if it provides some new information about the topic.</u> For instance:

(3) . Motorcycles are ridden. ⇐ Passive without an agent.

(4) . <u>The car</u> should be driven ***carefully at all times***.

       ⇑   ⇑

   topic   point of interest. – passive without an agent

(5) . WWW was invented in 1990's. ⇐ Passive without an agent

(6) . Some games are played.   ⇐ Passive without an agent

(7) . Mistakes have been made.   ⇐ Passive without an agent

(8) . Roses are planted.   ⇐ Passive without an agent

(9) . Nothing can be done now.   ⇐ Passive without an agent

(10) . New houses will be soon built. ⇐ Passive without an agent

. <u>The following sentences cannot be in the passive voice because each sentence has an intransitive verb element:</u>

(11) . I always ***sleep*** well.

intransitive verb ↵

(12) . It <u>happened</u>.

intransitive verb ↵

(13) . The hall has <u>warmed up</u>.

intransitive verb ↵

. <u>The passive voice is less common. It is considered as rather an impersonal and official style of writing. However, sometimes, you have to use it.</u>

. **Declarative sentences**

Declarative sentences are by far the most common sentences in the

English language. In a declarative sentence, the subject is followed by the verb, and its complement. The following examples illustrate this point further:

(1). <u>Ari</u> <u>is</u> <u>a father</u>.

⇑ ⇑ ⇑

S   V   O

(2). <u>Frank</u> <u>was</u> <u>a programmer</u>.

⇑ ⇑   ⇑

S   V   O

In these two examples **SVO** elements are obligatory. If you remove any one of these elements, the sentence will <u>not</u> be grammatically correct. On the other hand, the good news is that you can expand this basic structure in order to convey a wide range of information. This is illustrated by the following examples:

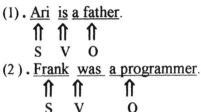

(1). *<u>Joan</u> <u>has studied</u> <u>at London University</u>*.

⇑   ⇑   ⇑

S + V   + <u>verb complement (C)</u>

prepositional phrase (PP)↵

We can analyse this sentence as follows:

. It has just one clause. This clause consists of *SVC* structural elements.

. The verb element in this clause *has studied* is *finite and active*.

. The absence of any of these structural elements will make this sentence grammatically incomplete.

. This sentence makes *a statement* which conveys some information. It is a typical example of an active voice.

. In fact, this sentence or a clause will not render the intended meaning, if you remove any **SVC** structural elements from it. On the other hand, you can extend this sentence so that it can give additional information. For example:

(2). <u>Joan</u> <u>has studied</u> **at** <u>London University</u> **for** <u>her PhD qualification</u>.

⇑   ⇑   ⇑

S + V   +   <u>verb complement (C)</u>

consists of two prepositional phrases (PP) ↵

. There are many different uses of declarative sentences for making statements. A statement may give just some information about something as illustrated above. Alternatively, it may give some information, which leads to an action or doing something. For instance:

(3). <u>I will copy this document and send it to you by post today.</u>

indicating action↵

The following examples of declarative sentences demonstrate a variety of statements.

****

(4) . I am ever so grateful for your help in this matter.

>> ***thanking someone*** ↵

(5) . Police ordered the crowd to clear the road immediately.

>> ***giving an order***↵

(6) . There were no injuries in this serious car crash.

> ***giving an account of an accident***↵

(7) . Everything seems to be in order.

>> ***indicating approval***↵

(8) . One of the capital cities, in the European Union, on both sides of the River Thames, is London.

>> ***describing a place*** ↵

(9) . I'm sorry to learn about floods, which have caused so much misery to your family.

conveying sympathy↵

(10) . Please let me know your decision by tomorrow.

>> ***seeking information***↵

(11) . They'd like me to have lunch with them today.

>> ***giving invitation***↵

Each sentence is conveying some information in the form of a statement or a declaration.

. Performative Verbs

Usually, a declarative sentence is constructed to make a statement as illustrated above. Some verbs in the first person present tense and in a declarative context indicate the action they perform. For instance: **'blame'** in 'I blame you'. For this reason, these verbs are called performative verbs. Here are some examples of performative verbs.

accept, advise, agree, apologise, blame, demand, forgive, guarantee, inform, insist, name, order, predict, promise, pronounce, propose, protest, recommend, request, suggest, swear, thank, warn.

The following statements illustrate the use of some performative verbs.

>> (12) . I promise to be there at the agreed time. ⇐ *promising*

>> (13) . I swear to tell nothing but the truth. ⇐ *swearing*

>> (14) . I thank you for the invitation. ⇐ *thanking*

>> (15) . I can not predict the outcome of this General Election.

>> ***predicting***↵

. A modal verb or similar expression may be preceded by the performative verb in order to make it sound somewhat polite.
Here are some examples:

(16) . <u>I would require a guarantee in the form of a small deposit.</u>

polite demand for a guarantee.⏎

(17) . I must confess my wrongdoing. ⇐ *confessing*

(18) . I have to *declare* that you are no longer a member of

this   club. ⇐ *informing about a formal decision*

. Some performative verbs such as *declare*, *order* and *warn* are used in formal writing and speaking. For instance:

(19) . I *warn / I'm warning* you for the last time, not to

both forms are possible.⏎   come late for work any more.

. Interrogative sentences

The basic use of interrogative sentences is to ask for information. The interrogative sentences/questions can generate answers in the forms of *yes/no* or some *specific information*. <u>The interrogative sentences which lead to yes/no answers are known as *yes/no questions*</u>. This is exemplified below:

(1) . Have you seen John this morning? *answer* ⇒ *yes/no*

(2) . Has your wife returned from her shopping trip? *answer* ⇒ *yes/no*

(3) . Have you ever had such an enjoyable outing to London?

answer ⇒ *yes/no*

(4) . Do you sell fried chicken? *answer* ⇒ *yes/no*

It is possible that answers to any of the above questions may be given more fuller than just *yes/no*. For instance, the answer to example (1) can be given as *Yes, I have seen him/John*. Even so, it is still a yes/no question.

. <u>The interrogative sentences which generate some specific information are known as *wh – questions*.</u> The following examples illustrate this type of interrogative sentences and answers.

(5) .Where were you yesterday at about 2 p.m.?

answer ⇒ *I was at home.*

(6) . When will we go for a long walk by the sea?

answer ⇒ *We will go now.*

(7) . Who can give me a lift by car to the station this afternoon?

answer ⇒ *I can.*

(8) . What's the matter with you?   *answer* ⇒ *I lost my hat.*

(9) . Why were you late this morning?

answer ⇒ *My car broke down on the way to work*

(10) .Whose is this car in my place? *answer* ⇒ *It is my car.*

. The structure of an interrogative sentence differs from the structure of a declarative sentence. The subject and the verb in an interrogative sentence do not occur in the same positions as in a declarative sentence. Here are some examples in order to illustrate these differences:

(11) . You live in this area. ⇐ *declarative sentence*
⇑   ⇑   ⇑
S   V   C

(12) . *Do* you live in this area? ⇐ *interrogative sentence*
⇑   ⇑   ⇑   ⇑
Aux   S   V   C   Aux = Auxiliary Verb
⇑

primary auxiliary verb *do* is used to express simple present tense

(13) . We worked all night to finalise the annual accounts.
⇑   ⇑   ⇑
S   V   C   *declarative sentence*

(14) . *Did* we work all night to finalise the annual accounts?
⇑   ⇑   ⇑   ⇑
Aux   S   V   C
⇑

primary auxiliary verb *did* expressing simple past tense

. In simple tenses the auxiliary *do* is used to form a question. It comes before the subject. If you compare example (11) with example (12) and example (13) with example (14) you can see there is *inversion* - changing word order of the subject and auxiliary.

. In example 15, *be* is used on its own as an ordinary verb. This example is converted to a question. This question is example(16). This example demonstrates that there is an inversion of the subject and *be* as an ordinary verb. Examples (17) and (18) also illustrate the same rule.

(15) . She is somewhere in the town centre now.
⇑   ⇑   ⇑
S   V   C   *declarative sentence/statement*

(16) . Is she somewhere in the town centre now?
⇑   ⇑   ⇑
V   S   C   *interrogative sentence*
⇑

be is used as an ordinary verb on its own

****

(17) . He was in Germany last week.

⟰ ⟰   ⟰

S   V   C   *declarative sentence/statement*

(18) . Was he in Germany last week?

⟰ ⟰   ⟰

V   S   C   *interrogative sentence*

⟰

be functions here as an ordinary verb on its own

. If there is more than one auxiliary verb, then there is inversion of the
first auxiliary verb and the subject. Examples (19) and (20) illustrate
this rule:

(19) . I could have finished that job by now.

⟰   ⟰   ⟰

S   V   C *declarative sentence/statement*

(20) . Could I have finished that job by now?

⟰   ⟰ ⟰   ⟰   ⟰

Aux S **Aux** V   C

⟰   ⟰

first auxiliary   second auxiliary   *interrogative sentence*

. Here are *wh-question* **words**:

what, who, whom, which, whose, where, when, why, how

Whom is rather formal and old-fashioned. Use **who**.

In addition, a **yes/no question** is used to seek **yes** or **no** answer.

. A question word may be the subject, object, complement or adverbial in
a sentence as demonstrated below.

. Examples (21) and (22) show that the *wh-question* word generates the
subject *John Smith* in the declarative sentence. There is no inversion.

(21) . *Who* will lunch with you today?

⟰   ⟰   ⟰

S   V   C

wh-question⤶   *wh-question sentence*

(22) . *John Smith* *will lunch* with me today.

⟰   ⟰   ⟰

S   V   C   *declarative sentence*

(23) . *What* has John made? *interrogative sentence*

⟰   ⟰ ⟰   ⟰

O   Aux S   V

wh-question⤶

. Example (24) shows that the *wh-question* word generated the object '*five boxes*' in the declarative sentence below. **There is no inversion**.

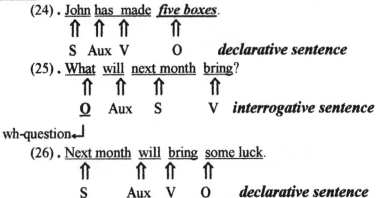

(24) . John has made *five boxes*.

    S Aux V   O   *declarative sentence*

(25) . What will next month bring?

    O Aux S   V *interrogative sentence*

wh-question↵

(26) . Next month will bring some luck.

    S   Aux V O *declarative sentence*

. Examples 25 and 26 exhibit that the *wh-question* word relates to the object *some luck* in the declarative sentence. There is inversion of the subject *next month* and the modal auxiliary *will*.

. Examples (27) and (28) exemplify that the *wh-question* word refers to the object *my car* in the declarative sentence. There is inversion of the subject and auxiliary verb.

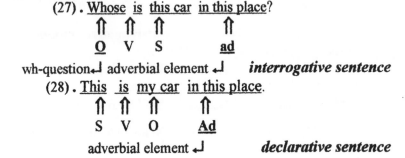

(27) . Whose is this car in this place?

    O V S   ad

wh-question↵ adverbial element ↵ *interrogative sentence*

(28) . This is my car in this place.

    S V O   Ad

    adverbial element ↵   *declarative sentence*

In this case, the preposition *in* is before the noun *place*. Therefore, it is a prepositional phrase of place and an adverbial (or adverbial element). See⇒ adverbial

. Examples (29) and (30) show that the *wh-question* word refers to the adverbial element in the declarative sentence. There is inversion of the subject *you* and modal auxiliary *will*.

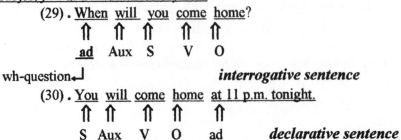

(29) . When will you come home?

    ad Aux S V O

wh-question↵   *interrogative sentence*

(30) . You will come home at 11 p.m. tonight.

    S Aux V O ad   *declarative sentence*

. Example (32) is derived from example(31). There is no inversion, except that the **wh-question** word is placed to the front in it. It makes perfect sense:

(31) . Annemarie Kling likes short stories most.

⇑   ⇑   ⇑   ⇑

S   V   O   ad

(32) . Which short stories does Annemarie Kling like most?

wh-question↵   ⇑   ⇑   ⇑   ⇑   ⇑

O   aux   S   V   ad

NOTE

In examples (11) – (32) above, the predicate of each sentence is analysed into its components /elements in order to explain the word order and the grammatical structure of each sentence.

. **Interrogative Sentences without Inversion**

An interrogative sentence has the same word order as in a declarative sentence. This happens in informal conversation when the question follows on from what was said before. Here are some examples:

(33) . I may leave you. **You are leaving now?** ⇒ *Not just yet*

(34) . I must visit my mother to see how she is now.

Your mother is not well? ⇒ *yes*

(35) . My friend met me at the airport.

Anne Kling met you ? ⇒ *yes, she did*

(36) . I bought a new house.

The house is which type? ⇒ *It is a semi-detached house*

(37). I have not completed this task.

You haven't completed this task yet? ⇒ *no*

(38) . We had a nice holiday in France.

You had a nice holiday in France? ⇒ *Yes*

(39) . Rachel and Ari became parents.

Rachel and Ari became parents? ⇒ *Yes*

. Negative interrogative sentences are also exemplified below.
. You can include an appropriate *negative word* in an interrogative sentence. For instance:

(37) . Did he tell you *never* to do it again?

negative word ↵

(38) . Why does your father allow _**no**_ one to visit you?

negative word ↵

(39) . Does she say _**nothing**_ about her previous marriage?

negative word ↵

. Imperative Sentences

The imperative is the base form of the verb. A sentence with an imperative verb element is an imperative sentence. An imperative sentence enables us to make an earnest request, give an order or a command. In fact, you can use it to make someone act on your wishes whether it is under any prevailing condition or without any condition. You can also use the imperative to offer someone your good wishes. It is always in the present tense and refers to the second person, singular or plural form. Normally, an imperative does not have a subject. Here are some examples:

(1) . _**Take**_ a seat, please.

⇑ - imperative form of the verb

an earnest request for an action resulting in sit down

It refers to 'second person singular' (= _you_). There may be several persons, but each person is requested to take a seat.

(2) . _**Through**_ this entrance, please.

an instruction↵ - imperative form of the verb

(3) . _**Be**_ careful.

an instruction/advice↵ - imperative form of the verb

(4) . _**Do be**_ quiet.

strong order/more emphatic ↵

(5) . _**Do**_ sit down.

an order/more emphatic↵

In examples 4 and 5, the auxiliary _do_ helps to soften the effect of the imperative on the listener. In other words, the use of _do_ sounds less authoritative.

(6) . **Don't** talk so loudly. ⇐ *an order*

In example 6, the auxiliary _do_ is essential in order to construct the negative imperative.

(7) . _**Stop**_. ⇐ *an order – remember traffic/road sign*

(8) . _**Don't**_ talk. ⇐ *an order*

(9) . _**Don't be**_ absurd. ⇐ *emphatic*

(10) . _**Come**_ in. ⇐ *permission* **But**

(10A) . _**Do**_ come in. ⇐*more emphatic*

(11) . _**Go**_ away. ⇐ *an order –* rather impolite

(12) . ***Shut*** the door at once ⇐ *strong order*

(13) . ***Get out*** of here. ⇐ *an order* - sounds rude

(14) . If you can't afford to pay, ***don't*** come.

    conditional instruction↵

(15) . If you *are coming* late, **take** your keys.

    conditional instruction↵

(16) . If you drive to London, ***don't drink*** for a day.

    conditional order↵

(17) . ***Enjoy*** your meal. ⇐ offering of good wishes

(18) . ***Let's*** have lunch. ⇐ *suggesting to perform an action together*

  ⇑

imperative form of the verb ⇒ ***let + us = let's***

It implies that the speaker and the listener perform the action together. It is in plural form.

(19) . ***Let's not*** keep arguing about it. ⇐ *negative form of the order*

. You can also construct the negative imperative with ***do let's***.

   (20) . ***Don't let's*** lose any of our clients.

    ⇑

negative form of the order (informal)

. **When there are two persons, *you* can be the subject.** For instance:

   (21) . ***You be gentle*** when she meets you.

    an emphatic piece of advice ↵ - you ⇒ subject

   (22) . ***You watch*** the traffic, I climb the ladder.

    an emphatic instruction↵ - you ⇒ subject

. <u>Exclamative sentences</u>

The purpose of exclamative sentences is to express a variety of feelings. These can be joy, sorrow, anger, shock, surprise or any other emotional feeling. The construction of exclamative sentences is based on ***how*** and ***what*** words. An exclamation mark is placed at the end of the sentence instead of a full stop. Exclamative sentences are not as flexible as other types of sentences. We use them for the sole purpose of expressing emotions. The following examples demonstrate their construction and usage:

   (1) . How ***intelligent*** your son is!

It means that your son is very intelligent. It expresses the writer's or speaker's feelings about the degree of intelligence.

. Examples 2 - 8 show that the wh-word can be followed by an adjective. The adjective can be with an article *a* or *an*:

  (2) . How *wonderful* the scene is!

  (3) . How *lucky* you were!

  (4) . How *kind* those people are!

  (5) . What *a lovely* person your wife is!

  (6) . What *a simple* style it is!

  (7) . What **a** *memorable* show we watched!

  (8) . What *an enjoyable* weekend we had!

. Examples 9 -17 illustrate that an exclamative can be a phrase. The phrase can also be just a short phrase:

  (9) . How *generous*!

  (10) . How *foolish*!

  (11) . What *a charming* evening!

  (12) . What *a mess* !

  (13) . What *fun*!

  (14) . *Oh*!

  (15) . *Look out*!

  (16) . *Excellent*!

  (17) . *Well done*!

. Examples 18 - 19 demonstrate that **how** can be followed by an adverb/adverbial:

  (18) . How *slowly* Elena talks!

  (19) . How *carefully* Yuonne handled the glass!

. Examples 20 –21 demonstrate that **how** can modify the verb:

  (20) . How they *run*!

  (21) . How the girls *giggled*!

. Simple sentences

In the last chapter, a distinction between simple, compound and complex sentences is made. In this section, we examine each type of sentence in detail. Some points made in the last chapter are repeated here in order to develop each topic further.

. **A simple sentence has at least one clause.** Here are some examples:

  (1) . *Margaret   enjoyed   her meal*.
          ⇑   ⇑   ⇑
          S   V   O

  transitive verb type↵

(2) . It was a warm afternoon.

transitive verb type⤶

. the structure of each sentence is stated in terms of SVO
. each sentence has a finite form of the verb
. each sentence can not be broken into smaller sentences because each
  sentence has just one verb
. each sentence has just one clause
  . each sentence is grammatically a complete unit

Each sentence is a ***simple sentence***. It can be said that each sentence has a
main clause with a *finite verb* in each sentence. Now consider the
following examples:

(3) . *She laughs*.   (4) . *Susan comes*.

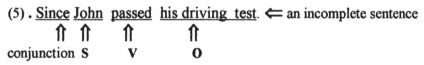

In examples (3) and (4):
. each sentence has an SV structure
. each has <u>an intransitive verb</u> – can not take an object
. each sentence can not be broken into smaller sentences because each has
  one verb element
. each sentence is grammatically a complete unit irrespective of its size

Each sentence is a ***simple sentence***. It can be said that each sentence has a
main clause with a ***finite form of the verb***.
. <u>A structure may have a clause but it is still not a simple sentence.</u>
  For example:

(5) . Since John passed his driving test. ⇐ an incomplete sentence

conjunction S   V   O

This sentence contains a clause, but it is not a simple sentence. It begins with
a conjunction, which requires further information. Thus, this is not a simple
sentence as it is grammatically incomplete. If we can remove the adverbial
since from this sentence, it will become a simple sentence containing a main
clause as shown below.

(6) . John passed his driving test.

(7) . It has been very cold all day. ⇐ *simple sentence*

. Compound sentences

This above sentence has only one verb. It can not be split into smaller sentences. It is a clause as well as a simple sentence. We can re-write this sentence as a complex sentence by adding to it some other structural parts as shown below:

(1) . It has been very cold all day **and** *I have stayed at home*.

sentence/clause 1↵   ⇑   sentence/clause2 ↵
                                        coordinating conjunction
                                        indicating clauses of equal status

Example (1) consists of two shorter sentences or clauses joined together with a conjunction *and*. In this example, each clause can stand on its own. In other words, grammatically, these clauses are of *equal status*. For this reason, this sentence is a compound sentence. A compound sentence can have two or more clauses of equal status. In fact, each clause is a main clause in its own right, and thus can stand alone. In order to form compound sentences by linking clauses, we use the following:

. **coordinating conjunctions/ coordinators:** *and*, *or* and *but*
  are mainly used. See examples (1) – (7). *For* is seldom used.
   See examples (8) and (9).
. **coordinating coordinator** *or* with *not* and *nor* can be used with
  the negative clauses. See examples (13) and (14).

. **correlative coordinators:** *either --- or* are used for emphasizing an
  alternative course of action. See examples (15) – (17).
. Conjunctions *and, or* and *but* must be placed between the two clauses
  (short sentences). In fact, you can not place them anywhere except
  between the clauses. Here are some more examples of compound
  sentences:

(2) . Jane wants to work in England, **but** *she doesn't like to be away*

clause 1↵   coordinating conjunction ↵   *from home.*
                                        clause 2↵

(3) . I like fried chicken ***but*** my wife likes grilled chicken.
(4) . They went out to go swimming ***and*** we walked to the local
     shopping precinct.
(5) . I wanted to travel to Paris ***but*** there is no direct train to Paris
     from here.
. When the subject is the same in both main clauses, we don't have to
  repeat it in the second clause. When an element of a clause is left out, it
  is called an ***ellipsis***. The reason is that the left out element can be
  inferred from the meaning and grammatical context of the sentence.
  The following examples illustrate the use of ellipsis:

(6) . You can take a taxi to Heathrow _or_ go by airbus from Victoria.

(7) . I may travel to France by car _or_ may fly to Paris by Air France.

(8) . Police caught John breaking the speed limit on the M1 _and_ charged him.

. A compound sentence can have more than two clauses. The coordinating coordinators _and_ and _or_ are used to link more than two main clauses in a compound sentence. For instance:

(9) . You can borrow my umbrella _or_ buy a new one _or_ you don't care about it.

(10) . You asked for some money _and_ I had no money _and_ the bank was already closed.

. The coordinating coordinator _but_ can not join more than two main clauses. The reason is that it is used only when two main clauses are expressing contrasting meaning in a compound sentence. See examples (2), (3) and (5) above.

. Now we can examine the use of _for_ through the following examples:

(11) . We were dancing _for_ the music was played.

    ⇑   ⇑   ⇑

main clause 1   coordinator   main clause2

The coordinator occurs in the same position where _and_ coordinator is placed in a compound sentence. Indeed, _for_ coordinator functions just like _and_ in a compound sentence.

(12) . We couldn't hear very well _for_ it was noisy.

For = because↵

. When the first clause in a compound sentence is conveying negative meaning, _nor_ coordinator is used as the negative complement of _or_ to link clause 1 to clause 2. This is illustrated below:

(13) . He could _not_ understand the question, _nor_ did the teacher

in clause 1 ↵   ⇑   repeat the question.

               joining clauses 1 and 2

(14) . I **wasn't** able to turn left or right on the motorway, _nor_ were other motorists.

. We can use _either — or_ in a compound sentence to express an alternative. The coordinator _or_ begins the second clause. Here _or_ places emphasis on the alternative – second part of the compound sentence. This is illustrated below:

(15) . _Either_ Team A bat first _or_ Team B bowl first.

    ⇑   ⇑

starts first clause   joins second clause with the first clause

Here are two more examples to confirm that *Either* can commence the first clause:

> (16) . *Either* you fix it as per our agreement, *or* we employ another
> joiner to do it.

> (17) . *Either* Frank will drive the car back home from the pub,
> *or* Sarah will not drink alcohol.

Warning!

Two pairs of correlative coordinators *neither ... nor* and *both ... and* can grammatically link phrases but not clauses. Therefore, these can not form part of compound sentences.

. Complex sentences

Like the compound sentence, a complex sentence also has two or more clauses. The difference between the complex and the compound sentences is that in the complex sentence clauses are **not** of the same equal status (main clauses). In a complex sentence, one clause is a main clause with one or more subordinate clauses. For instance:

> (1) . *I came home immediately* <u>when</u>   *I received this good news.*
>
> main clause /clause1⏎   ⇑ subordinate clause/clause2⏎
>   main clause   conjunction

In this case, the main clause can stand alone. For this reason, it is also called an ***independent clause***. It is not dependent on the subordinate clause, which begins with the adverbial element *when*. Clause 2 cannot stand alone. Therefore, it is a ***dependent clause***. Dependent clauses are subordinate clauses.

See ⇒ Clauses

> (2) . *When Antonia visited us, we made some Hungarian food.*
>   ⇑   ⇑
>   subordinate/dependent clause   main /independent clause
>
>   begins with an adverbial *–when*

<u>The presence of the subordinate clause makes this sentence complex.</u> Here are some more examples:

> (3) . <u>Soon</u> after we arrived home, <u>our grandmother greeted us with</u>
>   ⇑   <u>a smile and kisses.</u>
>
>   <u>adverbial</u>   main clause ⏎
>   ⇑
> started subordinate clause

In this complex sentence, the subordinate clause begins with a multi-word subordinator *soon after*, an adverbial element.

(4) . *He found himself in a hospital bed* **because** he was involved in

    main clause ↵   adverbial element ↵   a car accident.

              subordinate clause ↵

. As shown above, we can start a subordinate clause with **when** and **because**. Similarly, **if** and some other adverbials can do the same. See the last chapter on adverbial clauses.

(5) . *He will help you* **if** you approach him gently.

     ⇑   ⇑   ⇑

  main clause adverbial   subordinator clause begins with

               if - a subordinator

. The following examples demonstrate that a complex sentence can have more than one main and subordinate clause.

(6) . *I remember* **that** you visited us some years ago **and** stayed with

main clause↵   ⇑   ⇑   us in Paris.

       conjunction   subordinate clause 1   ⇑

                                 subordinate clause 2

Here *that* started a subordinate clause 1. Clause 2 is started with *and*. In subordinate clauses 1 and 2, the subject (*you*) is the same. We can leave out the subject in clause 2.

In each of the next three examples, there is one main clause in **bold style** and two subordinate clauses.

(7) . *Although* she was out of work, *she made a return trip to Switzerland because* her mother paid for it.

(8) . *Liz Taylor was married to Richard Burton who* died some years ago *because of* his heart failure.

(9) . *I went to Germany and* stayed with some family friends *because* it was interesting.

(10) . *A thief,* who brandished a gun and raided a bank, got away with a lot of money.

In the last example:

  . *A thief* got away with a lot of money   ⇒*main clause*

  . who brandished a gun   ⇒ *subordinate clause -1*

  . and raided a bank   ⇒ *subordinate clause -2*

(11) . Ursula thought *that* Ralf was a millionaire **when** she saw him *coming* in a chauffeur driven Rolls Royce, *but* she was mistaken.

We can analyse this sentence into the following clauses:

. Ursula thought ⇒ *main clause 1*

. that Ralf was a millionaire *subordinate clause 1* ⇒ *noun clause*

. when she saw him ⇒ *subordinate clause 2* ⇒*adverbial clause*

. coming in a chauffeur driven Rolls Royce ⇒*subordinate clause 3*
participle clause

. but she was mistaken ⇒*main clause 2 - but* joins two main clauses

This is how main clauses can be joined together, when there are two subordinate clauses between them.

> (12) . She was very tired when she returned from Poland, but went to work the next day, *where* she caught the flu, as it was a very stormy, cold, winter's day.

The structure of this sentence in terms of clauses can be analysed as follows:

. She was very tired   ⇒*main clause 1*

. when she returned from Poland   ⇒*subordinate clause 1*

. but went to work the next day   ⇒*main clause 2*

. where she caught the flu   ⇒*subordinate clause 2*

. as it was a very stormy , cold, winter's day   ⇒*subordinate clause 3*

. Here are two more examples of complex sentences with non-finite clauses:

> (13) . Sarah wishes to return home by car *because* there is no train
> main clause↵   service tonight.
> subordinate clause↵

(14) . I wanted to travel by air **but it was not possible** *to fly from the*
main clause 1↵   main clause 2↵   *nearest airport.*
subordinate clause↵

In summary, a sentence does not have to be short to be simple. What makes it simple is the presence of a single clause which is grammatically complete.

A compound sentence has two or more clauses of equal status. A complex sentence has at least one main and one subordinate or sub clause. Both compound and complex sentences can be broken down into smaller sentences or clauses. We often use the same tense in the main and subordinate clauses in both compound and complex sentences. Very long sentences should be avoided for the sake of clarity. Usually, in a short sentence, a comma is not placed between two main clauses.

Part 3
Punctuation

. Introduction

Punctuation enables the writer to clarify the meaning of a piece of writing. Punctuation has a set of rules and corresponding marks. These marks are inserted in writing in accordance with these rules. Punctuation also denotes specific points of grammar in a piece of writing. The misuse of punctuation marks or absence of punctuation can lead to misreading and ambiguity. The following punctuation marks* with their rules of usage are discussed in this chapter:

. apostrophe	. dash	. paragraph
. asterisk	. ellipses /three dots	. question mark
. brackets	. exclamation mark	. quotation marks
. capital letters	. footnotes	. semicolon
. colon	. full stop	. slash/ bar/diagonal/
. comma	. hyphen	oblique mark

. **word-processing marks - bullets, bolds, _italics_, underlining and arrows, etc.**

You may come across some other punctuation marks which are not listed above. On the other hand, you may find that some of these punctuation marks are not discussed in some other books. For instance, some people do not consider the paragraph formation and capitalisation as punctuation marks. In this book, these are considered as equally important punctuation marks and their application is outlined.

---

* The above punctuation marks are not discussed in the next chapter in a strict alphabetical order.

Chapter 13
Punctuation

. apostrophe

An apostrophe has the following two major functions:

> . to indicate possession or genitive case
>
> . to mark contractions or show contractions or omissions of letters or syllables in the spelling of some words

Each of these functions is exemplified below:

1. To indicate the possessive or genitive case or possession in the following ways:

    a . When a noun is singular, an apostrophe and 's' are added to the noun. Here are some examples:

        (1) . The *accountant's* office
        (2) . *Anne's* wedding dress
        (3) . *Robin's* car
        (4) . The *company's* management team
        (5) . *London's* red buses
        (6) . My German *friend's* name is Sabina
        (7) . It is *John's* chair.

    b . An apostrophe and 's' are also added to indefinite pronouns that do not end in s.

        (8) . This is *__nobody's__* fault.

indefinite pronoun ⌐⏊- *nobody = no one*

        (9) . *__Someone's__* car is parked in my driveway.

indefinite pronoun ⟹ *someone = somebody or a person*
                      unknown or not mentioned by name

      (10) . We hope that this year *__everyone's__* dreams come true.

indefinite pronoun ⟹ *everyone = all persons = everybody*

****

c . An apostrophe is added to plural nouns ending in *s*.

This is demonstrated below:

(11) . This is a *students'* computer laboratory.

(12) . Our *doctors'* surgery hours are between 6 –8 p.m.
on Fridays.

(13) . Our *neighbours'* dog barked all night.

(14) . Primary school *teachers'* trade unions help new teachers.

(15) . Our car is parked in ***Tesco's customers'*** car park.

's with the singular proper noun ⤶ ⇑
to indicate possessive case   an apostrophe is added to a plural noun
to show possession

(16) . *The hostages'* release at Frankfurt Airport came unexpectedly.

**d . An apostrophe and *s* are added to plural nouns that do *not*
end in *s*.**

Here are some examples:

(17) . There is the young *women's* hockey club.

(18) . She reads *children's* short stories.

(19) . I think *people's* opinions are important to politicians.

(20) . No one other than parents are allowed in a *children's*
playground.

**e . An apostrophe can be used to show the possessive form
without mentioning the noun to which a reference is made.**

For instance:

(21) . I met John outside the *barber's* (shop).

(22) . Julie works for a local *optician's* (practice).

(23) . We would like to have an Indian meal at *Taj's*
(Restaurant).

You do not have to mention the nouns shown in brackets. Here are some
more examples:

(24) . I saw Janet at **Lyon's** *(sports club)*.

omitted ⤶

(25) . We have our current account at the **TSB-Lloyd's***(bank)*.

omitted ⤶

**f . An apostrophe is used with some units of measure to denote
possession.**

For instance:

(26) . I think in a *week's* time she will arrive here.

(27) . My father retired after *forty years'* service as a Civil Servant.

(28) . Just imagine how you will look in *twenty years'* time.

(29) . I must take a *fortnight's holiday* before 31 December.

(30) . I don't think this shirt is *ten pounds'* worth.

g . When a genitive (possessor) consists of more than one noun, the apostrophe is marked on the last noun. A genitive shows possession.

For instance:

(31) . *The Lord Chancellor's* office is in the Palace of Westminster.

(32) . *The British Prime Minister's* country residence is not too far from London.

(33) . *The Duke of Edinburgh's* Award Scheme, to foster the leisure activities of young people, began in 1956.

h . When possession is shared by more than one noun, the apostrophe and s are added to the last noun.

This is illustrated below:

(34) . *Webster and Lancaster's* books can be seen on ADR web site.

(35) . *Brinkman and Blaha's* Data Systems And Communications Dictionary is a well known book.

i . When possession is not shared by more than one noun, the apostrophe and 's' are added to each noun, e.g.

(36) . *Earnest's* and *Klieg's* insurance training manuals are in our library.

(37) . I have *Hornby's* and *Webster's* dictionaries.

j . Use an apostrophe and s with personal names ending with s or z.

For instance:

(38) . **Prince Charles's** ideas on the environment are serious.

(39) . According to *Leibniz's Law,* if A is identical with B, then every property that A has B has, and vice versa.

k . An apostrophe and *s* are used with nouns which are preceded by the word *sake.*

For instance:

(40) . *For God's sake*, you must not lie during the interview.

(41) . *For pity's sake,* help your aged and sick parents.

(42) . *For heaven's sake*, allow her a day off with pay.

In examples 40 – 42, *bold words (idiomatic expressions)* are used to emphasize that it is important to do something. *God, pity* and *heaven* are singular nouns.

l . An apostrophe can be used with plural nouns which are preceded by the word *sake*:

For example:

(43) . *For old times' sake*, Anne forgave him and invited him for a meal.

If you do something for *old times' sake (idiomatic expression),* you do it
because it is connected with something good that happened to you in the past.

m . <u>Use an apostrophe with abbreviations functioning as verbs,</u> e.g.
(44) . I submitted my application for a day off and my boss ***OK'd*** it.

Ok'd =okayed ↵

(OK! in present tense)
In this context, it means my boss officially agreed to let me have a day off
work. It is rather an informal expression.

(45) . He was ***KO'd*** in the first round.

KO'd = knocked out ↵ - *it is connected with boxing.*

n . <u>Usually business names do not include an apostrophe in their business titles.</u>
For example:

(46) . I work at ***Sainsburys.*** ⇒ *should be Sainsbury's*

(47) . My wife used to work for ***Browns.*** ⇒ *should be Brown's*

(48) . I bought this CD from ***Victorias.*** ⇒ *should be Victoria's*
Sainsbury, Brown and Victoria are business names.

o . <u>In hyphenated compound words the apostrophe is added to the last word.</u>
For instance:

(49) . My wife's ***brother-in-law's*** home is not far from our home.

(50) . A ***well-dressed lady's*** car is parked in your place.

2 . <u>To mark contractions or indicate omissions in spelling certain words.</u>
For instance:

(51) . ***We'll*** see you soon.

we will = we'll ↵

(52) . She ***won't*** go there today.

will not = won't ↵

(53) . It is a lovely spring morning, ***isn't*** it?

is not = isn't ↵

(54) . ***I'd*** love to come with you.

I would = I'd ↵

(55) . We arrived here at the beginning of Spring ***'02***.

2002 = '02 ↵

(56) . He left home at 8 ***o'clock*****.   ⇐ *omitting* f *and* <u>the</u>

o<u>f the</u> clock = o'clock ↵

---

* o'clock:

. It is <u>not</u> used with a.m. and p.m.

. Use it only for telling the time in an exact hour

. In this example, it means that he left home at exactly 8 as shown or reckoned by the clock.

. <u>**Some specific cases where an apostrophe is used or omitted:**</u>

    a . <u>Use of an apostrophe *with a pronoun + an auxiliary verb* to contract them</u>.

For instance:

    (57) . I'm = I am

    (58) . We're = We are

    (59) . They're = They are

    (60) . She's = She is **or** She has

    b . <u>An apostrophe is also used with an *auxiliary verb + not* to contract them.</u>

Here are some examples:

    (61) . haven't = have not

    (62) . wouldn't = would not

    (63) . mightn't = might not

    (64) . couldn't = could not

    (65) . oughtn't = ought not

    (66) . needn't = need not

    c . <u>An apostrophe is used to indicate the omission of figures in dates.</u>

For example:

    (67) . They wanted to stay with us in *'02*.

       referring to the year 2002 ↵

    (68) . Thank you for your letter of 9th Jan. *'03*.

    d . <u>An apostrophe is not used with the possessive pronouns.</u>

For instance:

    . *its* . *ours* . *yours* . *theirs*

    e . <u>An apostrophe is not used when referring to wars, plans, projects and similar notions related to a specified length of time.</u>

This is exemplified below:

    (69) . *Six-Day War*

    (70) . *Hundred Years' War** (this does not obey the rule)

    (71) . *Five –Year Plan*

(72) . *Ten –Year Projected Savings*

---

* There are exceptions to the above rule as shown by example 70.

---

f . An apostrophe is not used with abbreviations and numbers which create plurals*:

For instance:

(73) . *the 1980s. For instance:*

(74) . *In the 1950s, she was very young and pretty.*

---

* There is some controversy surrounding it.
  Some writers place it before adding 's', e.g. ⇒ In the 1950's.

---

g . Sometimes the insertion or omission of an apostrophe is surrounded by uncertainty.

For instance:

(75) . 12 St. James's Square London SW 11.

(76) . *St. John's Wood* Underground station is in London.

(77) . He was seen in the *Earls Court* area yesterday afternoon.

An apostrophe is usually used with names of places, when possession is involved. See (75) and (76). However, this rule does not always apply. See⇒ example (77).

. Brackets

There are several types of brackets. In British English for writing purposes the round brackets ( ) which are known as parentheses are used. Square brackets [ ] are used in the USA. Of course, other types of brackets are used for mathematical and scientific work.

. Round Brackets or Parentheses

Round brackets ( ) can perform the following functions:
  . to enclose some additional or optional information without affecting the flow and meaning of a sentence, a paragraph or a piece of writing
  . to show alternatives
  . to include abbreviations and refer to something by figures or letters

Here are some examples:

(1) . Gandhi *(1869-1948)* was the foremost spiritual and political leader of the twentieth century. He was called the Mahatma

(Great Souls – in Sanskrit). Gandhi was a pacifist and a great champion of non-violence.

The removal of parentheses and their contents will not affect the flow and meaning of this paragraph. Here are some more examples:

(2) **.** Any *student(s)* who would like to join this trip must see me today.

(3) **.** Only 2 *(two)* delegates are allowed free of charge during the book fair.

(4) **.** (1) Introduction
(2) Objectives
(3) Who should attend

In this book, examples are numbered as (1) **..** The purpose of this "**.**" is to highlight each example for the ease of readers. You do not have to adopt this method.

. <u>Square Brackets</u>

Square brackets [ ] are used to supplement or append to an original text, some information which may be a correction, an explanation or some translation by a person other than the author. For instance:

(5) **.** During the Second World War, the British Prime Minister
[Churchill] made great and memorable speeches.

additional information appended by the editor

(6) **.** In Germany, during the Second World War, the Führer
[leader, Hitler] also made highly nationalistic speeches.

translation and additional information by another person

(7) **.** The first woman party leader in British politics
[Margaret Thatcher] became the longest serving 20th
⇑   century female Prime Minister in 1988.
added to the original text by the editor

. <u>Capital Letters</u>

The use of capital letters is governed by the following punctuation rules:

a **.** <u>Use a capital letter at the beginning of a sentence.</u>
For instance:

(1) **.** Punctuation enables us to write clearly.
(2) **.** Use punctuation to improve your writing.

b **.** <u>Use a capital letter after a colon.</u>

****

In the following examples, direct speech is within the inverted commas:

(3) . The British Prime Minister, Margaret Thatcher, said:

'I am extraordinarily patient, provided I get my own way in the end.' (The Observer 4 April 1989)

(4) . Once Mahatma Gandhi said:

'There is enough for the needy but not for the greedy.'

(4A) . Once Goethe (German poet, novelist, and dramatist) said:

'Boldness has genius, power and magic in it.'

c . <u>The pronoun I is written as a capital.</u>

For instance:

(5) . **I**'m pleased to meet you.

(6) . It's a pity **I** missed your birthday party.

d . <u>Use a capital letter to begin a proper noun.</u>

This is exemplified below:

(7) . Silvia Plew is here from Germany. ⇐ *both names began with capital letters*

(8) . Mrs Johnson has arrived.

e . <u>A title of a person and proper names begin with a capital letter.</u>

For instance:

(9) . <u>Dr</u> <u>Robertson</u> is our <u>General</u> <u>Practitioner</u>.

⇑　　⇑　　　　　⇑　　　　⇑

title   proper name   first word + second word = **title**

(10) . <u>Mrs</u> Taylor will see her <u>doctor</u> today.

⇑　　　　　　　　　　⇑

title   it is not functioning as a title here but as a common noun

(11) . <u>Aunt</u> Kay lives in Nottingham.

⇑

title (Auntie or Aunty is informal for aunt)

(12) . My <u>**aunt**</u> lives in Nottingham but <u>Uncle</u> Tom King died

⇑　　　　　　　　　　　　　⇑　　some years ago.

aunt is not a title but a common noun   it is the title of Tom King

Words like doctor, aunt, grandfather are titles only when they are used with proper nouns.

f . <u>Nouns for religions, scriptural books and related titles begin with a capital letter.</u>

For instance:

(13) . Islam means submission to Allah. A Muslim is someone who
         has submitted to Allah, believing in Muhammad as a prophet
         of Allah. Allah is God in Islam. The Holy Qur'an (also
         known as the Koran) is the holy book of Islam.

(14) . Christ, the Holy Bible, the Prophet Muhammad, Buddha,
         Judaism, the Talmud, Hindu and Hinduism are all
         connected with different religions.

In examples (13) –(14), Islam, Muslim, Allah, Muhammad, God, the Holy
Qur'an, the Koran, the Prophet Muhammad, the Holy Bible, Buddha, Juda-
ism, the Talmud, Hindu and Hinduism all began with capital letters. Here
these are considered as proper nouns. However, in the phrase 'as a prophet',
prophet is a common noun, not a title. For this reason, it does not begin with
a capital letter.

   **g . Capitals are used to begin the names of places, rivers,
        mountains, books, newspapers, plays, films, trains, ships,
        spacecraft, aircraft and other such things.**
These are exemplified below:

(15) . London, Berlin, Moscow and Paris are all capital cities
         in Europe.

(16) . The longest span bridge in the world is Akashi-Kaiyo. It is
         in Japan. Its length is 1990 metres.

(17) . The longest railway tunnel in the world is Seikan.
         It is 54 km long. The second longest railway tunnel in the
         world is the Channel Tunnel UK- France. It is 50 km long.

(18) . The largest desert in the world is the Sahara in northern Africa.

(19) . The highest mountain in the world is Everest in Asia.

(20) . The longest river in the world is the River Nile in Africa.

(21) . The largest country in the world by area is Russia.

(22) . The largest city by population in the world is Tokyo, in Japan.

(23) . The Himalayas are the highest mountain range on Earth. They
         are in Asia.

(24) . The distance from the Earth to the Sun is about
         150 million km.

(25) . "The Times" is a daily newspaper for well-informed readers in
         the UK.

(26) . "The Diamond Sūtra" is the oldest surviving printed book in
         the world. It is a Chinese translation of Buddhist scripture,
         printed in AD 868.

(27) . The Orient Express is a famous train.

(28) . Apollo 11 made the first lunar landing.

(29) . The actress Elizabeth Taylor played the title role of the 1963
         film "Cleopatra."

(30) . "Java Simplified"is a computer programming book from ADR.

h . Capitals are used for abbreviations of names of some organisations and countries. These are formed from the first letter of each word in the name.
Here are some examples:

(31) . **UN** is an abbreviation for the **U**nited **N**ations.

(32) . **UK** is a short name for the **U**nited **K**ingdom.

(33) . **EU** stands for the **E**uropean **U**nion.

(34) . **BBC** is an abbreviation for the **B**ritish **B**roadcasting **C**orporation.

(35) . **BP** is short for the **B**ritish **P**etroleum company.

The correct use of both capital and small letters has been muddled by the arrival of the Internet. Often proper names are written either in capital or small letters and joined together. This practice is not recommended in this book.

. A Word of Warning

. The Hilton Hotel / Hilton Hotel ⇒**correct**

. a Hotel ⇒**wrong** – it should be ⇒ **a hotel**

. River Indus ⇒**correct** as river is a part of the full name

full name ↵

. There are many Rivers in England.

incorrect ↵ - correct form ⇒ **rivers**

. Hyde Park is in London. ⇒*correct*

. There many Parks in London.

incorrect ↵ - parks because it is the second part of this name.

. Colon

A colon is used for the following functions:

a . To introduce a list or a series of items.
For instance:

(1) . The following students must register their proposals today before 16.00 hours:
James Walker, Joan Smith, Elizabeth Wood and John Baker.

(2) . We can travel to London by any of the three means of travel: by car, by train or by coach.

(3) . These are unused product code numbers: BA 00012C, CC 18919X and CC 18920 X.

b . To identify a speaker in direct speech and quotations.
This is exemplified below:

    (4) . Joy said: 'It was my handbag.'

    (5) . Silvia shouted: 'Leave my home now!'

    (6) . Tony Blair promised: 'Education, education, education.'

    (7) . She asked me immediately: 'Who told you about my illness?'

c . Use a colon for introductory remarks.
For example:

    (8) . Ladies and gentlemen: allow me to present tonight's guest speaker.

d . To add information to a clause so that it is elaborated.
This is exemplified below:

    (9) . This group has students from six countries: Germany, Russia, India, China, Ireland and the United Kingdom.

    (10) . We specialise in selling technical books: engineering, computing and physical sciences.

    (11) . The inner city has been neglected by the authority: derelict buildings, dirty streets, lack of public transport, hardly any footpaths and ill-equipped hospitals are some of the things that local residents reported to the media.

e . To supplement information to a phrase so that it is expanded.
For example:

    (12) . Lots of books: computing, engineering, gardening, short stories and other topics.

f . To start a clause which contains an explanation of the previous clause.
This is demonstrated below:

    (13) . Today our town is very busy: there is an annual festival and a procession along the promenade.

    (14) . Our train was full of overseas visitors: many passengers were travelling to London Heathrow Airport.

g . To introduce a subtitle.
For example:

    (15) . Essential English: Grammar, Structure and Style of Good English.

                subtitle ↵

    (16) . C++ Simplified: A practical C++ Programming Manual.

                subtitle ↵

h . <u>To form numerical ratios and other number systems.</u>

For instance:

(17) . Profit and expenditure ratio **4:1**

(18) . Our train left London Victoria at 15:30 sharp.

i . <u>Another use of the colon is in the electronic mail(email/e-mail)</u>

Here is an example:

(19) . From: John Smith
　　　To: James Taylor
　　　Sent: write date here
　　　Subject: Delivery by car

Before to the arrival of email/e-mail, in the office memos 'Dated' was used instead of 'Sent'. <u>Colons are also used in mathematical, scientific and engineering expressions.</u>

. <u>Comma</u>

The comma and full stop are the most common punctuation marks in the English language. The correct use of the comma is not a mystery. Its usage is fairly well documented and understood, yet there is a tendency either to use too many commas or to use too few commas in a piece of writing. Indeed, there is a wide variation in the use of commas. Sometimes, a comma as a separator is essential. There are occasions when the use of a comma may be considered as optional for the sake of clarity. The following discussion illustrates its use for some specific aims:

a . <u>To separate items in a list of three or more items. These item may be words, phrases or clauses.</u>

Here are some examples:

(1) . Anne, Wolfgang, Elena, and Frank went to Austria for a skiing holiday.

(2) . You can have one more portion of potatoes, peas, or cabbage.

(3) . John is energetic, ambitious, and rich.

---

*　　<u>A comma before a conjunction is debatable</u>

In examples 1-3, a comma is placed before the coordinating conjunction. These coordinating conjunctions come before the last item in each list. The placing of a comma before the coordinating conjunction which indicates the start of the last item is often called the '**Oxford comma**'. However, there is a growing trend towards the omission of the comma <u>before the last coordinating conjunction.</u> On the other hand, when the last item in the list has **and** in it, the comma is necessary to avoid ambiguity.

****

(4) . My children used to enjoy watching television game shows, children's programmes, **and** the *Little and Large* comedy show.

essential comma ↵   ⇑

                              compound noun joined by *and* ⇒conjunction

(5) . He went to Fulham, Putney, **and** *Kensington and Chelsea* by bus.

a comma is essential here ↵ compound noun ↵

b . If the list ends with such phrases as *etc.*, *and the like* and *so on*, a comma is needed to indicate continuity of the same thing.

For instance:

(6) . Gull, golden eagle, finch, duck, ***and the like*** creatures with feathers and two legs are birds.

(7) . Tesco, Safeway, Morrison, etc. stores have been attracting customers of small corner shops to their own big retail outlets.

c . To join main clauses if they are linked by the coordinating conjunction *and*, *but* or *so**.

For example:

(1) . Our staff room is situated on the first floor, and the students' room is on the third floor.

(2) . You can attend our meeting today, but you must not come more than five minutes late.

(3) . She has declined our invitation, yet there is still plenty of time for her to accept it.

---

* The comma can be omitted when the clauses are short. This is exemplified below:

(4) . She cooks and I clean.

(5) . We ran very fast but still missed the last bus.

(6) . Susan is married yet she is known by her maiden name.

---

d . To separate a subordinate clause or phrase from the main clause, the use of a comma may be justified to avoid misunderstanding. The comma is more desirable and helpful, when the sentence is long.

For instance:

(7) . *After three hours of the skiing session*, they returned to their hotel

adverbial phrase↵   for a hot meal.

(8) . *At the end of the long working day*, I didn't receive my wage.

adverbial phrase↵

(9) . *As soon as they left home,* we had to cook our evening meal.

subordinate clause ↵

e. The use of a comma is less common, when the subordinate clause follows the main clause. For this reason, the comma is enclosed within the [ ] to indicate that its use is optional.

This is illustrated below:

(10) . I did not travel with my wife to London [,] *because I had to attend an important meeting.*

subordinate clause ↵

(11) . She wrote short stories as well [,] *so that she could support her family.*

subordinate clause ↵

(12) . We left home in the morning [,] *soon after our breakfast.*

subordinate clause ↵

f . Use commas to separate an adding /non-restrictive*/non-identifying clause from the main clause.

For instance:

(13) . My son, who is a soldier , has left the army.

⇑

adding/non-restrictive/non-identifying clause

(14) . Miss Jones, who is our store manager, grew up in a foster home.

In examples 13 and 14, both relative non-adding clauses are specifying the head nouns. If you remove the adding/non-restrictive/non-identifying clause from the sentence, it will still make sense.

---

* No commas are needed to separate identifying (restrictive) and classifying clauses from the main clause. See clauses for examples.

---

g . Use commas to separate the speaker from the direct speech.

This is exemplified below:

(15) . The head teacher said, 'No one is allowed to use a mobile phone in class.'

direct speech within single quotation marks ↵

(16) . John Smith shouted, 'You are breaking speed limits. Reduce your speed now.'

Note the use of single quotation marks. Single quotation marks are often used to report direct speech. You can use double quotation marks.

For instance:

(17). "Ian, I don't agree with you," he said angrily, "you are not thinking clearly."

(18). Franklin D. Roosevelt said, "The only thing we have to fear is fear itself."

h. Use commas to separate a question tag from the rest of the sentence.

For example:

(19). This is your new car, isn't it?

(20). Your wife is a doctor, am I right?

(21). Your complaint was dealt with by me to your satisfaction, wasn't it?

i. Use commas to separate parenthetic remarks from the rest of the sentence.

Words and phrases such as: *indeed, certainly, oh, by chance* and *incidentally (adverbial elements)* are not necessarily essential parts of a sentence in order to render its intended meaning. Indeed, they give additional information. Such words and phrases are also known as parenthetical remarks or parenthetic remarks. In a sentence, these are marked by commas, brackets or dashes. Here are some examples:

(22). *Indeed,* she came with her two children.

(23). I promise you, *sir,* I will pay back my tax by monthly instalments.

(24). *By the way*, do you know where John lives?

(25). *Now,* what can I do for you?

(26). *Lords, ladies and gentlemen**, allow me to present our honourable guest speaker, the Lord Mayor of Westminster.

---

* within a pair of comma as it is in the middle of a sentence. Here a pair of commas is functioning as parenthesis.

---

j. Use commas with numbers in accordance with the following rules:

. Write non-technical numbers, by placing a comma after every three units, commencing from the right of the number: For instance:

(27). 10,000   105, 111, 456   88,000,789

(28). The population of Bridlington is around 65,000.

---

*The comma is not used in numbers smaller than 10,000.

The following three numbers show the misuse of a comma in each number:

    (29).   1,267   2,345   9,999

Reason: *Commas are used with numbers 10,000 and above.*

- When dealing with the British currency, the whole pounds should be written with the pound symbol £. For example:

    (30). £1   £5,349*   £24   £1,009*

---

* Comas are essential here in such cases.

- When the British currency involves both pound and pence, write **pence** in numbers after the decimal point. The comma is also used if the number is £1,000 or greater. For instance:

    (31). £34.05   £467.99   £ 9,789.75

These examples are indicating two places after decimal point for pence.

- When the money is in pounds and pence, do not use the abbreviation *p* for pence. Mixed currency is extended to two places after the decimal point. This is illustrated by example (31).

- When the amount of money is less than the whole pound, it is written as:

    (32). 66p   99p   5p   1p Or write as:
        .66   .99   .05   .01

- Large amounts involving a million or a billion or a trillion can also be written with their respective symbols/abbreviation or without it: For example:

        . **m**   is an abbreviation or a symbol for million
        . **bn** is an abbreviation or a symbol for billion
        . **trillion** is written as trillion

    (33). 1,000,000   or   1 m   1,000,000,000 or 1 bn

        178,000,000   or 178 m   1,500,000,000 or 1.5 bn

- We say **a, one, two** or **several** billion or million. There is no need to say millions or billions. We say these without the final 's'. For example:

    (34). At the end of the first six months of this year, our sales reached between 2.6 m and 1 bn.

- When there is no quantity or a number before million or billion, we say millions or billions. For example:

(35). Millions/billions of pounds were invested in the London Dome.

The following examples on the use of million give further information.
.You can say:

(36). Our government has wasted ***tens of millions*** on advertising

plural numbers ↵   their failed policies.

. Always use a plural verb with million or millions and billion
  or billions: For instance:

(37). One million ***pounds*** were spent on this building project.

plural form ↵

(38). Three million ***pounds*** have been deposited in his bank account.

plural form ↵

(39). Some gangsters make ***their millions*** by selling drugs.

make their millions = all their money ↵

. *Currency in the USA*

Money is written in the same way as pounds and pence in the UK, except
with the dollar sign. For instance:

(40). $ 5,567   **$1.6m** $ 10.66   **50¢**

. Dash

The prime function of a dash is to separate a part of a sentence from the rest
of a sentence. There may be one or more dashes in a sentence. The dash is
used for a variety of aims. Some of these are exemplified below.

. In the following examples, dashes have added some excitement and
  informality:

(1). Annabel loved Rex so much – and she left her husband.

(2). Here is a bouquet of flowers – my sweetheart.

. In examples 3 and 4, the dash is used to place emphasis on a phrase
  towards the end of a sentence:

(3). He only has one thing on his mind – his girlfriend.

(4). Their car is just six months old – and rather expensive.

. In examples 5 and 6 dashes are used to separate list items:

(5). All the team members – John, Carl, Carol, Barry, Derek,
     Susan and Anne – left.

(6). Today we have sold – 20 copies of C++, 20 copies of Java,
     54 copies of XHTML – and taken orders for 45 copies of

English Grammar – the forthcoming title.

. In example 7 a dash is used to comment on a phrase which preceded it:

(7) . *Frankfurt, Vienna and Budapest* – these cities are well served by

phrase ↵   fast trains throughout the year.

comment on the phrase   ↵

. Examples 8 -10 demonstrate that when the dash is used parenthetically, a pair of dashes must be used:

(8) . The Himalayas – the highest mountains in the world – are the ultimate challenge.

(9) . Martin Luther King Jr – the US civil-rights campaigner, black leader, and Baptist minister – was awarded the Nobel Peace Prize in 1964.

(10) . Muhammad Ali – three times World Heavyweight Champion – was the most recognised person in the 20th century in the whole world.

In these examples, a pair of dashes is used instead of brackets in order to enclose the information. This parenthetic use of dashes is equivalent to brackets. For the parenthetic use, a pair of brackets is preferred as information within the brackets stands out better and makes a stronger impression on a reader. Therefore, it is suggested that you avoid using a pair of dashes for brackets.

. Examples 11 and 12 show the use of dashes to separate the additional clause from the main clause:

(11) . **Charlie Chaplin was a film actor and director** – *who made his reputation as a tramp with a smudge moustache, bowler hat and twirling cane.*   (main clause is shown in **bold**)

(12) . Berlin is smaller than London – *where underground trains*

main clause↵   *are too crowded during the rush hours.*

additional clause informing more about London/head noun   ↵

We usually separate the additional clause with commas.

. Examples 13 and 14 demonstrate the use of a dash to indicate different types of ranges:

(13) . World War I 1914 – 1918 caused the death of an estimated 10 million people.

(14) . World War II 1939 – 45 caused the loss of an estimated

last two digits ↵ 55 million lives.

When on both sides of the dash the dates are in the same decade, it is conventional to write only the last two digits on the right side of the dash.

    (15) . Queen Victoria 1819 – 1901

Here full dates are given on both sides of the dash because there is a change of century.

    (16) . See pp 210 – 220 **or** See pages 210 – 220

    (17) . A – K

    (18) . volumes I– V

Some writers use dashes to imitate spoken English, to place emphasis, to indicate a missing   word or words (maybe a rude word or phrase), incompleteness or uncertainty. Comic writers and tabloid journalists use dashes frequently. In formal writing and in academic work, commas and round brackets (parentheses) for parenthetic use are generally preferred. It should be noted that after a dash, only a proper noun begins with a capital letter.

. Ellipses(dot dot dot)

Ellipses (singular ellipsis) are a series of usually three full stops, or points, or dots. In essence, ellipses indicate:

        . omission of one or more words from a sentence

        . a sentence or paragraph is missing from the writing

        . withholding of something for whatever reason

These are exemplified below:

    (1) . They were thirsty, but also **...** and penniless.

        a word (hungry) is omitted ↵

    (2) . You must tell the panel nothing but **...**

        a phrase (the truth) is omitted ↵

In example 2, ellipses occurred at the end of the sentence. When ellipses are utilised at the end of a sentence, there is *no* need for the fourth dot or full stop. On the contrary, in example 3, the ellipses are used to separate two complete sentences. In this case, there is a need for the fourth dot. Here ellipses indicate that at least one complete sentence has been withheld. The missing or withheld sentence or further sentences should have been where ellipses are shown.

    (3) . I have never said that **... .** I don't use that sort of language.

    ------------------------- ⇑ -------------------------------------

complete sentence 1↵   ellipses   complete sentence 2 ↵
                  and a full stop

    (4) . They visited us in 1996,1997, 1998 **...**

        omission of some subsequent years↵

. Exclamation Mark

The exclamation mark is represented by **!**. It is a terminator just like the full stop; but it is used for the following specific purposes.

a . <u>To denote strong emotional feelings</u> – *<u>anger, happiness, sorrow, etc.</u>*

For instance:

> (1) . You are a bloody fool!
>
> (2) . How wonderful the party was!
>
> (3) . Didn't they cry!
>
> (4) . We won! Hurrah!

b . <u>To mark emphatic phrases</u> - *scorn, insult, swearing, irony, <u>command</u> , etc.*

Here are some examples:

> (5) . She must be silly!
>
> (6) . You're a mess!
>
> (7) . Get out of my class! And wait outside until I call you back!
>
> (8) . Get lost!
>
> (9) . You have no money! And you buy a new BMW !

c. <u>To mark the end of interjections</u>

For instance:

> (10) . *Cheers!*
>
> (11) . *Blimey!*
>
> (12) . *Be quiet!*
>
> (13) . *Ow!*   (*Ow! That hurt me!*)
>
> (14) . *Ouch!*   (*Ouch! That hurt me!*)

See ⟹ Interjections

d . <u>To indicate the importance of a specific statement</u>

For example

> (14) . What a difficult journey she faced!
>
> (15) . Didn't I call your name? Sorry!
>
> (16) . John is only twelve!

e . <u>Some other uses of exclamation marks</u>

Sometimes people use multiple exclamation marks in order to make a piece of writing more interesting. Unless you are writing comic material or working for the tabloid press, try not to use them.

In mathematics, the exclamation stands for the factorial sign. e.g., five factorial = 5!. As a matter of interest, its value works out as:

> $5! = (5 \times 4 \times 3 \times 2 \times 1) = 120$

There are other less common uses of exclamation marks. For instance (!) and
[!]. These are used in the publishing world.

. Footnotes

A footnote is written below the text at the bottom of the page. It may be an
explanation, a comment, some additional information or reference. The most
common symbol used for footnotes is the Arabic numeral written as a superscript figure. A superscript number/figure is
written above the normal line of writing. For instance:

> "Object Oriented Programming (OOP) is not new. What is
> new is the application of its concepts in modern programming
> languages such as C++ and Java."1
>
>   1 Java Simplified, Adam Shaw, ADR, 2004.

Some people use other symbols such as asterisks and oblique.

. Full Stop

The full stop is the most commonly used punctuation mark. It is also known
as a *full point*. In the United States of America, it is called a *period.* It is a
terminator that is used for a variety of situations as exemplified below:

> (1) . Rose is engaged to Russell. ⇐ full stop at the end a sentence
>
> (2) . Would you kindly leave this room now.
>
> (3) . What you should do is to listen to your mother.
>
> (4) . May I ask you to show me your current pass.

Example 2-4 are not questions but polite requests and thus a full stop is
placed at the end of each statement.

a . Use a full stop at the end of indirect speech that sounds like a
   question.
For instance:

> (5) . I would very much like to know where your manor in
>   Yorkshire is.
>
> (6) . The office manager wanted to find out why the monthly report
>   was delayed.

b . Many abbreviations end with a full stop.
For example:

> (7) . Joan Smith Ph.D.
>
> (8) . Dr. A .Williams is away this week.

There is a tendency not to place full stops after initials. Some people do
not use the full stop at the end of any abbreviation. For instance:

> (9) . Jan ⇐ *January*
>
> (10) . e.g. ⇐ *for example*

It (e.g.) is derived from the Latin words *EXEMPLI GRATIA*. For instance: e.g. red colour.

  (11). et al. ⇐ and other people or things
It is derived from the *Latin 'et alii or alia' or 'aliae'*. It is usually used after names. For instance: discovered by John Major et al., 2001

   (12). etc. - it indicates that in the list there are other items that could have been included.

It is an abbreviation '**for** *et cetera*' or '*et ceteri* ' For instance: Colin, Robin, Jane, etc.

   (13). www.adrlondon.ltd ⇐ known as 'dot' in an e-mail address

   (14). Mr and Mrs Blair have arrived. Or
     Mr. and Mrs. Blair have arrived.

   (15). The UN offices in the UK are in London. Or
     The U.N. offices in the U.K. are in London.

c . Use full stops for both British and American currencies.
For example:

    (16). £45.76 ⇐ pounds . pence

  seventy-six pence↵

    (17). $ 45.90 ⇐ dollars . cents

  ninety cents↵

In both examples, the full stop is used as a *symbol for the decimal point.* In the UK, less than a pound is usually written as a number with p.
For instance: *96p*

d . No comma is added to abbreviations for metric measurements,
 e.g. cm, mm, kg, l, km, etc.

e . Full stops are used between days, months and years when dates are
 written in numbers.
For example:

  (18) . 01.03.03   (19). 31.05.01

f . A full stop is placed between the hours and minutes when time is
 written in the UK.
For instance:

  (20). 3.45 a. m*.   (21). 8.15 p. m**.

 ante meridiem ↵   post meridiem ↵

---

 * There is a full stop after m in 'a.m.' 'p.m.'
 * * There is a full stop between 'a' and 'm' and 'p' and 'm'.
 Some people do not insert a full stop where it is required.

. **ante meridiem** ⇒ before noon. It is from Latin. It starts at 10 a.m.

. **post meridiem** ⇒after noon. It is from Latin. It starts at 3 p.m.

g . <u>A full stop is placed at the end of a footnote irrespective of its grammatical status.</u> For instance:

(22). 1 pp. 12-33.

(23). 2 Adam Shaw in Java, pp.* 10-12.

---

* 1. **pp.** is an abbreviation for pages. It is written in lower-case letters followed by a full stop. A **lower-case** abbreviation cannot begin a sentence.

2.It is written in a business letter in front of a person's name when someone signs the letter on behalf of another person, i.e. **pp Sarah Baker**. It means it is from Sarah Baker but signed by somebody in Sarah Baker's absence. Also **'pp.' is written** in a business letter.

. <u>Hyphen</u>

It can be said that hyphens are used for two main functions:

. to join two words together

. to split the word at the end of a line of print

In British English, hyphens are more commonly used than in American English. The following examples illustrate some of the purposes for using hyphens.

(1)   . He went to see his ***mother-in-law*** in the Bahamas.

hyphen forming a compound noun↵ - compound noun containing

a preposition ⇒ **in**

a. <u>The following examples also demonstrate the use of the hyphen in forming compound words:</u>

(2). He is a ***jack-of-all-trades*** who takes on almost any work he is offered.

In example 2, the compound noun is formed by including two prepositions – *of* and *all*.

(3). You can travel by an ***inter-city*** train anywhere in France.

(4). His ***ex-wife*** is a hairdresser.

(5). She paid <u>*seventy-seven*</u> *pounds for this beautiful dress.

hyphen ↵

---

* <u>Compound Numbers</u>

1. The hyphen is used in writing out numbers in words between twenty-one and ninety-nine.
2. Do not use hyphens when writing out numbers in words such as three hundred.
3. In compound numbers hundred, thousand, etc. <u>do not</u> end with –s.

****

    (6) . Your bill comes to *two hundred* and *thirty-four* pounds.

        not hyphenated ↵   hyphenated ↵

b . The following examples show that when a compound word is formed with a verb form, it is written with a hyphen:

       (7) . John couldn't think of a *put-down* fast enough.

a remark to make someone look /feel stupid ↵

      (8) . Natasha gave a *record-breaking* performance last night.

      (9) . It is a *well-thought-out* idea.

    (10) . Barbara is always *well-dressed*.

c . Some other compound words formed with well + hyphen and verb forms are as follows:

well-advised, well-aimed, well-behaved, well-born, well-built, well-connected, well-deserved, well-desired, well-documented, well- earned, well-founded, well-groomed, well-heeled, well-informed, well-intentioned, well-known, well-looking, well-made, well-off, well- preserved, well-respected, well-rounded, well-spoken, well-tempered, well-thought-of, well-tried, well-to-do, well-wished, well-won, well-worked-out.

These are compound adjectives. The use of hyphens in compound words is often debatable.

d . The following examples illustrate that some nouns preceded by a letter are hyphenated:

      (1) . On British motorways a *U-turn* is prohibited.

      (2) . Our hospital is short of chest *X-ray* machines

      (3) . A *T-junction* is a place where one road joins another but does not cross it, so that joining roads form the shape of the letter **T**.

      (4) . A bend in a pipe or road like the shape of the letter *s* is called an *S-bend*.

compound noun ↵

e . The following examples show that some compound nouns with adverbs or prepositions are usually written with or without hyphens:

      (5) . motorway **or** motor-way

      (6) . phone card **or** phone-card

f . The following examples show that in some words with prefixes, hyphens are used to separate the prefix from the root word:

      (7) . Our home telephone number is *ex - directory*.

               prefix ↵ root word↵

(8) . A *post-dated* cheque will be treated as payable immediately.

(9) . Please *re-enter* the office from the side entrance.

(10) . There is no *multi-storey* car park in our town.

(11) . At present, there are plenty of *semi-skilled* jobs in our area.

g . The following examples demonstrate that adjective compounds preceded by *self* are hyphenated:

(12) . The enclosed document is *self-explanatory*.

(13) . In some Indian villages, *self-help* community projects have transformed villagers' lives.

(14) . Last summer, we rented a *self-contained* flat in a small sea-side town in France.

(15) . Don't be too self-critical because such an attitude can be *self-destructive*.

(16) . Professor Burkhardt is a *self-styled* professor of the German language.

(17) . He is a *self-taught* software designer.

(18) . Anne-Marie always seems so calm and *self-possessed*.

(19) . You shouldn't allow fear and *self-doubt* to rule your life.

h . The following compound words formed with self + hyphen + root word:

self-access, self-appointed, self-appraisal, self-assertive, self-assured, self-awareness, self-catering, self-centred, self-confessed, self-confident, self-congratulation, self-conscious, self-contradiction, self-control, self-criticism, self-deception, self-defeating, self-defence, self-denial, self-destruction, self-determination, self-discipline, self-derive, self-educated, self-employed, self-esteem, self-evident, self-examination, self-fulfilling, self-government, self-image, self-important, self-imposed, self-indulgent, self-inflicted, self-interest, self-made, self-opinionated, self-pity, self-preservation, self-reliant, self-respect, self-restraint, self-righteous, self-sacrifice, self-satisfied, self-seeking, self-service, self-serving, self-worth.

i . Hyphens are also used in double-barrelled family names as demonstrated below:

(20) . Mr. and Mrs. *Douglas-Home* are here.

(21) . Lord *Baden-Powell* founded the Boy Scout movement in 1908.

j . Some British names of places are also hyphenated, e.g.

(22) . *Southend-on-Sea* is in Essex near London.

(23) . *Stratford-upon-Avon* is where William Shakespeare was born in 1564.

. The word after the preposition begins with a capital letter as in
Examples 22-23.

k . Hyphens at the end of a line (word division)

We are in the age of Information Technology (IT). Typewriters have virtually
been replaced by keyboards and word-processors. Generally speaking, word-
processing software truncates a word at the end of a line in accordance with
its own rule. Increasing numbers of books are created by using word-
processing software. It is the word-processor which formats the document,
hence inserts the hyphen at the point of a word division at the end of a line.
This is shown below:

There are two subject areas, namely *etymology* and *phonetics*, which deserve
mention here. *Etymology* is the study of word origin and *phonetics* is the
study of speech and sounds. **Etymology** has a set of rules for dividing the
word into syllables, prefixes and suffixes. Phonetics suggests the division of
a word based on its sounds. If you are keen to explore word division, it is
suggested that you pay a visit to your local library to consult reference books
or search the Internet for further information on these topics.

. Paragraph

There are no hard-and-fast rules that regulate a paragraph's size and content.
In any piece of writing, paragraphs enable the writer to lay the text in its most
appropriate order so that the reader is at ease with the text. A paragraph contains a main theme. The main theme may have one or more related points.
The whole idea is to place related points in a paragraph so that the reader is
helped to grasp what is being written. Of course, the main theme may have
several related paragraphs.

For instance, the main theme of the above section is the use of the hyphen. It
has two related paragraphs. The first paragraph talks about the way words are
divided by a word-processor these days. In the second paragraph, an example
is given in order to demonstrate how the word-processor has divided the
word *Etymology* at the end of a line (see above).

These paragraphs are short and concise. In fact, the length of a paragraph is
dictated by the amount of the text in the main theme and related points. As in
this example, the sizes of both paragraphs are based on the amount and flow
of the text in each paragraph.

Some people write long paragraphs. For instance, a letter from a solicitor
(lawyer) usually has long paragraphs. There are other experts such as phi-
losophers who also construct longer paragraphs as longer paragraphs provide
them with plenty of space to develop their ideas and argue their opinions.
Nowadays, the widespread tendency is to write shorter paragraphs.

Paragraphs are also visual aids. Some writers prefer to leave at least one blank line between two paragraphs. This is the style of this book. Some writers have other preferences. For instance, they start a paragraph by indenting the first word by a number of letter spaces, usually 3 to 5. They do not allow a blank line between two paragraphs. Hardly ever, writers indent and allow a blank line space at the same time. If you are interested in fiction and poetry, consult some relevant reference materials for paragraphing techniques. It is worth mentioning that publishers have their own house style for paragraphing.

Example of paragraphing by indenting the first word

> This is an indented paragraph.....
> you said that---------------
> ....
> This is the second indented paragraph.....

Example of paragraphing with a blank line between two paragraphs

> This is a paragraph...............
> --------------------------------------
> --------------------------------------
>
> This is the second paragraph --------

. Question Mark

The question mark (**?**) is a terminator like the full stop. The main purposes for which it is used are exemplified below:

. The following examples indicate that what precedes the question mark is an interrogative sentence:

(1) . Are you related to this woman?

(2) . What are you carrying in that heavy suitcase?

(3) . The policeman asked me first, 'Is this your car?'

(4) . I asked him, 'Where were you at the time of the accident'?

The purpose of the interrogative question is to get an answer from the respondent. An interrogative question or a *direct question* always ends with a question mark.

a . Direct *question-like* a statement ends with a question mark(question tag):

For instance:

       (5) . It is a lovely morning, isn't it ?

       (6) . She looks very pretty in her wedding dress, doesn't she?

       (7) . They look disappointed, don't they?

       (8) . Joan's mother is always nagging her, isn't she?

       (9) . You are a footballer, aren't you?

     (10) . They are always <u>as busy as bees</u>, aren't they?

               idiomatic expression ↵ - it means very busy

b . <u>The short question also ends with a question mark:</u>

The following example shows that instead of asking a full question, you can make it short.

    (11) .

    . What is your name ? ⟹ short form   ⟹ First name please?

    . What is your surname? ⟹ short form   ⟹ Surname please?

    . What is your home telephone number? ⟹ short form ⟹ Home
                                    telephone please?

    . What is your permanent address? ⟹ short form ⟹ Permanent
                                    address please?

<u>The above example illustrates that a short question may only be a word or
several words</u>

c . <u>When there is uncertainty about the fact, a question mark is usually used to indicate it.</u>

Here are some examples:

    (12) . Socrates (?470 –399 BC) was a Greek philosopher.

    (13) . Friedrich Engels (?1820-95) was a German philosopher who
         collaborated with Karl Marx on *The Communist Manifesto*
         (?1848).

    (14) . Albert Einstein was born in Berlin(?)*.

---

    * Often a date or place of birth is doubtful or unverified.

---

d . <u>The question mark is not used with an indirect question:</u>

For instance:

    (15) . We would like to know what your thoughts are on capital
         punishment.

    (16) . I was wondering if you could give my wife a lift to the town
         centre.

    (17) . We would like to know what the cost is.

. The following question words always end with a question mark:

	Question Word	**Example**
(18).	What	What is your question?
(19).	When	When did you order the goods?
(20).	Where	Where is your mother?
(21).	Which	Which is your desk?
(22).	Who	Who won the election in our area?
(23).	Whom	Whom did you invite?
(24).	Why	Why were you late this morning?
(25).	Whose	Whose book is this?
(26).	How	How are you this morning?

e. In chess, the question mark is used by itself and with other symbols, e.g.

(27).   ? means a bad move

(28).   ?? stands for a serious blunder

f. Some writers use two question marks (??) or a question mark with an exclamation mark (?!) to imply scepticism or strong feeling :

For example:

(29). Do you really think he is telling us the truth??

(30). What made you believe her??

---

* Some people repeat question marks several times with or without the exclamation mark. The use of more than one question mark is not recommended for formal writing.

. Quotation Marks

Quotation marks are also known as inverted commas, speech marks and quotes. There are single quotation marks (' ') as well as double quotation marks (" "). In Britain, single quotes are preferred. The main purposes of using quotation marks are exemplified below.

a. The following examples illustrate that quotation marks are used in order to enclose direct speech:

(1). 'How do you like the flowers I sent you through Interflora?' Emma asked Anne.

(2). 'War is always a sign of failure,' said the President of France.

Punctuation   **241**

****

The rule is that the words within the quotes must be exactly those spoken.

(3) . 'We will always remember Jill as a kind person,' said Mrs.
Jones. 'She was ever so friendly and generous to us.'

This example illustrates:

. When a quoted speech is interrupted at the end of a sentence, instead of a full stop a comma is used to mark the end of the sentence.

. The word which resumes the quoted speech begins with a capital letter as shown above.

. **Direct Speech** is someone's exact spoken words. When direct speech is reported or quoted, the words actually spoken must be within quotation marks. The writer must also give the precise source of the words actually spoken. The reader should know to whom quoted words are attributed.

b . When words *where, why, yes* and *no* are part of direct speech, these are enclosed within quotation marks (but not in reported speech).

This is demonstrated below:

(4) . Veronica said to him, 'Yes!'

(5) . 'Yes,' Tom replied, but Monica shouted, 'No! It is not for me.'

(6) . Joyce asked, 'Where?'

(7) . Gary said, 'Why?'

(8) . When we asked him to come along with us, he replied, '<u>No.</u>'

direct speech↵

. **Indirect Speech** is when instead of reporting someone's exact words, the meaning of words is expressed in the third person form using a past tense.

(9) . When we asked Derek to travel with us, <u>he said no</u>.

indirect speech not within quotes↵

(10) . She has just left home. <u>She did not say where she was going.</u>

indirect speech↵

c . When a quotation is within another quotation, double quotation marks are used to enclose the quotes within quotes.

It is illustrated by the following examples:

(11) . 'What do you mean by **"late"?**' I asked him.

a quote within a quote↵– within double quotation marks

(12) . I asked the speaker, 'Could you please give an example of "willy-nilly"?'

In example 12, *willy-nilly* is a quote within a quote. It is an adverb (informal). It means irrespective of whether someone wants to or not, e.g.

. We were forced willy-nilly by the policeman to turn left.

It also means doing something carelessly without planning or thinking, e.g.

. She spends her money willy-nilly.

d . When the direct quotation has several paragraphs, it is customary to start each paragraph with an opening quotation mark, and place the closing quotation mark at the end of the entire quotation.

For instance:

(13). 'Tagore also believed in learning by doing. For this purpose, a garden and a handicraft shop were part of his school. He had great interest in ecological matters. He used to have tree planting ceremonies.

'Tagore also founded a university. At his university, he established an international faculty in order to teach unity in diversity.'

(Rabindranath Tagore – the first Asian to receive the Nobel Prize for Literature 1913)

e . When a phrase or a word is quoted, it is enclosed within quotation marks.

Here are three examples:

(14). Colin told me 'certainly no deal', which I conveyed to my boss.

(15). My doctor declared my health was 'excellent'.

(16). The hyphenated word 'willy-nilly' has two different meanings as explained above.

f . Titles of lectures, book chapters, articles, short stories and short poems, television and radio programmes and musical writing are shown in quotes.

For instance:

(17). The title of our annual lecture is ' The Role of Neighbourhood Watch'.

(18). 'Fruit Gathering' is one of Rabindranath Tagore's poems.

. The following rules should be observed for quotes:

g . Punctuation marks (comma, full stop, question marks, etc.) connected with quoted words are placed *inside the closing quotation mark*:

For instance:

(19). 'I am fine. How is your wife?' he said to me.

(20). 'We have been trying to compromise for three days. Can someone suggest another idea which may appeal to all of us? Let's see who has a bright idea. First, let's have a drink!' The chairman remarked.

h . When a statement or a sentence finishes with a quotation that ends with a full stop, or a question mark, or an ellipsis, or an exclamation mark, the full stop to stop the entire statement is not required:

(21) . She said, 'I sent you my CV yesterday.'

(22) . Sarah shouted, 'It's marvellous!'

(23) . Alan said to his wife, ' I never agreed to your ... '

(24) . My teacher asked me, 'How long do you need to finish this essay?'

i . Punctuation marks (comma, full stop, question marks, etc.) connected with the entire sentence are placed outside the closing quotation marks:

This is demonstrated below:

(25) . A few days ago, I read a book ' Napoleon Bonaparte – The French Emperor'.

(26) . I wrote a letter to a friend and told her about 'White Teeth by Zadie Smith'.

. Semicolon

A semicolon (;) indicates that there are two separate pieces of information in a sentence. It is used for the following purposes:

. To join two related clauses:

(1) . Alexander is a well-known local businessman; he is also mayor.

(2) . Anne went to Austria from Frankfurt; she stopped en route in Stuttgart for a few hours.

In these examples, clauses could have been joined by *and* - a coordinating conjunction. You can also write each example as two separate short sentences, ending each with a full stop. A semicolon, like the full stop, indicates that these are separate but related short sentences.

a . To join clauses that are linked by a conjunction in order to place greater emphasis on the following clause.

For instance:

(1) . All motor cars must be fitted with seatbelts; and both the driver and passengers must fasten their seatbelts correctly.

(2) . It is not true to say that poverty is man-made; but it is the result of many complicated and inter-related factors.

b . To separate groups within a list which may have a number of commas in each group.

(3) . We publish computer programming, Web design and

>   information technology books; we represent American and
>   Australian medical, engineering and science book
>   publishers; we also supply technical, medical and IT
>   periodicals through the post to our regular subscribers both
>   at home and abroad.
>
> (4) . You should demonstrate both written and spoken working
>   knowledge of German and French; explain how European
>   Union laws are incorporated and implemented at
>   governmental levels in France and Germany; and the way
>   industry and commerce operate in these countries.

In these examples, semicolons have created groups within the list. The elements in each group are separated by commas. In essence, semicolons eliminate the overuse of coordinating conjunctions and refine long sentences by balancing them well.

c . To create a pause when preceded by an adverb or conjunction such as *nevertheless, moreover, hence, besides, also, consequently.*

This is demonstrated below:

> (5) . In city centres car speed is limited; moreover, honking your
>   car horn aimlessly is prohibited.
>
> (6) . She is really self-motivated; hence, she always completes
>   her task on time.
>
> (7) . Elizabeth is friendly, rich and generous ; therefore she has
>   many friends.

. Slash

A slash functions as a separator. It is also known as bar, diagonal, oblique mark, solidus, and stroke. Some of its uses are as follows:

a . To indicate alternatives.

For instance:

> (1) . Tea/Coffee ⇐ instead of *or* a slash is used
>
> (2) . Dear Sir/Madam
>   This phrase may be ended with or without a comma.
>
> (3) . We vote now/adjourn the meeting for lunch.
>
> (4) . True/False
>
> (5) . He/she can stand for the election of club secretary.

b . To indicate fiscal (connected with the government's financial year), academic, accounting and similar fixed periods of time.

Here are three examples:

> (6) . Tax Year 2008/09
>
> (7) . Academic year 1999/2000

(8) . Balance Sheet for the Period 2009/10

c . To form part of certain abbreviations.
This is demonstrated below:

(9) . I/O ⇐ Input – output in the computing world

(10) . A/C No. 1200   ⇐ Account = A/C

(11) . Send it to me c/o John Smith ⇐ c/o = care of

(12) . We must **w/o** these long outstanding bad debts.
      write off ↵

d . The slash is also used for some specific purposes in scientific, technical and Information Technology (IT) fields.

It has two forms in IT. These are a forward slash (**/**) and a back slash(****). Personal Computers and Internet users deal with these types on a regular basis.

. Asterisk

The symbol for the **asterisk** is a star (*****). It is used for the following purposes:

a . To indicate a reference, a footnote or an explanation given at the bottom of the text or elsewhere on the same page
For example:

(1) . First-degree burns affect the very top layer of the skin.*
      * Hazel Courtney with Gareth Zeal in
        500 of the Most Important Health Tips 2001

---

*Some people prefer to use superscript numbers instead of the asterisk.

---

b . To indicate omission of letters in taboo words.
Here is an example:

(2) . He is really a gentle person who rarely loses his temper. He was understandably annoyed and shouted, 'F *** off!'

c . To show the importance of a particular word or phrase.
For instance:

(3) . The items out of stock are marked with an asterisk and should be re-ordered by tomorrow:
              ISBN 19011 97808
              ISBN 1901197 883*
              ISBN 1901197 700*

It is used in some dictionaries to indicate important points.

. <u>**Word-Processing Symbols (or Marks) - Bullets, Bolds, Italics, Underlining and Arrows, etc.**</u>

We are in the age of IT and increasingly using word-processors. There are many symbols now that were not available on typewriters. These symbols or marks should be used sensibly.

. **Bullets** have been increasingly appearing in printed material. In this book bullets are used in order:
   . To begin a heading so that it can stand out as the start of another section.
   . To form part of numbering system for examples.
   . To show the importance of the text to follow.
   . To summarise points made or show conclusions.
   . To use bold, italics, underlining techniques, and arrows which can help the reader in the following ways:

. **Bolds, Italics, Underlining and arrows** <u>are used for the following functions</u>:
   . To highlight the importance of a word, phrase, or a larger piece of text by means of **bold,** *italics* and <u>underlining</u> tools.
   . To pinpoint a particular word, phrase, or a clause in a sentence by means of an arrow ($\Leftarrow \dashv \Downarrow$). In many places in this book, this technique is applied.
   . To clarify the pinpointed text by giving further information. on its nature and function. You can also make the pinpointed text larger so that it can stand out.

These techniques can only be applied if you use a word-processor. These means of marking text are new and on the periphery of punctuation. With the passage of time, they will be well recognised and used, especially by science, technical, and text books writers. Use them if you think they will help you clarify the text.

In summary, punctuation marks enable us to join, separate, and manipulate words, phrases, clauses, and paragraphs. In addition, these marks can enhance the meaning of a piece of writing irrespective of its size.

Part 4
Written Communication

. Introduction

' Someone somewhere wants a letter from you!'
(an old slogan used by the Post Office)

Good written communication is required in all aspects of life. Indeed, the knowledge acquired in the preceding parts can enable you to construct both social and business written communication, i.e. letter, application, invitation, etc. The fact of the matter is that one cannot effectively communicate by simply writing correct clauses, sentences and idiomatic expressions. What is desirable for good communication is to know or imagine the recipient of your written communication, so that you have an idea what they will be thinking when they receive and open your written communication. On receipt of a written communication, instantly, consciously or unconsciously, the thought that often enters our minds is *what's in it for me*?

This leads to an interesting conclusion that is, you should write it in such a way that they read the whole written communication attentively, and respond to your communication positively. For instance, if it is a social letter, it must create a better mutual understanding between the writer and the recipient. If it is a business letter, you want them to do business with you whether they buy from you or you buy from them. In both cases, it is important that you understand what the recipient wants from your letter.

Good written communication requires not only knowledge of English grammar but also the skill of putting it into practice in written communication. It raises a fundamental question:

What should you put into practice to construct a good written communication?

You should construct your written communication which demonstrates:
- . the clarity of your thought about the main theme/subject matter
- . the order or arrangement of points or events in their order of occurrence or importance
- . the explanation of each theme/point/ topic in paragraph form
- . the connectivity of paragraphs in the logical sequence events occurred and stated in each individual paragraph and within paragraphs leading to the completion of the whole written communication

. the appropriate writing style for social and business communication,
meaning the particular forms* in which social and business written
communication is done respectively.

---

* Written communication forms have been established over a long
period. The neglect of them, in the age of the Internet, is a sign of not
only carelessness but also ignorance. The World Wide Web(WWW)
has led to the growth of written communication, and the growing fear is
that many people across the Internet are distorting well established forms
and customs of written communication. a

. Style of addressing the reader

In this day and age, formality in addressing people is somewhat relaxed, but
it is still desirable that we are courteous and address people correctly. When
you write to a large organisation, it is not always possible to know the name
of the recipient. If you try to find the name of the person by telephone, you
spend time and money on telephone charges. They can still tell you to write
to their company, or a particular department. It is, therefore, common practice to use in business letters the following address:

Salutation remark – it is the opening remark: 'Dear Sir/Madam'
                                   and conclude the letter with the
Complimentary remark - closing remark : 'Yours faithfully'.

. Usually, letters from business to business have names of individuals. In
  this case, it is customary to address them as follows:

Salutation remark: 'Dear Mr Broomfield' and conclude the letter with
the
Complimentary remark: 'Yours sincerely'

The salutation and complimentary remarks for social letter writing is discussed later.

. The superscription

It means the name and address that is written on the envelope. If you know
the recipient's academic awards, titles, honours or any other distinctions,
these should be included in the superscription.

If it is a business letter, and you know the name of the recipient, it is polite to
mark the letter for the attention of the individual by writing the name. In addition, if you know the post the recipient holds, write it as well. For example:

For the attention of Mr G B Smith MSc(Computing)(London)*

Managing Director
Smith Sportswear PLC
1 Smith Road
Edinburgh
EH1 1BB

---

* For important letters do not use **F. A.O**. for: 'For The Attention of'
both in the letter and on the envelope.

The above superscription has **open punctuation***. This is increasingly
becoming the acceptable style of addressing correspondence. It is the
omission of commas and full stops in both salutation and complimentary remarks and address. It is common practice to do so in order to save time
and space when using a word processor. On page 250, you can see both
open and fully punctuated examples of address on an envelope.

. In a workplace, academic and professional awards and other distinctions
  awarded are important. These should be included in the superscription,
  if they are known to you.

. Some women prefer not to be known as 'Miss' or 'Mrs'. In a business
  letter, if a woman does not want to state whether she is married or not,
  she prefers to be addressed as '**Ms**', e.g., Ms Barbara Castle. Thus, write
    . in the salutation section: 'Dear Ms Castle' and
    . in the complimentary section: 'Yours sincerely'.

. If there is no need for preference, address her in accordance with her
  status, e.g. 'Professor/ Dr/ Mrs/Miss Sara Brooks', or any other status.

. In important business letters that are usually typed/word processed by a
  secretary, salutation and complimentary marks may be handwritten by
  the person signing the letter. Often, a greeting such as 'kind regards' is
  also added and handwritten. This is a good idea as it shows a personal
  touch and interest. However, it is not necessary to write it by hand. I
  would prefer to write these lines myself. It is better to be courteous.

. If you write a business letter to husband and wife: In the salutation
  section write:
    . 'Dear Mr and Mrs John Taylor' or
    . 'Dear Mr and Mrs J Taylor' and in the
    . complimentary remark section: 'Yours sincerely'

One initial of the husband's first name is written after 'Mrs' as shown
above. In the complimentary remark section write: 'Yours sincerely'.

. Often people address a wife as ' Mrs Pamela Taylor' that is **incorrect**.
This is a common error. It should be her husband's first name, not her
own first name, followed by her married surname (husband's surname).
The growing trend is that a married woman mentions her first name
followed by her husband's surname. It is slowly replacing the customary
form of addressing a married woman.

. For two or more **business women,** write in the:
    . salutation section: 'Dear Ladies' and
    . complimentary remark section: 'Yours faithfully'

. For **one woman** whose surname is not known to you, state in the:
    . salutation section: 'Dear Madam' and

    . complimentary section: 'Yours faithfully'

. A **professor**, even if he/she is a doctor and professor:
    . 'Dear Professor Brown"

. To find out how to address people with titles such as Sir, Lord,
Bishop, etc. consult a reference book.

In this part, we are concerned with social and business written communication. Thus, it is divided into two chapters. These are Chapters 15, on Social
Letter Writing and Chapter 16 which is on Business Letter Writing.

. Qualifications

In a social letter, it is customary not to list **qualifications** below the grade of
doctor after the name in the superscription (on the envelope). These days, it is
not wrong, if you write the recipient's qualifications, whatever they are, irrespective of their grades, after the name.

---

* open punctuation address on an envelope

  Mrs Gordon Brown
  23 Palace Gardens
  London
  SW11 2AA

* Fully punctuated address on an envelope

Mr. L. M. Smith,
10, Manchester Road,
Salford,
Greater Manchester,   (some people use full stop after the county/area)
MN12 6BN

****

Chapter 14
Social Letter Writing

. Introduction

Social letters are written to relatives, friends and acquaintances. A get well letter is a social letter. Letters of invitation and sympathy are also examples of social letters. These are informal letters.

. Stationery

Ordinary writing paper is good enough. Some people like to use *Letterhead paper* designed especially for social communication. A letterhead has the name and address of a person (for business its name, address, etc.) printed at the top of their writing paper. Nowadays, for social letter writing, it is becoming acceptable to include telephone, fax and even email details in a letterhead.

Letterheads designed for purposes other than social ones have other information as well. There are local printers who can provide you with a variety of paper types, colours and design of letterhead papers. Some letterheads for social writing include imaginative graphics.

For social letter writing, letterheads do not usually include names. If you correspond with some friends overseas, it is a good idea to start your letterhead with your name, because it will help your overseas friends to write your name correctly. Often foreign names prove difficult to spell correctly.

Usually, printers offers *envelopes* of the same colour as letterhead paper, where your name and address are printed at the left-hand top corner of the envelope, or at the back* of the envelope with the message:
If undelivered, please return to——'

---

* As nowadays the post is processed by means of electronic devices, it is best to print your name and address at the back of the envelope. This will avoid the possibility of your letter being delivered to your own address.
Why is it so?
The electronic device starts reading the address from the left side of the envelope/card/packet and directs the post to the address being read first, which may be your own address.

Indeed, the use of personal computers has made it possible to design your own letterhead. It is not necessary to get your personalised letterhead printed. It depends on individual preference and willingness to spend money on one's serious interest in letter writing.

For overseas correspondence, it is a good idea to use both thin paper and an envelope. In the UK, you can buy from any post office an *aerogramme*, which is a thin writing paper for foreign correspondence. It is designed to be folded and sent as a letter by air. An aerogramme has a limited space for writing, and you cannot insert any item such as a photo in it.

For many devoted social letter writers, the ***presentation style*** of letter writing is very important. These letter writers also pay special attention to choosing a ***writing instrument***, such as ***a fountain pen and ink*** in order to match it to the paper colour. Of course, choosing the colour of paper, envelope and ink is very much a matter of individual taste. Most regular letter writers would not use pencil for writing a letter. Nor would they expect to receive a letter written in pencil. I receive personal letters from my friends who stick pictures and similar colourful decorative labels on both the letter and its envelope. All these things show keen interest, mutual respect and a special kind of relationship between two correspondents.

You can also purchase ***ready made cards*** without any writing. These are also known as ***blank-inside cards***. I find these cards very useful for exchanging message with my friends. In a decent stationery shop, you can get well designed and attractive cards of many different styles, with or without graphic designs. These cards are not the same as holiday postcards.

It may be that your handwriting* has deteriorated. In this case, it is better to type your letter by using your word processor(typewriters are now almost museum pieces). Most social letter writers avoid word processing (or typing) a letter. A ***word processed/typed letter*** is considered as impersonal and unfriendly. If you have word processed/typed a letter, for whatever reason, it is polite to add an apology or explanation for doing so. It will be appreciated by the recipient of your letter.

---

* The hand-written letter, which has indented paragraphs, is always much valued. It is worth mentioning that social letter writing, especially to friends, is a hobby that requires warmth and respect.

. <u>Means of sending letters</u>

The traditional means of sending a letter is through the postal service in the world. Since the advent of **<u>electronic mail</u>**, young people are especially enthusiastic about e-mail. Most serious social letter writers still use the postal system for sending letters and consider email as impersonal and unfriendly. There is no doubt about the speed of electronic mail, convenience and cost, but I would consider it only if I had to send an urgent message such as informing my friends about my arrival at their local airport.

. Parts of a Letter

The visual presentation of a good written letter means that it must be set out neatly and in a logical manner. This is achieved by dividing the letter into the following sections:

. **Head section** – This is your printed letterhead part of the paper, followed by the date. If it is not a letterhead paper, write your address in the top right-hand corner, followed by the date. In informal letters, such as letters to your mum or dad, the address is left out altogether.

For overseas correspondence - write your name, address and the date. After exchanging a few letters, you may start with the date written in the top right-hand corner. There is no harm if you start with your name and address or the name of your city followed by your country and the date. There are no rigid rules about it. It is a matter of preference. If you are using a printed letterhead for overseas correspondence, write the date beneath your printed information, in the right-hand side of the paper. If you use an aerogramme - start with the date in the right-hand corner, as there is a box for your name and address on the reverse side of the aerogramme.

. **Salutation remark** – this is where you write, 'Dear…,' or other suitable words. This is also known as the opening section. Below you can find salutations for different relationships. It may be that a relative, boyfriend, girlfriend or even your close friend has a "pet name or nickname". If so, use it in an informal letter (Dear followed by "pet" name).

. **Body section** – this is the main part of your letter. It is divided into paragraphs. The number of paragraphs depends on the length of your letter.

. **Complimentary remark** – this is the closing section, where you finish as 'Yours ….'. A list of complimentary remarks is given below. You can use the one you think is most suitable for your relationship to the recipient of your letter. It also depends how you feel about the person at the time of writing.

. **Signing off** – put your signature under a complimentary remark.

. **Your name** – there is no need to write your full name under your signature when you write to your relatives and close friends. However, if you write to someone with whom you are not on first name terms, write your name under your signature. Once you have exchanged a few letters with your **pen friends**, there is no need to write your name under your signature.

. **Pages** — some people write on only one side of a sheet of paper. It is also perfectly acceptable to write on both sides of the same sheet of paper. When your letter has more than one sheet, it is better to number the pages, so that it is easy to read. Usually, the first page is not numbered. So, start the numbers from 2. Some people write page numbers in the centre of the page, just above the head section. Some writers prefer to write it in the right-hand top corner, also above the head section. Some people have their own way of writing page numbers.

. Salutation and complimentary remarks

In fact, how to begin and end a letter depends on the following:
> . your relationship with the person
> . how well you know the person
> . how you feel about the person

The following suggestions are based on many years of letter writing experience. It is worth remembering that social letter writing is informal. Therefore, the basic rule for this type of writing is **informality** as opposed to formality. Thus, you can use any of the following suitable remarks without any hesitation.

Relationship: Parents, Grandparents, Sisters, Brothers

Salutation Remarks: "Dear Mum,", **"Dear Dad,",** "Dear Mum and Dad,", "Dearest Dad,", "Dearest Mum,", "Dearest Mum and Dad,", "Dear Brother,", "Dear John,", "Dearest Brother,", "Dearest Sister,", "Dearest Anne,"

Complimentary Remarks: "Love,", "With all my love,", "With much love,", "With very best wishes and love,", "With all the best,", "Lots of love,"

Relationship : Aunts and Uncles

Salutation Remarks: "Dear Auntie Jane,", Dearest Sally,", "Dear Uncle John,", " Dearest John,"

Complimentary Remarks: "Love,", "With all my love,", "With much love,", "With very best wishes and love,", "With best wishes,"

Relationship : Wife, Husband, Fiancée, Fiancé, Girlfriend, Boyfriend

---

Salutation Remarks: "Dear David,", "My Darling Susan,", "My Darling John,", "Dearest Angelica,"

Complimentary Remarks: "Love,", "With all my love,", "With much love,", "With very best wishes and love,", "With best wishes,"

Relationship: Sons, Daughters, Nieces, and Nephews

Salutation Remarks: "Dearest Alexander,", "Dear Aristotle,", "Dear Rachel,", "Dearest Sophia,"

Complimentary Remarks: "Love,", "With all my love,", "With much love,", "With very best wishes and love,", "With best wishes,"

Relationship: Youngsters to adults

Salutation Remarks: "Dear Mr Clarke,", "Dear Mrs Clarke,", Dear Mr & Mrs Brown,"
When allowed to call by first name:
"Dear Barry,", "Dear Barbara,"
Addressing very close old family friends:
"Dear Auntie,", "Dear Uncle,"

Complimentary Remarks: "Love,", "With all my love,", "With much love,", "With very best wishes and love,", "With best wishes,"

Relationship: Very close unrelated old friends of your family - if you call them as "Auntie", "Uncle"

Salutation Remarks: "Dear Auntie Sandra,", Dearest Claire,", "Dear Uncle Jim,", " Dearest Jim,"

Complimentary Remarks: "Love,", "With all my love,", "With much love,", "With very best wishes and love,", "With best wishes,"

Relationship: Close friends

Salutation Remarks: "Dearest Anne,", "My Dear Sigrid,",
"My Dear Beata,", **"**Dearest Beata,",
"Dearest Jolanta,", "Dear Ines," ,

"My Dear Yvonne,"

Complimentary Remarks: "Love,", "With all my love,", "With much
love,", "With very best wishes

and love,", "With best wishes,", "Lots of love,",
"Kind regards and lots of love,"

Relationship: Acquaintance, or anyone with whom you are not
on first name terms

Salutation Remarks: "Dear Mr Taylor,", "Dear Mrs Taylor,"

Complimentary Remarks: "Yours sincerely,"

Relationship: Pen friends

Salutation Remarks: "Dear Wolfgang,", "Dear Ines,", "Dear Anne,"

Complimentary Remarks: "Yours,",
**After an exchange of a few letters, you don't
have to say** "Yours,",
Just write:
"Best wishes,", "Kind regards,", "Best wishes
and kind regards,"

. Think about the recipient

The above information lays the foundations for written communication.
When you write a letter, think about the person to whom you are about to
write. if it is a social letter, the recipient of your letter must be pleased to receive it, and enjoy reading it. It is not always possible to give some good and
exciting news, but the way you describe things can be interesting. Therefore,
try not to impress the recipient with too many words which need explanation,
but be polite and honest.

There is no need to be afraid of writing a long letter, because some people
enjoying reading such letters. Usually, older people like to read and write
long letters. They have time for this activity. Young people also enjoy reading such letters. Older children especially like some sort of drawing, such as
a smiling face. The content of your letter will reveal how much pleasure you
have had in writing it. **Here are some examples of social letters**:

(1) . <u>Congratulations on passing exams from an uncle</u>

12 Bond Street
Manchester
M11 1BB

(date here)

Dearest Simon

I'm delighted to hear the good news that you have passed your final exams for your Bachelor of Science degree. I congratulate you whole-heartedly on your well-deserved success.

It is wonderful that you have gained an upper second class pass, which was required by the company who have conditionally offered you the post of Systems Analyst. Your achievement in the exams has met the employment condition, and it has opened the door for future prosperity. Indeed, you have gained your objectives. It is great news, as you can start your career right away with a reputable large software company. Well done!

I will return home from Switzerland next month, a few days before your double celebration party. Most certainly, it'll be a great pleasure to join you on this happy occasion.

I'm very much looking forward to seeing you all and joining the celebrations.

Love and very best wishes

(2) . <u>Congratulations on passing exams from a friend of the family</u>

The oaks
20 Star Street
London
SW11 1AA

(date here)

continued on the next page----

> *Continued from the last page*
>
> Dear Barbara
>
> It is really very pleasing to hear from your mother that you have passed your Pitmans Advanced Level Secretarial exams and that you're going to to start a new job at our local Town Hall. We send you our warmest congratulations.
>
> You worked so hard for a long time to gain this qualification of secretarial proficiency. This is what you've always wanted and now you have got it. Very well done!
>
> It will help you to make good progress in the future.
>
> With best wishes

. Congratulations on an engagement

Examples 3-4 show two letters of congratulations. The letter in Example 3 is written to an acquaintance. In this letter, the letter writer has not given any personal assessment or opinion about the engaged couple. If you know the engaged couple, you can add more to the basic letter. The letter in example 4 is sent to a close friend. As it is to a close friend, the letter writer has said more than just accepting an invitation.

(3). Congratulations on the engagement of an acquaintance

> 10 Beach Street
> Birmingham
> YO10 2BB
>
> (date here)
>
> Dear James
>
> I was very pleased to see your engagement announcement in " The Birmingham Times". Congratulations! Perhaps, one day, your fiancée will come with you to our tennis club. It would be nice to meet her with you.
>
> I'm curious to know when you will be married.
>
> Best wishes

(4). <u>Congratulations on the engagement of a close friend</u>

10 Beach Street
Birmingham
YO10 2BB

(date here)

My Dear Jane

Thank you so much for inviting me to your engagement party on 1 May, which is only three weeks away, It's great news that you have become engaged to John Russell. I have known him for many years, as we both went to the same school. He is really a charming , honest and kind person.

I have seen you and John happy together for nearly two years, and can say that you were made for each other. We can talk about it when we meet soon, but I must add that I sincerely believe that you have made the right decision.

I'm very much looking forward to joining your celebration party.

With very best wishes and love

. <u>Child's birthday</u> – this is to congratulate friends on the birth of their child.

(5) . <u>Birthday of a child</u>

1 London Road
York
YO1 1AA

(date here)

Dear Colin and Kay

We were overjoyed to hear from Mrs. Smith that you had became happy parents on the arrival of your healthy baby son Alexander – you must be delighted. Congratulations!

continued on the next page ----

---

continued from the last page

We were very pleased to learn that there were no complications and that Kay and Alexander are both doing fine.

Once Kay and Alexander are home, one evening we will call on you to have the pleasure of seeing your lovely son with his proud parents.

With all our love and best wishes

If you wish to expand this letter, you can do so. For instance, you can ask them about the weight of their son. Of course, you can start it with "Dearest Colin and Kay," if you feel particularly close to them.

(6) . <u>Wishing a colleague good luck in a new post</u>

---

3 King Street
Leeds
LE 1 8XX

(date here)

 Dear Alistair

I have just found out from Jane that you have accepted the post of Systems Programming Manager at People's PLC in the City, and you will be soon leaving us. I am ever so pleased that at last you are successful in getting a job which you wanted for a long time. Certainly, it is a promotion at this time in your career. Congratulations!

This is, indeed, a step in the right direction. I hope this chance of working for an international financial institution will give you every opportunity to progress towards becoming Director of Information Systems. This is your final goal, and now you are one more step nearer to it. We all know how hard you work and how much energy you put into it. Obviously, you have done very well.

We will miss you at XYZ, but your new work place is close to us. Once you're settled down in your new post, we could meet, whenever possible, for lunch or a drink, after work, in the same old place as usual.

Let me know how you are coping with your new responsibility, and how you are getting on in general. Do keep in touch!

 With very best wishes

Social Letter Writing   **261**

****

. <u>Good luck in a new job</u>

People often change jobs. Sometimes, you feel you must wish someone good luck in their new job. Two letters in examples 6 and 7 are designed to give an idea of what you can write to a colleague with whom you have worked for a long time, or a friend or someone in your own family.

The letter in example 6 illustrates a good friendship and understanding between the letter writer and the recipient of the letter. Their friendship and the informality between them are indicated by both the opening and closing remarks.

(7) . <u>Wishing a relative good luck in a new post abroad</u>

The Rose Cottage
The Village Green
Stamford Bridge
YO2 1AB

(date here)

My Dear Roger

Your sister Jane just telephoned giving me the news of your success at a job interview. I'm ever so pleased to hear that you have been promoted within the Civil Service and that your new post will give you the opportunity of working abroad in association with the British trade Mission in the USA. Well done!

This is a marvellous chance for you to travel abroad, and I'm sure it will broaden your horizons. This is what you have always wished and I'm glad you have succeeded in doing so.

Since you were at school, you were destined for a Civil Service career, like your loving father. I knew from your school days that you were a bright young man in our family, and that you would always strive for the achievement of your goal. This new direction, hopefully, will strengthen your self-confidence, and I'm pretty sure that you'll soon be making your presence felt in the UK and the British Trade Mission in the USA.

It's such a long time since I saw you. I know how busy you are, but do pop in soon to see your Auntie.

With love and best wishes

. <u>Letters of sympathy</u>

In all our lives, there are occasions when we have to write letters of condolence, following a bereavement. Some years ago, people used to write lengthy letters about the deceased's life. In this day and age, the tendency is to write a short letter in order to convey your sincere feelings of sympathy to the deceased's relatives in simple words. Any other matters should <u>not</u> be included. You may add a few words about the deceased person, if you feel that you ought to do so.

You may have to write other letters of sympathy on some unfortunate happenings such as a car accident, illness, business failure, etc. Examples 8 and 9 demonstrate this aspect of letter writing. <u>Such letters should be handwritten and the use of punctuation marks in salutation, complimentary marks and address is preferable.</u>

(8) . <u>Letter of condolence - the death of an acquaintance</u>

                                                20 Grove Close
Nottingham
NT4 5LD

(date here)

Dear Mrs. Blanket

I was deeply saddened to read in today's local paper that your beloved husband Lesley was involved in a fatal car accident. Lesley's sudden death has shocked my husband and I. How horrendous for you to lose him, so tragically, so young and so suddenly.

My husband and I offer our sincere sympathy on your loss.

With kindest regards.

Yours sincerely

(9) . <u>Letter of condolence – the death of a close friend's wife</u>

35 Cross Road
London
NW1 9 QL

(date here)

My Dear John

Last night, my mother broke the dreadful news of Jane's death over the

continued on the next page —

continued from the last page

telephone. Anne and I are shocked. I can't imagine how sorrowful you are on your beloved wife's death. If it's any consolation, she has been finally released from her painful illness.

Anne and I enjoyed her friendship for so many years. She was always ever so kind, honest, cheerful and helpful. Jane was always very hospitable to friends and strangers. We will miss her very much.

If there is anything at all which we can do to help, please ask us without any hesitation.

We send you our deepest sympathy.

Love

The letter in example 9 is slightly longer than in example 8. The reason is that we know how much the recipient would like to hear from us, as we knew our friend's wife well.

(10) . Letter of sympathy – a colleague in hospital

12 Camden Road
Stockport
ST5 12 MV

(date here)

Dear Simon

I was sorry to hear that you had been admitted to Chelsea & Kensington Hospital for an emergency operation, but luckily, there were no complications. It is such a big relief to learn that the operation was successful and you're making satisfactory progress.

There is no need to worry about work, as the manager has already organised cover for you for as long as you are away due to illness. If there is anything at all which I can do to help, please let me know.

I hope that you will be fully recovered from your operation soon.

With kindest regards.

Yours sincerely

. <u>Hospital visit</u>

When you write to a colleague, an acquaintance, or a friend with whom you do not have a very close relationship, it is not easy to say whether you should visit them or not. The problem is that for some reasons, they may not want visitors other than their relatives and intimate friends. On the other hand, they may appreciate your visit as very few people visit them. Anyway, it is a good idea to indicate that their work has been taken care of and there is no need to worry about it. Furthermore, it is advisable
to add that you will be happy to help if they ask you.

<u>The letter in example 10 is an example of such a letter. You can write a similar letter to someone who has had an accident and is unable to work.</u>

. <u>Get well messages</u>

If a friend or relative is ill, you can send a get well message. You can buy specially designed get well cards with a variety of printed messages. It is a matter of taste and how you feel about the sick person. These cards have sufficient space to write a short personal note. So, you may send a card with your handwritten note on it. If you do send a card, it is recommended that you choose a card which does not refer to an illness on its front, as it may prove to be depressing. It is better to buy a card with some sort of alternative picture or design. If you don't send a card, you can still send a message written on a sheet of ordinary writing paper. Here are examples:

(11) . <u>Get well message from colleagues sympathising about illness</u>

<u>Work Place address Printed</u>

(date here)

Dear Ray

Here in the IT Department, we are all very sorry to learn that you are unwell and wanted to let you know that we are thinking of you.

Sarah and Barbara are providing cover for you until you are back. Therefore, don't worry about work, just look after yourself. We will be pleased to see you back at work, when you are fully recovered from your illness.

With best wishes.

Signed by colleagues in Accounts

Social Letter Writing   **265**

****

(12) . <u>Get well message to a close friend</u>

(date Here)*

Dear Cherie

I met your sister by chance and she told me that you had broken your leg during a hockey match. I'm very sorry that you were hospitalised for a couple of days, but the good news is that you were soon back home in the comfort of your own home.

I am sure your leg will heal soon. Don't worry too much about it, and keep yourself occupied with something interesting. Well, now you have time to read some of your favourite novels.

Knowing how much you love bright colours, I have sent you this colourful card with my get well wishes. It may cheer you up a bit. I'll pop in over the weekend to see you and have a chat over your mother's nice cup of tea. I wish I could make tea as well as your mother. Keep smiling!

Lots of love

---

* The address is left out, because the message is from someone who knows the recipient very well.

. <u>Invitations</u>

Many people still send invitation cards, despite the fact that nowadays, an increasing number of people send fax, text messages or exchange email(e-mail) messages. All modes/means of communication except the ordinary telephone involve some writing. It also depends on the nature of the invitation. If you want to invite a few close friends for a drink in a local pub, you can still telephone them. For other occasions, it is a good idea to have something in writing because it is still valued. Here are some examples:

(13). <u>Invitation to stay to a couple overseas with us</u>

20 Scarborough Road
York
YO1 5MN

(date here)

continued on the next page - - ―

continued from the last page

Dear Sylvia and Ralf

It is very pleasing to hear that you are now happily married. We asked you to visit us before you got married, but at that time both of you were busy organising things for your wedding celebrations. Once again, we invite you to visit us whenever it is possible. It would be a great pleasure to have you with us for at least one week, although you can stay with us as long as wish. Our guest room is ready – waiting for your arrival.

It would be our pleasure to show you our part of England. Yorkshire is the largest county in England. It has many attractions including secluded bays, rolling hills, undulating moors, interesting cities, towns and villages. It has many historical places and the largest national park in England – the North Yorkshire Moors.

We live by the sea, where the air is really fresh, clean and good for your health. Our local area has cliffs, woodlands and is also well-known for all kinds of birds. We can have some leisurely walks together along the impressive picturesque Yorkshire coastline.

We look forward to hearing from you regarding when you can visit us.

With our best wishes

(14) . Invitation to a house-warming party

(date here)

Dear Alison and Arthur

Last month, we moved to our new home. It wasn't quite as simple as we thought it would be. It was rather a hectic experience but we are glad that it's all over now. Our new address is:
    Sea View Cottage, The Square, Flamborough, YO18 6JJ

Telephone: 01262 500 5000   Fax: 01262 500 5001

Albert and I invite you to join us to celebrate the move and to toast our new home on Saturday 4 June. A bit of knees-up will kick off at about 21.00 hours. We would be delighted if you could come along! Hope to see you on Saturday.

With best wishes,

The above letter, indeed, is very informal.

(15) . <u>Invitation to a wedding</u>

Mr & Mrs John Smith

request the pleasure of the company of

Mr & Mrs Philip Taylor

at the marriage of their son

Mr James Smith

to
Miss Marion Henderson

at the Catholic Church Bridlington

on Saturday May 20 XXXX

at 13.00 hours

Reception afterwards

at

The Carlton Hotel
Promenade
Bridlington

2 James Street
Bridlington
YO1 2AC

RSVP*

---

* **RSVP** is an abbreviation for the French word:

" **Rèpondez s'il vous plaĭt**", meaning ⇒ please reply

. <u>Invitation to a wedding</u>

If you know lots of people and can afford to invite them to your wedding party, you will most likely send them formal invitation cards. Your printer will offer you a selection of cards to choose from. In fact, you can buy already printed cards and just fill in the spaces where some information is needed.

If you wish to invite only a few close friends and relatives, you can send them a letter of invitation. Example 15 shows an invitation to a wedding party which may be used for printing formal wedding invitation cards. You can also simply write it on good quality writing paper, as an invitation to relatives and close friends. It has the same effect as the printed formal wedding card. In addition, it has a personal touch, as it is hand written, and it would be more economical. It can be prepared using a word processor, with guests' names written in by hand.

. Replying to invitations

It is straightforward to accept an **informal invitation**. You should reply as soon as you can, so that the host has a good idea of the number of people who will participate in the event. This is illustrated below:

(16) . Acceptance of an invitation to a house-warming party

> 50 Queens Gate
> Bridlington
> YO1 10BB
> (date here)
>
>
> Dear Edna and Albert
>
> Thank you very much for inviting us to your house-warming party. Indeed, we would be ever so pleased to come. We know the area where your new house is situated very well. It is a really nice district. Well done!
>
> Look forward to seeing you at about 8.30 p.m. on Saturday 4 June.
>
> With our very best wishes.

If you have to **decline** an informal invitation for whatever reason(s), it is important that you do so politely without any unnecessary delays. Your friendly letter will not offend them. **See example 17.**

If you receive a formal wedding invitation, you can send your **acceptance** or **refusal** on a printed card, which you can buy from a quality stationery shop. Or you may prefer to write a short note of acceptance or refusal on quality paper. **See examples 18 and 19.**

(17). <u>A letter of refusal to join a house-warming party</u>

> 50 Queens Gate
> Bridlington
> YO1 10BB
>
> (date here)

Dear Edna and Albert

Thank you very much for inviting me to your house-warming party. I'm very sorry that I will not be able to attend it, as I have already bought my train ticket to visit my parents in Blackpool.

As they are anxiously waiting for my long overdue visit, I cannot give it a miss. Your social gatherings are always joyful and I hope that you and your guests have a great time on Saturday 4 June.

When I'm back from Blackpool, I'll ring you up so that we can arrange to meet for a drink.

With my very best wishes

(18). <u>Acceptance of an invitation to a wedding party</u>

> 1 Wellington Gardens
> Chelsea
> London Sw1 1AA
>
> (date here)

Dear Mr and Mrs Major

Thank you for your kind invitation to Brian and Christine's wedding and reception on Sunday 2 June.

Jim and I would be delighted to attend the celebrations and we very much look forward to congratulating you, the bride and bridegroom.

Yours sincerely

If you have received a formal invitation in the form of a printed invitation card, it does not mean that you should reply using a similar card. A hand written letter is, in fact, a better idea because it shows your personal interest.

(19) . Declining an invitation to a wedding party

> 10 Clifton Road
> Brighton
> BN 21 4QQ
>
> (date here)
>
>
> Dear Mr and Mrs Smith
>
> Thank you for your kind invitation to James and Sarah's wedding and reception on Saturday 1 July.
>
> It is, indeed, very much regretted that due to an important prior engagement arranged some time ago, we will not be able to attend.
>
> We wish you a very enjoyable occasion*
>
> Yours sincerely

> * You can still send them a good luck and congratulations card with your letter or separately.

. Far away friends

Many people in the world enjoy writing to their friends. I'm one of them. These friends may be in the same country or other countries. You don't have to be a member of a pen club to have **pen friends**. You may meet people through newspaper advertisements, travel and sometimes in public places(restaurants, airports, etc.) or the Internet. In all circumstances, irrespective of how long you have been in contact with each other through writing, in the interest of your personal safety, you must make sure that you (especially females) have taken all the necessary precautions, if you are invited by your pen friend to meet up.

You may start as a pen friend, and steadily develop your friendship into a family friendship. It all depends on trust and a genuine desire to understand each other, to exchange points of view and life experiences in general. Indeed, it is a very pleasing hobby. It can brighten your day when

****

you hear from a far away friend. It can enable you to relax, as you learn to share your feelings, etc. with your friends. Indeed, through letters, one learns that we can be united by a sense of common humanity.

(20) . <u>A letter from a friend in France</u>
(A retired energetic person)

> Address
> in
> France
>
> dated
>
> Dear Mark
>
> Thank you for your nice letter and the enclosed photo. The garden looks beautiful. You haven't changed much since we met some years ago. My enclosed snap was taken last month in Carcassonne on my way to Aix en Provence. See what happened to me? You know how thin I was! Well, that's rich French food!
>
> I suppose, at some time in one's life, everyone puts on some weight. That's true! This must be the reason, I think! Don't you? That's good living. I'm not going to starve because it will not do me any good. I have no plans to seduce anybody, not at my age, anyway!
>
> I was supposed to visit some friends in Carcassonne, but I sprained my ankle badly and went back to my cousin's in the Pyrènèes, where I came from originally. I had to rest at my cousin's home before coming back to Paris. Three days after my return, I suffered from a stiff back for two weeks. As I couldn't walk much, I read a lot, but I was anxious to move again normally.
>
> As soon as I felt better, I booked my passage to New York, where I will be on 18 September. I'm hoping that nothing happens to me in New York. I think I'll return home totally broke as the exchange rate for dollars is too high. Who cares? You have to keep moving. **Voilà** (French), the story of my life during the summer---.
>
> Your own life seems less adventurous at present, but it is certainly more rewarding. You also take risks, but in a different way. I do hope that your hard work will bring positive results. How are Daniel and Adam? Are you still in touch with your friend about whom you told me some months ago.
>
> At present, you must be feeling a little lonely without Anne, as she is in
> *continued on the next page —*

continued from the last page

Russia. Like you, I enjoy looking at colourful pretty flowers. They are the symbol of harmony that appears to be vanishing from our world. Somehow, we must protect our natural environment. I do miss our 'Clamart Garden' – my family home, but I always have some flowers around me.

I may call you before leaving for the USA. Now I'm with a cheap phone company and I enjoy talking to my far away friends more than ever.

Best wishes

(21) . <u>A letter from a friend in South Africa</u>
(A young person trying to build a life)

Address
in
South Africa

dated

Dear Mark

Fondest greetings. My humblest apologies for not having written any sooner. I was wondering when I'd last heard from you and when I checked your last letter. I realised that I was, in fact, the one whose turn it was to write. So there you have my acknowledgement of guilt.

What has been happening in your side of the world?

Quite a bit has been going on here, but I don't have much time to tell you about it all. As you can see from the above address, I'm staying in a little flat in the university suburb of Rondebosch, and have been there for roughly three months. I'm looking to move at the end of the year, so if you are ever confused as to where to reach me, my parent's address is always a sure way to do so.

I promise to make my subsequent letters far more interesting and certainly longer. At the moment, work has been driving us all crazy and I have also been trying to study. My boyfriend and I broke up recently, and although it is not 'Heartbreak City', it has been a change in routine.

I've been giving some thought to my long-term future as I have very little

continued on the next page —

---

continued from the last page

trust in the situation here in a few years' time. It is not a place where I feel even slightly safe, or would like to see the end of my days, or my children grow up. However, there is still much to do before I can seriously contemplate a final decision of that nature.

I'm afraid I have to stop here, so I shall bid you farewell until next time. Please bear in mind that my examinations finish mid-November and I should be back to speed then, and be slightly more sociable and human!

Please write soon with all your news.

Love

---

(22) . A letter from a friend in Canada
(Someone who is interested in the natural world)

Address
in
Canada

dated

Dear Mark

Hallo! How are you?

Everyone and everything is fine here. There hasn't been a whole lot happening with me lately. I've just been basically existing. Doesn't that sound like the ultimate life style?

Can you believe that the present year is almost half gone? I can't. There is nothing I or any other person can do about it though, so I won't dwell on it anymore. I was listening to a really interesting radio programme this morning. The topic was the **Crop Circles**. They were saying, 'The number of these formations is around 3,000.' That's incredible. Don't you think so? Do you think there is another life form somewhere out there? I think there is one.

continued on the next page —

---

continued from the last page

Whether or not it's Martians, I can't really say. It definitely makes a person take a look at our world. Like they were saying during the discussion, it's exciting and interesting to think that there is more out there to learn about. It is also scary because it is something new and different from what we are used to. For people who were brought up with certain beliefs, in a way it makes them re-think those beliefs. Sitting comfortably and thinking about that, if you do strongly believe in what the Bible says about God creating the earth and all life as it is today, who's to say that God didn't create any other worlds not known to us?

The Bible is man's written account of how the human race was created. Isn't it possible that other worlds' aliens have their own account of how their world and race were created?

I realise that not everyone believes in God and those that do, may have a different version (for lack of a better word) of God or some higher being. I'm not a Bible reading church-goer, but I do believe there is something stranger out there.

Anyway, that is my thought venting for the day. I want to get this letter in the mail to you, so I will say bye for now, and hope that you will tell me something interesting in your next letter.

Take care.

(23) . <u>A letter to develop a friendship with someone you meet on holiday</u>

Address
in
England

(date here)

Dear Sylvia and Ralf

I just thought of you as I was working on my PC and vividly remembered everything about our short meeting. I decided to stop work, and write this short letter, so that I can convey my feelings to you. How wonderful it was to meet both of you!

continued on the next page ——

continued from the last page

The problem is that life on this planet is too short and we are very much involved in maintaining it. The human race is still loveable, no matter where one lives, and what nationality one belongs to. Nationalities are no more than political labels, which unfortunately divide the human race and erect psychological barriers between us. Despite these artificial partitions between people of this global village, it is so enjoyable to accept people from other parts of the world and to share this short life together, whenever an opportunity for meeting arises. We should avail ourselves of life's rare chances of bringing people together, despite geographical distances, different nationalities and gender.

Indeed, our words create a world as we see it. Therefore, we should speak those words, which bring us together as the people who belong to one human race, irrespective of some apparent differences.

I send you this short letter because I feel as if I'm still sitting next to you in that café and talking to you with great enthusiasm with a view to exchanging our experiences in this present life, and indeed, sharing world heritage as well as improving our mutual understanding.

To maintain our lives on this planet, as you may remember, I work for myself as a computer programmer and, therefore, I can work from home. My wife has a part-time job in a department store. I thought you would like to see where we live, thus I have sent you a few snaps. These will give you an idea of our simple but happy life style. We live in the Greater London area, just 10 miles away from Central London. We have the best of both worlds – the capital of the UK and the countryside. We consider ourselves lucky, as we are alive and healthy.

I sincerely hope that it will not be too long before I hear from you.

Kind regards and best wishes.

Yours sincerely

In summary, the social letter writing is an excellent way of keeping in touch with friends and relatives. It creates mutual understanding, removes prejudices between young and old, man and woman, especially of different cultural and religious divides across the world. It gives considerable pleasure when you send or receive a letter.

Remember: *Someone somewhere wants a letter from you!*

Chapter 15
Business Communication

. Introduction

The aim of this chapter is to exemplify some aspects of business letter writing. It is not a place to discuss in detail business stationery design and style aspects, except to say that a business has its own printed letterhead paper for business letter writing and any other communication purposes. Usually a business letterhead paper has a business logo, the full address, telephone and fax numbers. It may also include some other information. Many businesses may have their full name and address printed on the envelope, with the message, 'If undelivered, please return to.....'

Business letterhead paper is official paper which should only be used for official business letter writing, that is, for dealing with business matters. Nowadays, many businesses do not send letters with day-to-day documents such as invoices, accounts statements and the like. Any generalisation of business letter writing in terms of day-to-day routine letters and important correspondence does not apply to all kinds of businesses. For instance, many firms of solicitors send a letter with an invoice to their clients. Owing to a small volume of invoices and the type of work, it appears to be important, practical and traditional for this type of business. On the other hand, a busy wholesale electrical goods firm may find it impractical and costly to send letters with its many daily sales invoices. As far as business courtesy is concerned, at one time in the business world, it was almost universal to enclose a compliments slip with day-to-day correspondence (e.g. a sales invoice), but it is less common than it was some years ago because of the increasing cost.

A compliments slip is a small piece of paper which contains a complimentary remark and the company's name and address. It is similar in style to that of the letterhead. The complimentary remark is 'With compliments' or 'With our compliments'. Sometimes, it is also used to write a short note and send it with some other business documents.

Some businesses keep ***copies*** on files of all correspondence for a specified period for the purpose of internal department communication, and to prove that action has already been taken. Some firms, particularly small concerns, consider copies of letters unnecessary, if they are not part of accounting records for tax purposes. However, it is wise to keep copies of letters that you think may be required as evidence in any legal dispute.

. Letter Format

It is possible that your company has a business letter format. If so, you are expected to adhere to it. However, there are the following three formats:

Blocked Format	Semi-blocked Format	Indented Format
. all lines start at left-hand margin	. date and references start at right-hand margin	. paragraphs are indented by some spaces
		. the entire layout may follow either blocked or semi-blocked format

. Examples of Letters

It is of paramount importance that the writer should have precise *factual information* relating to the letter being written. In order to establish all facts, it may be necessary to check all relevant records, telephone conversations or seek information and advice from any other colleague(s) who might have dealt with the matter before.

Depending on the nature of the business and the content of the letter, the writer should use *the English language style* that is most suited, and which matches the knowledge and understanding of the recipient. It is wasteful and confusing to the recipient if you use too many words and jargon/technical phrases or local expressions.

It should go without saying that *plain English* is preferred by most people. Of course, if you are a biologist writing to another biologist, your language will include technical phrases, which will not alienate the recipient. On the other hand, if you use technical words which are commonly used in your trade, and write long and verbose sentences, you can easily confuse the recipient who does not possess the knowledge of your trade or profession. Likewise, if you oversimplify your writing, the recipient may feel patronised. Therefore, the best idea is to use plain English, that is to use appropriate words and short sentences that make the point directly, clearly, accurately and briefly. [Note: Plain English is not for toastmasters.]

. Salutation & Complimentary Remarks

If you know the title (Mr/Mrs/Miss/Ms/Dr....) and surname, use an appropriate salutation and complimentary remarks. For instance:

Salutation: "Dear Sir/Madam"*
Complimentary remark: "Yours faithfully"
Salutation: "Dear Mr. Smith"
Complimentary remark: " Yours sincerely"

Sign it and underneath write your name. Under your name write your job status. If your company has its own style, you must adhere to it.

(1) . <u>Enquiring about supplies</u>

<u>Letterhead</u>
<u>Business name and address etc.</u>

date here

Sales Manager*
XYZ Limited
12 London Road
Birmingham
B1 2BB1

Dear Sirs/Madam

I understand that your company is the sole distributor for the **WWW** Publications, which we are interested in stocking.

I should be grateful if you would provide me with a current catalogue of WWW Publications, and a retail price list. Please could you also send your trading terms and conditions, together with your discount rates for book-shops, and credit account opening information by return of post.

Yours faithfully

Jane Brown
Manager

---

* **Business letters** – the use of open punctuation is common in salutation, complimentary remark and address, as it saves time.

. In Example 1, the idea is to obtain some relevant information on WWW Publications only. You are not interested in some other products which XYZ Limited may stock. Thus, the opening paragraph refers only to the publications from one publishing house.

. In case you decide to take this matter further, relevant commercial and payment information is requested in the second paragraph. There is no need to give any information on your business, as in the second paragraph the nature of your business is already stated -bookshop.

. If you wish, you can add 'With good wishes' on a separate line above the complimentary remark.

(2) . <u>Opening a credit account</u>

<u>Letterhead</u>
<u>Business name and address etc.</u>

date here

Mr Colin Smith
Sales Manager
XYZ Limited
12 London Road
Birmingham
B1 2BB1

Dear Mr Smith

Thank you for your letter of 12 June. We would very much like to stock some of the items listed in WWW Publications' current catalogue. We are pleased to send you the following two business contacts whom you can approach for references about our company:

. Mr H N Roberts, Manager, Hope Bank PLC, High Street, Rugby, RB1 2NW

. Miss A Johnson, Credit Controller, ABC PLC, Tree Street, White Cross
Reading , RE1 2BC

We await your reply and look forward to doing business with you to our mutual advantage.

Yours sincerely

Jane Brown
Manager

In Example 1, credit facilities were requested. Now you have decided to open a credit account at XYZ Limited. Since XYZ does not have a formal form for this purpose, you must send two references. One of these must be your business bank where your current business account is operated from. Example 2 illustrates how to write this simple letter.

(3) . <u>Confirming the opening of a credit account</u>

<u>Letterhead</u>
<u>Business name and address etc.</u>

date here

Ms Jane Brown
Manager
Vision Bookshop
3 Kensington High Street
London W11 4MN

Dear Ms Brown

<u>Reference: Current Account Number: 00123</u>

We are pleased to confirm that your credit account number is **00123** and that your monthly credit limit is **£1,500**.

At present, we do not accept payments by BACS (Bankers Automatic Clearing System). Therefore, all payments should be made by cheque within thirty days from our invoice date.

Yours sincerely

Miss Doris Day
Credit Control Manager

---

* **Ms or Ms.** - use this title when you do not know whether a woman is married or unmarried. It can be placed before a woman's surname name or before her first and surname.

In the above letter, the essential information is given in paragraph 1, so that the trade between these two businesses can commence. In the second paragraph, a polite advance notice is given so that the supplier is not approached for BACS method and delaying payment. There is no need to add any further information. Many small businesses still prefer cheques.

(4) . <u>Accepting a quotation</u>

<u>**Letterhead**</u>
<u>**Business name and address etc.**</u>

date here

Mr M R Dodd
Director
Dodd Building Services(London) Limited
1 Camden High Street
London NW1 7 AX

Dear Mr Dodd

<u>**Reference: Q123908**</u>

Thank you for your quotation for replacing the existing flat roof of our office extension at the above address. We are pleased to accept your quotation for the following work:

. to strip off the existing felt and decking
. to re-board the roof with 18 mm plywood
. to re-felt using 2-layers of built laid bonded hot bitumen, finish lay
  green mineral
. to supply and fix new wooden fascia to all three sides of the roof
. to re-fix all gutters
. to dispose of all waste materials

We understand that the work will commence at about 7.30 hours on
20 July. The job will be completed within three days. If there are any changes due to severe weather conditions before starting the work, you will contact me immediately, so that we can make some other arrangements to complete this job satisfactorily without any unnecessary delays.

The total cost for all materials and work is £3,500 plus 17.5% VAT. This price includes <u>five years' guarantee of labour and materials, if within five years any part or the whole flat roof need any repairs or replacement</u>. The total price three thousand and five hundred pounds plus VAT is payable on the day, when the job is satisfactorily completed as per your quotation and this letter. If you accept the content of this letter, please sign and date the attached copy and return it to me.

Yours sincerely

Carl Duncan
Purchasing Manager

. The acceptance of a quotation forms the basis of an agreement between two parties. Thus, it is advisable to clearly state the nature of your purchase, prices, terms and conditions. Without clear understanding of what is agreed, there can be some problems later on. Therefore, it is important to write a precise and concise letter stating all key points.

. In Example 4 above, the bullet-pointed list of items gives a job specification (nature of purchase). These are the things that must be done.

. The next paragraph relates to the date when the work should commence, days to be taken to complete the work and any problems that may arise because of unpredictable weather conditions.

. In the last paragraph, the price is written twice – in both numbers and words. The guarantee is underlined and payment time is stated with the payment condition. Finally, the recipient's attention is drawn to the attached copy of the letter which must be signed and dated by the recipient and returned to the writer.

. If a quotation is about a complex job or some expensive purchase, such as a property deal, it is worth paying a fee to a solicitor, so that the purchase agreement has a proper legal format.

. <u>Rejecting a Quotation</u>

The buying department may receive a number of quotations. Often many buyers do not write to prospective suppliers whose quotations are rejected, because it is both time consuming and costly. On the other hand, some buyers feel that it is in their business interests to acknowledge all quotations and inform each supplier why their quotation was unacceptable. By using this approach one can also avoid receiving further telephone calls, letters or even salesmen's visits from all those prospective suppliers of goods and services, enquiring and trying to negotiate about the outcome of their quotations. It is suggested that you write a letter to all prospective suppliers on the following lines:

. start by acknowledging the receipt of their quotation, and state the quoted price for the proposed goods and service.
. give your reason for finding their quotation unacceptable.
. tell them that at some point in time in the future you will contact them for some quotations.

Example 5 contains a letter rejecting a quotation. The tone of this letter is friendly, but its message is dismissive.

(5) . Rejecting a quotation

Letterhead
Business name and address etc.

date here

Mr M R Dodd
Director
Dodd Building Services(London) Limited
1 Camden High Street
London
NW1 7 AX

Dear Mr Dodd

Reference: Q123908

Thank you for your quotation of £3,500 plus 17.5% VAT for replacing the existing flat roof of our office extension at the above address.

We are very sorry to inform you that we feel that your price is in excess of what we have budgeted for this work.

Once again, we thank you for sending us the quotation and giving us the opportunity to consider it with great interest. We assure you that whenever we need similar repairs to our office
properties in the future, we will approach you for a quotation.

Yours sincerely

Carl Duncan
Purchasing Manager

. Sales Letters

Sales letters are not easy to write, yet many people consider them as junk mail and put them into the waste paper basket without opening them.

. Different Forms of a Sales Letter

The prime purpose of a sales letter is to persuade the recipient to buy some products or services offered by the writer of the sales letter. For
instance, a small hand written duplicated note from a window cleaner,

offering his services, pushed through the letterbox, is a sales letter. When you receive through the post a large white envelope containing a letter and some glossy leaflets from a large insurance company, it is also a sales letter. The range of sales letters is very large indeed. A sales letter may be disguised as an invitation, which is well designed and printed in colours on glossy paper. For instance:

> "An invitation to a wine and cheese party and to witness the launch of
> a new and exciting BMW business car at our purpose-built
> showroom in your town ...."

In some sales letters, some ridiculous claims are made. For instance, 'the most attractive place in the world', 'the cheapest and best', and similar phrases. You should describe your products or services in words which give correct factual information, and ensure that your products or services can match their descriptions and stand up to close scrutiny. Here are two examples of sales letters:

. Sales Letter 1

. Example 6 contains a sales letter about specialist bilingual dictionaries
  from Germany. In its opening paragraph, the writer has introduced the
  business as the sole distributor of these dictionaries. The writer has not
  given any other information about other business activities, because the
  main purpose is to sell these dictionaries.
. In the middle part of the letter two products are listed and their vital
  book information is given. The prospective customer is provided with
  two information sheets on these two products. These information sheets
  contain concise and precise information, and no wild claim is made
  about the products being introduced.
. In the next paragraph, the importance of these products is highlighted,
  but not over-stated.
. In the last paragraph, the writer expresses an appreciation in anticipation
  of an order by any of the four modes of placing an order.

This is a simple and honest sales letter. It informs the recipient about two products, from whom and how to purchase them. Its approach is friendly and its tone is polite. It is precise and concise.

. Sales Letter 2

. Sales letter 2 is in example 7.The communication approach in this letter
  is based on an observation. The first paragraph makes it clear.

. In the second paragraph, Linden Hall nursery's current system is <u>not</u>
  criticised. Here, the writer has briefly mentioned the product which was
  supplied to nurseries in the UK. Go on reading under example 7.

****

(6) . <u>Sales Letter 1</u>

Letterhead
<u>Business name and address etc.</u>

<u>date here</u>

DR R Angus
University Science & Technology Library
Newland University
Newland
NEW1 6AB

Dear Dr Angus

<u>Specialist bilingual dictionaries from Germany</u>

We are pleased to inform you that we are the sole distributors of reputable comprehensive specialist dictionaries from Germany:
. **Dictionary of Engineering & Technology - Wörterbuch der industriellen Technik**, Englisch -Deutsch

Ernst Richard, ISBN 3-87097-162-2, 6th edition 2004

. **Data Systems and Communications Dictionary – Wörterbuch der Daten-und Kommunikationstechnik,** Deutsch – Englisch and Englisch – Deutsch

Brinkmann, Karl-Heinz / Blaha, Herbert F. ISBN 3-87097-206-8, 6th edition 2006

Further information on each of these dictionaries and their prices is given separately on the enclosed two information sheets.

These dictionaries are indispensable for communication between the English and German speaking countries in the field of science and technology. Indeed, they provide authoritative coverage of science and technology subject areas in depth.

We would greatly appreciate your order by post, fax, e-mail or telephone, and look forward to hearing from you in due course.

Yours sincerely

Mrs Sarah Brown
Library Supplies Co-ordinator
Brown Brothers

286   **Business Communication**

****

(7) . <u>Sales Letter 2</u>

<u>Letterhead</u>
<u>Business name and address etc.</u>

date here

Mr G Spencer
Proprietor
Linden Hall Nursery
Linden Hall
YO1 8LH

Dear Mr Spencer

I visited your nursery last Sunday afternoon, as we were in your area. It is, indeed, a large nursery, as you have a wide range of all kinds of indoor and outdoor plants, shrubs, bushes and gardening accessories. At your cash desk, four persons were dealing with customers payments, and all chargeable amounts were worked out without the aid of any calculating machine. Customers paid by cash and transactions were completed without receipts given to customers. In fact, there was a long queue of customers, including myself, waiting to pay for their purchases.

I do not see anything wrong with this system, but I thought I should write to inform you that we have developed our computer based cash register and management system. This system has been supplied to many retailers, and our clients include a number of nurseries in the UK.

Once you have initially invested in this reliable, accurate and fast system, you will soon experience fast cash handling, dealing with credit card transactions, issuing sales receipts, improved and timely ordering of stock items, regular management reports, customer satisfaction and an increase in sales. After some time, the financial benefits will become apparent, as the cost of overall business administration will decrease gradually.

Our system is guaranteed and we service it on a regular basis. I would be happy to introduce you to one of our clients in the nursery business, and they would be happy to discuss our system with you.

Our systems consultant and a demonstrator can visit you at your earliest convenience and give you a demonstration without any obligation.

I look forward to hearing from you.

Yours sincerely

Alan Jolly
Managing Director

. In the third paragraph, a link is created between an initial investment in this system and some key benefits without too much unnecessary emphasis.

. In the fourth paragraph, an assurance is given to the prospective customer in terms of the guarantee, service and a reference so that the recipient takes a keen interest in the letter and the product.

. In the next paragraph, the recipient is invited to see a demonstration of this system at the recipient's own place without any obligation.

Like the sales letter in example 6, it is a simple, precise and concise letter. It does not make any wild claims about the system being offered for sale.

. Money Matters

For whatever reasons, sometimes customers do not pay for goods or services purchased, but continue sending orders. In the interest of your business, you do not wish to upset them, but at the same time you must get your payment from them before they even go bankrupt.

. Example 8

. In this example, the writer acknowledges the order from a customer, but politely and firmly rejects it. The idea is to refer to the order number/ reference and in simple words tell them the reason for not passing this order for completion.

In the second paragraph, the recipient is reminded of the terms and conditions of trade. Here the writer firmly informs the recipient that the order will be kept on file for only ten days. It is also stated that within this period, payment should be made, so that it can be processed.

. Example 9

. Example 9 is concerning a request from a customer to increase the existing credit limit. Since the customer's sales account shows that they have not paid for goods supplied two months ago, and have already bought goods equivalent to the agreed credit limit, it is not your company's policy to increase their credit limit in such circumstances.

There is no need to tell them something which does not sound right, when a polite and sympathetic reply is sufficient. However, tell them that you still value their orders, and you will continue to supply goods within the existing credit limit.

. Example 10

. It is generally understood that it is worth asking for a discount. Example 10 exemplifies the content of a letter asking for a discount.

. In the opening paragraph, the writer thanks the suppliers for sending them a copy of their current catalogue, and shows an interest in their goods.

. In the next paragraph, the writer tells them what they will buy immediately, and that they purchase IT products on a regular basis. It is better not to place too much emphasis on future purchases, because it may look as if you are trying to stress this point in order to get a discount. It is a good idea to ask for a particular percentage discount rate. If you don't, they may suggest a rate which may be lower than you would like to have, and that may be their final offer. See Example 10 on the next page.

(8) . <u>Declining a sales order</u>

<u>Letterhead</u>

<u>Business name and address etc.</u>

<u>date here</u>

Mr J M Simpson
Buyer
Bow Electronics Ltd
12 Clapham Common
London
SW12 8 VC

Dear Mr Simpson

Thank you for the order number A 00234 received today. Regrettably, your account is already two months overdue. Furthermore, you have already purchased goods equivalent to the agreed monthly credit limit of £5000.

In accordance with our terms and conditions of trade, we would very much appreciate your cheque for £5000 before we can complete this order. We will keep this order on our pending file for ten days. We hope that within this time you will be able to send us a cheque. As soon as we have received your cheque, we will release this order for completion.

Yours sincerely

Bruce Butler
Credit Control Manager

(9) . <u>Declining a request for increasing credit limit</u>

<u>**Letterhead**</u>

<u>**Business name and address etc.**</u>

<u>**date here**</u>

Mr A K Brown
Proprietor
Brent Bed Manufacturers
Industrial Park
Brent
BR1 9 MM

Dear Mr Brown

<u>**Account No. 0786**</u>

Thank you for your letter of 10 June, asking us to increase the credit limit from £5000 to £7500, and informing us about your company's capital investment and expansion plans.

As a small company, we do understand and appreciate your current difficulties and commitments. Indeed, we have a number of our own commitments to meet. Like yourself, we also operate within the financial constraints and cash flow problems.

In fact, you have already bought goods equivalent to the agreed credit limit, and the account is already two months overdue. It is our company policy, in line with general practice in the manufacturing industry, that no credit extension is granted when the account is already 60 days overdue.

Under these circumstances, regrettably, we are unable to increase your credit limit on this occasion.

Yours sincerely

Tim Clark
Credit Controller

(10) . <u>Asking for a discount</u>

<u>Letterhead</u>
<u>Business name and address etc.</u>

<u>date here</u>

Mr P N Smith
Sales Manager
London PC Centre
12 Old High Street
London
W11 7CC

Dear Mr Smith

Recently we received your product catalogue together with your price list, for which we are grateful. It is really good to know that you have a wide range of IT products.

We are a large commercial IT training provider in this area of London. We do buy IT products, on a regular basis, for both our training requirements and administrative purposes. At present, we would like to purchase four Deskjet 999 Cxi printers. According to your price list, the total gross cost will be £ 1,050 plus VAT @17.5%.

We usually get 25% discount on all our IT supplies. If you would like to match this rate of discount, we would be pleased to place an order immediately.

We look forward to hearing from you in due course.

Yours sincerely

Dr Frank Nödel
Director

. <u>Employment Matters</u>

It is really important to give serious thought to what you should say in your letter of employment and CV(Curriculum Vitae). A well-written letter of employment and CV can get you an interview, but cannot guarantee that you will be successful at the interview. However, your letter of application clears the first hurdle for you, if you get a call for a job interview. Therefore, it is important to prepare both the letter and the CV with great care and thought.

A well-written letter does not mean a letter composed as a super literary piece of writing, but something that is simple, polite, clear and concise that gives correct information. Here are some examples to help you develop your own style of presentation of your application for a job.

. A CV or *Résumé*

A CV is also known as a *résumé*. A CV will be read by a number of people. Each person will make an observation. Therefore, you should design a CV that keeps selling your attributes. Your attributes include your abilities, qualifications, experience, ambitions and personal qualities related to a particular job. It also includes your potential that can be developed further in the job or by means of further education and training. The best way to prepare your CV is to develop a personal data bank for collecting all information about yourself. Example 11 lists items on which you should start collecting information for your CV. As you gain more experience, you may need more headings to build your up-to-date CV.

(11) . <u>Personal data bank for preparing a CV</u>

Personal Information

Title (Prof/Dr/Mr/Mrs/Miss/Ms) ---

First Name(s) ------------------------------ Surname------------------------------

Address ---

Telephone (home) --------------------- Telephone(work) -------------------------

Mobile Telephone--

Fax------------------------------- Email --

Date of Birth --------------------- Place of birth --- ----------------------------

Age at last birthday----------Nationality -------------------------------

National Insurance No.---

Gender ------ Marital Status ------- Children ------------ Age(s) --------------

Current Passport -------------Driving Licence------------- Health.------------

Hobbies--

(11) . <u>Personal data bank for preparing a CV</u>
(cont. from last page)

Next of kin --------------------- Telephone ---------------- Fax -------------

Email------- --

Education & Training

School (from age 11 in the UK) --

Qualifications gained with dates

--- ---

College/University attended (start from the last course/ qualification gained/ professional training)	<u>Date</u>	<u>Course(list subjects)</u>	<u>Qualification</u> Gained
	------	------------------------	-------------
	------	------------------------	-------------
	-------	------------------------	-------------
	-------	------------------------	-------------
	-------	------------------------	-------------

<u>Membership of Professional bodies</u>	<u>Date</u>	<u>Methods of Joining</u> Exams passed/ exempted	<u>Membership Level</u>
	-------	------------------------	------------------
	-------	------------------------	------------------
	-------	------------------------	------------------

Employment History (start from your most recent job)

<u>Employers</u>	<u>Start</u> date	<u>End</u> date	<u>Job title and</u> brief description	<u>Salary & reason</u> or leaving
-------------------	-------	-------	------------------------	------------------
-------------------	-------	-------	------------------------	------------------
-------------------	-------	-------	------------------------	------------------
-------------------	-------	-------	------------------------	------------------

****

(11). <u>Personal data bank for preparing a CV</u>
(cont. from last page)

Any publications

Describe some other aspects of your current job or previous jobs which you initiated or developed leading to improved efficiency, better working environment, increased profitability, etc.

Objective (describe in a few words how you can make a contribution)

Interests & Hobbies (clubs, societies, charity work, etc.)

Any accomplishment from the age 11 at schools/college/university/ sport

----

Any special aptitudes/skills that can be developed at work and is useful to employers

----

References

Usually a minimum of two references are required. These are your last and present employers. If you are still a student, give the names of your present tutor and the head of department. Your tutor can advise you about this matter. It may be that you worked for many years for just one employer, and left school/college many years ago. In this case, give references from the same company where you were employed. You must ask for permission before listing them as your referees. Give full name, status, address, telephone (and fax) number and email address (if any).

. <u>CV styles</u>

There are a number of ways to draw up your CV. In fact, some companies offer a commercial service for preparing your general CV, which you can cir-
culate to prospective employers and employment agencies. This service is not
recommended in this book. If your letter of application and your performance
at the interview do not match it, you will be very disappointed after the interview. A general CV may not have the specific information for a particular
post or it may have too much information. If so, it will be difficult for the
reader of your CV to pick out the relevant information from it. This will not
help you to get an interview. Therefore, it is strongly suggested that you write
your own CV.

Once you have your personal data bank, you can use it to write your CV.
From your personal data, you can extract the relevant information for a CV
for a particular job. If you want to compete successfully with other applicants, you must write a CV that meets the requirements of the job for which
you wish to apply. It is worth knowing that a style of CV for a young person
will not be suitable for someone who has been working for some years, and
may have changed jobs many times.

It is best to use quality white paper of A4 size. It must be typed/word processed on one side of the page only. Allow left and right margins, as well as at
the top and bottom of the page. It is a good idea to avoid excessive use of underlining, or similar emphasis, as some people do not like
it.

Example 12 illustrates a CV drawn for a young graduate applying for the post
of a graduate trainee. The style is known as *historical*. It gives information in
a chronological order. It is most suited when someone's career or work experience is unbroken. Therefore, this style is ideal for young people, as it
shows continuity since they left school. It is also suitable for people who
have not changed jobs over many years of their lives, because it reveals their
career progress and continuity. The CV must be sent with a covering letter,
only when you are looking for employment.

If you are responding to an advertisement to fill a vacancy, you must apply
for this vacancy in accordance with the prospective employers' rules. It may
be that you have to fill in a formal application form and send it with a letter
of application. It is strongly recommended that a letter of application is short
and precise. It must not be more than two pages. Usually, prospective employers set the size - A4 one page, one side only.

Example 13 contains a letter of application written by an applicant in
order to send it with the CV shown in Example 12.

(12) . <u>A CV for a graduate</u>

****

<u>**Personal History**</u>

<u>**Title:**</u> Miss   <u>**Status:**</u> Single

<u>**Surname:**</u> Scott <u>**Other Name:**</u> Jane   <u>**Date of Birth:**</u> 12.12.1980   <u>**Age:**</u> 21 years

<u>**Address:**</u> 23 Home Street, London NW1 1BN   <u>**Telephone:**</u> 0123 456 987

<u>**National Insurance No.**</u> ABC/1334/ABN   <u>**Driving Licence:**</u> Full UK

<u>**Passport:**</u>   Full UK   <u>**Health:**</u> Excellent

<u>**Next of Kin:**</u> Mr and Mrs Scott (parents) at the address shown above

<u>**Objective:**</u>
A graduate trainee appointment in IT field. I possess BSc(Hons) Degree in IT and some part-time work experience. I can quickly learn and contribute towards the IT team work at Goldsmith Retail Stores.

<u>**Education:**</u>

1991- 98	Green Comprehensive School, Camden Town London NW1 2BB
1998 –03	Newland University Bristol BR1 6FD

<u>**Qualifications:**</u>

1996	GCSE in English Language (B), Maths (A), Computer Studies (A), Physics (C), British Constitution (B)
1998	A Levels in Computer Studies (A), English (B), German (C)
2003	BSc (IT), second Class Honours, Newland University

<u>**Work Experience:**</u>

1991–03	Part-time weekend, Shop Assistant, Foods & Drinks Store Camden Town London NW1 1SD Duties included filling of shelves, stock checking, checkout help and stock taking
2003-to-date	Part-time weekend, Shop Assistant, Friendly Stores Newton Street, Bristol BE3 5AC Duties included filling of shelves, stock checking, and checkout help

<u>**Interest & Hobbies:**</u>
I played hockey at school and university. I held the post of chairman, IT Society at Newland University

<u>**Reference:**</u>

Dr Peter Sellers	Miss J Smith
Head of Computing School	Store Manager
Newland University	Foods & Drinks Store
Bristol	Camden Town
BR1 6FD	NW1 1SD
Tel: 0126 44445	Tel: 0207 444 1234

(13) . <u>A letter of application for a trainee job from a graduate</u>

23 Home Street
Bristol
BR1 9AS

(date here)

Miss M B Jones
Personnel Manager
Goldsmith Retail Stores
Paddington
Peterborough
PE1 4AA

Dear Miss Jones

I have been informed by our Graduate Employment Officer at the University of Newland that annually you recruit some newly qualified graduates. This year, I completed my BSc (Hons) degree in IT. I would very much appreciate it if you would consider me as a candidate.

I am particularly interested in joining your company as I have had some part-time experience working in the retail business. During the last six years, I worked for two major retail stores in London and Bristol. This experience has given me some working knowledge of big store operations and the important role played by IT in the smooth running of a large retail store.

On my IT degree course, I have experienced theoretical computing and IT knowledge, and acquired some software development skills. I believe that my training at your company will enable me to extend my knowledge and skills as well as to take part in developing software for the company quickly.

 I enclose a copy of my CV and hope that you will grant me an interview.

I look forward to hearing from you.

Yours sincerely

Jane Scott

. The above letter is from a graduate who has just completed her course of study. Jane Scott's chosen career has not begun yet. Therefore, it is more appropriate to call her CV 'Personal History'. This CV format is most suited for someone who has not had much work experience. In your letter of application, avoid the use of long and complex expressions as simple and direct sentences will convey your meaning more clearly.

. In this application, it is relevant to list all part-time jobs. It does not matter if they are not related to the work you are seeking now. If you had any additional duties, over and above your normal responsibilities, you must state them. Part-time work shows your motivation to work as well as some experience of the world of work.

. The section on interests and hobbies is essential. You can call it 'Other Information', or give it another title. However, it is important to say something about your activities other than just learning to gain a qualification. This section reveals your social and sports activities, and gives an idea of any sign of leadership. Applicants who show signs of leadership and team work have something extra to offer. If you did not take part in any sports or societies, you could still mention something like gardening, charity work, etc.

. The lack of space in this chapter does not allow me to discuss another type of CV known as *functional* and a cover letter, except to add that this type of CV is most suited for an applicant who has had varied experience and held a number of posts over some years. The functional CV can also be called *'Career History'*. To write a functional CV, you still have to extract data from your personal data bank. When listing work experience in your CV, break it down into some functions. The following is a part of a functional CV:

Major Experiences during the last ten Years

Store Manager - 2003 –2009   World PLC, Kings Road, Chelsea, London W1 2SS
                             Under my control, the sales increased from
                             £14 - £17 millions during the last three years.

Sales Manager – 2000-003 Home Stores PLC, High Street, Nottingham NO1 3CV
                             I was responsible for 'Northern Sales Regions'.
                             My sales team had twenty sales representatives.
                             I re-organised our sales and goods delivery
                             procedures that led to an increase in sales.
                             Our sales steadily increased by 20% under my
                             supervision.

                                                       --------- **cont.**

Most employers will ask you to fill it in an application form. It is important that you fill it in. A CV and a letter of application are sent together when you are directly approaching a prospective employer for a suitable job. If you are granted an interview, it is highly likely that you will be asked to fill in a form.

. Holiday Arrangements

Holiday booking is fairly easy. Sometimes it can lead to serious problems due to a lack of clarity of information given by either party. It is, therefore, suggested that you give and receive precise written information prior to agreeing the terms and conditions of your booking. Here are two examples.

(14) . A letter to the manager of a hotel for holiday arrangements

Your name
and
full address

date here

The Manager
Bridlington Hotel
Promenade
Bridlington
Y016 4 AA

Dear Manager

I write to enquire whether you have accommodation for five nights for four persons. I list our requirements:

. Arrival on Saturday 11 June xxxx (early in the morning).

. Departure on Thursday 16 June xxxx.

. Accommodation in a large en suite bedroom which should have one double bed and two single beds. This accommodation will be for my wife, myself and my two sons 7 and 10 years of age (two adults and two children). We would prefer an en suite room on the front side of your building and located on the first or second floor. It must not be next to the lift or a staircase. The room must have a colour television set and its use must be included in your rates. Please inform us if the room is equipped with tea/coffee making facilities.

Cont. on the next page

(14). <u>A letter to the manager of a hotel for holiday arrangements (cont.)</u>

Cont. from the last page

. If you do not have a large en suite bedroom for a family of four, then I would be interested in two small adjoining/connected rooms, one must be an en suite bedroom providing their total cost for five days does not exceed the cost of one large en suite bedroom, as long as they have the same facilities as outlined above.

. We will arrive at 3.30 hours at Edinburgh Airport from London Heathrow Airport.
. Can you please tell us the best way to travel from the airport to your hotel?
. Will we be able to have access to our room as soon as we arrive early in the morning? If not, when can we do so ?

By the time we arrive at your hotel, our children will be rather tired, and therefore, we would very much appreciate your help if we could occupy our accommodation on our arrival, or as soon as it is ready for us. If we have to wait for some time before our room is ready:

. Will it be possible for us to relax in your reception area until our accommodation is ready for us, and buy our breakfast at your hotel? If so, please inform us of the cost of breakfast per person. Will it be English breakfast or continental?
. We would also need breakfast during our five nights' stay.
. Can we please book our evening meals on a day-to-day basis, when we are staying with you?

If for some unknown reason(s), I have to cancel the booking, please tell me:
. What notice should I give you to avoid losing my deposit?
. Are there any recreational facilities for children at the hotel or near the hotel?

I would be grateful to hear whether you can accommodate us. If so, please send me your rates, how much deposit you would require, and how you would like to be paid, together with the other information requested above.

I look forward to hearing from you in due course.

Yours faithfully

John R Smith

This is not really a social letter. It is better to word process/type it and write your name below your signature; otherwise, print important information such as date of arrival.

****

(15). <u>A letter to the manager of a hotel for further information</u>

Your name
and
full address

Mrs Anne Blair
Manager
Bridlington Hotel
Promenade
Bridlington
 Y016 4 AA

Dear Mrs Blair

Thank you for your letter of 15 May in response to my enquiry of 10 May. I am pleased that you have provisionally booked for my wife, myself and my two sons one large en suite bedroom which has two single beds and one double bed for five nights, from 11 June to 15 June inclusive, leaving on 6 June. It is good to know that a full English breakfast is included in the rates you quoted, and we can book our evening meals each morning, if we wish to do so.

 I'm glad to learn that on our early morning arrival, we can stay in your reception area, if our accommodation is occupied by some other guests until 11.00 hours. We can also buy either an English breakfast or a continental breakfast. I understand that 20% of the total cost is payable as a deposit on booking, and that it can be paid by cheque or by a credit card (visa card only).

I should be grateful if you would answer the remaining point raised in my last letter concerning cancellation notice without losing the deposit.

On receipt of your prompt reply, I should be able to decide about my booking and inform you without any delay. Thanking you in anticipation of your prompt reply.

Yours sincerely

John R Smith

In summary, business letter writing is for the purpose of achieving business objectives. Depending on the nature of the business and the content of the letter, the writer should use the language style that matches the knowledge and understanding of the recipient. It is wasteful and confusing to the recipient when you use too many words and jargon/technical phrases or local expressions. Of course, if you are a biologist writing to another biologist, your language will include technical phrases, which will not alienate the recipient. Indeed, most people prefer plain English. Just remember it!

<u>Test Your Knowledge</u>

1. <u>Explain to a friend with the help of an example how a word can be recognised.</u>

2. <u>Read the following passage in order to identify proper, common and collective nouns:</u>

> Mr. John Smith, the secretary of the UK Branch of the International Association of Booksellers chaired a special conference. It was attended by 350 delegates from many countries.
>
> It was held in the Forest Hotel situated in the heart of our beautiful Epping Forest, on the edge of London. The hotel was built some ten years ago. It has 400 bedrooms, each room with bathroom *en suite*. Its high standard facilities include:
>
> a restaurant, a cafeteria, a large and well equipped conference hall, a number of seminar rooms and plenty of recreation amenities for adults and children.
>
> At this conference, British delegates exchanged ideas and information about the book trade, and how to cope with the changing trading conditions and requirements both nationally and internationally.
>
> The increasing pressure from multimedia electronic book publishers to sell their products have forced booksellers to form a forum called Multimedia Book Forum. The aims of this group are:
>
> to agree an international trade discount structure with the representatives of multimedia publishers, distributors and wholesalers;
> to discuss and agree goods ordering facilities; and
> to settle their accounts with all the major multimedia publishers, distributors and wholesalers through the Booksellers Clearing House.
>
> Mr. John Smith of Smith Booksellers, England, was appointed as its secretary and Miss Jane Clarke of Clarke Bookshop, Ireland, as its president. A team of ten persons drawn from ten countries was appointed as the forum's members.

3. Complete the following writings by inserting the correct pronouns. Also indicate the type of each inserted pronoun:

a) We sell most national newspapers. ----- are also printed outside London.

b) My friends wrote to me last month at the same time I wrote to -----.

c) We have just received a copy of John's new publication. ------ has 500 pages.

d) They telephoned us twice today. I cannot guess ------- reason for doing so after such a long time.

e) He was here a few minutes ago. We were enjoying talking with -----.

f) Certainly, this old car is not ---------. I have a new motorcycle.

g) At last, we bought this house. It is ----.

h) This job is not new for me. I have done ------- before.

i) My wife and I have just entertained some guests. They were ----- old friends.

j) There is a big difference between our opinions and ------.

4. The following incomplete sentences contain phrasal verbs. Fill in the blank spaces in order to complete the sentences:

a) Can you ----------- up a meeting?

b) We were looking ------ the photo.

c) Their car's noise woke us ------.

d) Please do not ----------- away these papers.

e) Mary -------- after her sick mother.

f) Fame has crept ------ on him after just one television appearance.

g) Don't just fool ------.

h) I do not wish to hang ------- here.

i) I cannot put --------with this sort of behaviour.

h) You ought to get ------- of the house more.

i) She gave ---------- one million pounds to charity.

j) We must set ----- a new system for dealing ----------so many claims.

Test Your Knowledge   **303**

****

k) He is so humble that he always talks --------- his own achievements.

5. The following sentences contain finite and non-finite verb phrases. Identify these verb phrases. Give two reasons for the identification of these types of verb phrases.

a) Please leave this room.

b) Our manager took action to remedy the situation.

c) The suspect murderer has been interrogated for the last three days.

d) He tried to help us.

e) Definitely, we want to know the truth in this matter.

f) She categorically denied her involvement in that car accident.

g) He wished to come home tonight.

h) They wanted to be assured of their place in the semi-final.

i) Our shopping centre was crowded with day trippers.

j) They had been trying to telephone us from Moscow.

k) A passer-by found an elderly man bleeding on the roadside.

l) Jane reported to work twenty minutes late twice last week.

m) He prepared his speech very carefully to deliver it tonight.

n) He wondered what to do next for a living.

o) Neither Anne nor I recalled ever having seen them.

6. Each of the following sentences has one or two blank spaces. Your task is to fill in these spaces. These completions will result in different tenses. Identify each completed tense.

a) I ----- happy.

b) They ------ going to the beach now.

c) Two years ago, she ------- in England for three years.

d) Recently, Harry ------ written to us from Cambridge.

e) On my arrival, I ------ write to you from Spain.

f) Now we ------ watching a film.

g) Last week they --------skiing in Switzerland.

h) Not long ago, they --------- travelled to France.

i) Last year, we -------- the Indian summer in the UK.

j) She -------- never ridden a horse before she joined our club.

k) You must believe me I did not think that I ----- come First
    in London Marathon Race this year.

l) The Indian summer --------- returned today.

m) We will ------ arriving at 14.000 hours at Victoria Coach Station.

n) Most certainly, I --------- be staying at The Regents Hotel in Paris.

o) By that time, we will have retired.

p) The weatherman told us that it --------- going to rain all that day.

q) He had ----- talking to me.

r) At that time our train will ------- been travelling through
    the tunnel.

s) By that time, We ----- have returned to France.

t) At the end of this year, we -------- -------- been living in this house
    for ten years.

u) Indeed, she promised that she --------- be writing to me soon about
    our plans for the future.

v) During our visit to Paris last year, you indicated that you ------ ----
    been moving to another flat.

w) We all knew Jane would ------- working at the post office.

x) Your father told me you -------- served your country in Bosnia.

7. In the following sentences pick out modifiers(words which are before nouns) and adjectives.

a) I am so tired today.

b) In my opinion, she was absolutely right in accepting his sincere
   apology.

c) I must say that the lecture was not at all informative and interesting.

d) It was really the nicest place I ever visited in that part of the world.

e) He is by far the best candidate for this job.

f) She is feeling no better today.

g) We were warm enough that night.

h) In Paris underground trains were somewhat crowded.

i) I am pretty sure that they will accept our offer this time.

j) We quite enjoyed travelling by train to Paris.

8. The following statements contain adverbs and adverbials. If you find any of these either in the wrong place or incorrect, you should correct them and give a reason for doing so.

a) Often one can buy fruit cheaper in the market.

b) She told the grocer that she could buy this cheaply at a supermarket.

c) On the left, the gentleman is my uncle.

d) Usually this car park is full

e) He probably does not care very much about her health.

f) He purposely did not exchange greetings with his opponents.

g) How is she? She is kind and we like her very much.

h) The business conditions improved themselves even more rapidly than was expected.

9. The following sentences have some **highlighted** words. List these under adjective, adverb and preposition.

a)
Although there is no right or wrong way to apply this technique, it does help to have a **basic** understanding **of some applied** principles.

b)
Kissing and worshipping the feet **of** divine or eminent souls is **still** a sign **of** respect that was, **for** centuries, evident in cultures **worldwide**.

c)
The social smile is **quite distinct from** the genuine smile of pleasure. **For** a start, the one you conjured **up just now** has **almost certainly by now** disappeared **without** trace. A **spontaneous** smile lingers, and fades **more evenly** and **slowly**.

d)
With life **constantly** changing, and people striving to progress, this understanding makes it easier to be **hard working** and **healthy**.

e)
Just as you shouldn't take a polite letter **for** an **encouraging** one,

don't let a harsh letter do more damage **than** necessary.

10. The use of both definite and indefinite articles in the following sentences requires correction. Correct these sentences.

a) We all know that the bicycle does not run on petrol.

b) You should get a parcel on Friday as it is a special delivery.

c) There is a lot to show the visitor.

d) She was a only woman I loved.

e) He is a right person for this job.

f) We invited some friends for a lunch. Luckily sun was brilliantly bright in the afternoon.

g) In the dark, I was searching for switch button of my radio.

h) Suddenly, the car in front of us stopped and a driver of this car ran fast to escape arrest by the police.

i) A night Mary was taken ill.

j) Our new car is as big as a jeep we saw the other day.

11. Your task is to make meaningful statements in order to demonstrate the usage of the following interjections/exclamations:

dear me, oh blast, good grief, good heavens, goodness me, nice, ow, surprise, whoops, yuck.

12. Complete the following sentences. Name the type of each conjunction inserted in the appropriate place in each statement.

a) The traffic lights changed to amber ------I approached.

b) It is possible ------Yvonne has not received our letter.

c) Our tutor said ---- we can leave ------ we answered the question.

d) My wife went to the Chelsea Flower Show ----she enjoyed her visit.

e) Our tutor was unhappy ------- we came fifteen minutes late.

f) She was very kind to us, ---- ------ she hurried us.

g) Milk ----- sugar.

h) Our roof leaked --------- it rained last year.

i) We can finish early ---- ---- -----get ready for the dinner and dance tonight.

****

j) He is working very hard ---- --- the report can be submitted in time.

k) I liked her very much, ---- ----- I did not have much chance to
to meet her after work.

l) Hurry up , ----- you'll be late for work.

m) I have no car , ---- I'll hire one just for tomorrow.

n) She is not a racist ------ a feminist.

o) Some of the overseas students are very hard working -----
others aren't.

13. In what specific way does a prepositional phrase differ from a noun, a verb, an adjective or an adverb phrase? Illustrate your answer with the aid of an example.

14. Which of the following sentences consists of subordinate clauses namely noun, relative, adverbial and comparative?

a) I am looking for a young man **who** used to live in this house
with his girlfriend.

b) I told you **that** it happened on a Christmas Day.

c) This new car is not as smooth to drive **as** the salesman told us.

d) When I rang this number, no one answered my call.

15. Identify simple, compound and complex sentences. Give your reason(s) for your identification of each type.

a) Rebecca is a shy young lady, but she knows her job well.

b) How long is it since you left China for England?

c) Peter is kind and friendly.

d) Some people drive their own cars to work, but many people
travel to work by public transport.

e) Although it was really hard work, I enjoyed it because it was a
challenge.

f) I operate my business from a rented small premises.

g) Software business made John bankrupt.

h) We went to Scarborough and came across Colin Smith, who was
with his family on a day trip to the seaside.

i) As soon as, our stores' gates were open, sales hunters(shoppers)
rushed in and grabbed high quality merchandise at the lowest prices.

****

j)   Visit our local store or phone or visit our website.

16. Punctuate the following passages:

a)   The importance of language skills in a literate society can hardly
     be exaggerated. People are judged on how they speak, **and** nearly
     all academic teaching is done by means of language. so anyone who
     has not achieved an average standard in literacy is likely to be
     seen as deficient across a wide range of skills.

b)   humour is a diffuse fuzzy sort of thing a matter of taste and
     something you do not expect to find in even the most sophisticated
     computer unless it has been programmed in by human beings

c)   unlike space time as we understand has a direction there is
     an asymmetry between the past fixed and the future yet to exist
     times arrow is whatever gives time this direction

d)   its my nature to be like i am she said I was fated to be
     unhappy I believe you can learn to be happy and healthy
     i replied

e)   the man mr Joe Bloggs, was reported present when the morning
     roll call was taken though officials are not sure now whether it was
     he in fact who replied present

f)   did people really speak this way of course they did but as with
     many other aspects of the language the words and phrases which
     people use change and change again as the years go by

g)   this woman was still unemployed she had neither money nor
     prospects even so her world was relatively good for she was
     at peace with herself she was not eating away at her health her
     resolve and stamina with angry self-defeating thoughts she was
     not filling her mind with negative ideas positive thinking helped
     her to take great strides she could sleep at night her stomach
     was better and she didnt blow her top like she used to in
     other words she was learning how to make the world a great
     place to be with her positive attitude soon she found a new
     job a well paid job in fact well done!

h)   The following members have won prizes sarah dean first prize
     £1000 one thousand pounds robert mcDonald second prize £200
     two hundred pounds natasha robinson third prize £50 fifty pounds
     our annual membership fee in accordance with the cost of living
     index will rise to £55 fifty-five pounds from £50 from 1st January
     next year finally our revenue for the year just ended amount to
     £550 000

Glossary

A

absolute adjectives – adjectives which exist in their basic form only, e.g. ⇒ wrong.

abstract nouns – nouns that are used for concepts, which have no material existence, e.g. ⇒ anger. They describe ideas or qualities instead of something physical such as a house(it is a concrete thing).

active clause – a clause in which the action or doing of something is taken by the agent (subject), e.g. ⇒ John is writing a letter.

active participle – the -ing form of a verb in the continuous form, used after **be**, e.g. ⇒ I am reading.

active verb – when the subject performs the action or experiences the state or condition, e.g. ⇒ I write a letter.

active voice – same as active verb. Here is another example: she has won the first prize. She ⇒ subject and performs the action of winning.
See ⇒ active verb.

adding relative clause – it is separated from the main clause by two commas. It gives some additional information about the headword,
e.g. ⇒ Frank, **_who is Elina's friend_**, is working abroad
        relative clause ↵

adjective – a word that modifies/qualifies the meaning of a noun, or pronoun, e.g. ⇒ she is **kind**.

adjective phrase – a phrase which has an adjective in it,
e.g. ⇒ she is very beautiful. In this sentence:
very beautiful ⇒adjective phrase **and** the headword ⇒beautiful
                            adjective ↵

adjunct (adverb) – an adverb or phrase that adds meaning to the verb in a sentence or part of a sentence or clause e.g. ⇒ he screamed loudly. Here, loudly ⇒ adverb is acting as an adjunct and adds meaning to the verb - **scream**. It shows the extent to which something happened. Thus, it adds information about manner, time or place.

adverb – the most common function of an adverb is to modify the main verb in a sentence, e.g. I can do it *easily*. easily ⇒ adverb.

adverb phrase – it can be an adverb on its own e.g. ⇒smoothly. It can also be part of a phrase, which has an adverb as its headword **(see ⇒headword),** e.g. very abruptly ⇒ very ⇒**headword.**

adverbial clause – in a complex sentence, it modifies the main clause, e.g. I will talk to you when I meet you tomorrow. An adverbial clause is joined to the main clause by the conjunction ⇒ when.

adverbial element (or phrase) – a part of a sentence which gives the least compulsory information in a sentence,

> e.g. ⇒ I wrote this letter <u>in a great hurry</u>.
> adverbial element ↵

agent – in an active clause/sentence, the subject is doing the action. It is known as the agent, e.g. ⇒I write it. Here, agent ⇒ I. In a passive clause, an agent comes after *by*, e.g. the letter is signed by *Anne*.

agreement (or concord) – it is a rule in accordance with the verb form which is agreed with the subject and number of the subject (singular/plural), e.g. ⇒ she sings. On the other hand, e.g. ⇒ they cry.

apostrophe – a punctuation mark, e.g. ⇒ Joan's father is a phrase in which the apostrophe is placed between Joan and s to indicate the possessive case. For other usage, see punctuation.

apposition – when in a sentence or clause, two *noun phrases* come one after the other and both refer to the same thing, then phrases are in apposition, e.g. ⇒ *Mr Brown, our director*, is retiring today.

article – there are two types of articles: *a* and *an* ⇒ indefinite article and *the* ⇒ definite article.

aspect – there are two verb aspects: progressive aspect, e.g. ⇒ I am writing and perfect aspect ⇒ I have written. These two aspects can be combined together, e.g. ⇒ she has been living in the UK.

asterisk '*' – it is a star symbol used as a punctuation mark to indicate the omission of letters, the importance of a particular word , a reference or a footnote at the bottom of the text, or elsewhere.

attributive adjective – it comes before a noun or clause, e.g. ⇒ my **new** car has arrived.

 auxiliary verb – a small number of verbs such as *be, will, have* are used with ordinary verbs, such as *work*. These are divided into modal and primary auxiliaries. See ⇒ modal.

B

bare infinitive –   verbs without the particle *to* e.g. ⇒ talk . Bare infinitive is the base form.

base form ,(*root form* or *stem*) – verbs as listed in a dictionary, e.g. ⇒ walk.

brackets – in British English, for writing purposes, the round brackets ( ) which are known as parentheses are used. They indicate alternatives, include abbreviations or show additional information.

c

cardinal numbers – a whole number, e.g. ⇒ 1,2,3.

classifying relative clause – it describes the head noun in the main clause by its nature or type. It does not have commas around it, e.g. ⇒ she likes John *who is very intelligent*. John ⇒ head noun.

clause – it is a group of words containing a finite verb, and any other verb complement, e.g. ⇒ he went home early tonight. See ⇒ main clause and see ⇒ independent clause.

clause elements – there are five clause elements: subject, verb, object, complement and adverbial. A clause may have some or all of these elements.

clause of manner – it tells us the way something is done or someone's behaviour, e.g. I don't work **like he does**.
      clause of manner.⌐

collective noun – a noun that refers to a group of objects, or things or people e.g. ⇒ team, committee, government.

colon ':' – a punctuation mark. It is used for different purposes.

comma ',' – like the full stop, it is a common punctuation mark. There is a tendency to use too many or too few commas despite the fact that it is well. documented and understood.

common noun – nouns that that refer to many of the same type of things, places, objects or people, e.g. country ⇒ there many countries in the world. People ⇒ there are millions of people in the world. Common nouns are divided into abstract and concrete nouns. See ⇒ proper nouns for a comparison.

comparative clause – this is used to express comparison, e.g. Anne is less interested in eating out *than her husband*. It is introduced by the subordinators *than* or *as*. It is a subordinate clause.

comparative form of adjective – for comparing two things or people, e.g. ⇒ he is older than me. old ⇒ adjective and older ⇒ comparative form (oldest ⇒superlative form).

complement – a noun or adjective phrase that follows a linking verb, e.g. ⇒ she is the *champion*. See ⇒ copular verb and **see** ⇒linking verb.

complex sentence – in a complex sentence, one clause is a main clause, with one or more subordinate clauses, e.g. ⇒ I telephoned my wife when I arrived at Heathrow Airport. Main clause ⇒ underlined.

compound sentence – a compound sentence has at least two clauses of equal status which are joined together with a coordinating conjunction, e.g. *he lives downstairs* and *I live upstairs*.

compound word – it is composed of two or more words, e.g. mother-in-law.

concessive clause – it is a subordinate clause which begins with a conjunction (although, despite, whilst, while, much as, in spite of, even though, even if). For instance: Although we get on well, I don't want to marry her.

concord - see ⇒ agreement.

concrete noun – a tangible thing that can be seen or touched is a concrete noun, e.g. ⇒ book. These are common nouns. see also ⇒ abstract noun.

conditional clause – it is constructed when you want to talk about a possible situation and the likely outcome. It usually begins with **if, e.g.** ⇒ if she comes, she will try to take over.

conjunction – a conjunction functions as either a coordinating or subordinating conjunction, and joins clauses, e.g. ⇒ when in:
I will meet you *when* you are upstairs.

coordination of phrases – it means joining together two phrases or clauses of the same status.

coordinator – a coordinator is a coordinating conjunction, e.g. ⇒ *and, but, or*. It joins clauses of the same status.

copular verb – it links the subject with a complement. The basic linking verb is '**be**'. There are only a few copular verbs. These include *be, appear, become, seem.*

countable(count) noun – it has singular, and plural forms and can be pre- ceded by a determiner such as *the*, *a*, *an*, *every*, *many*, *one*, *two*, *three*, *four*, etc. For instance: She has a cat. She has several cats.

D

dash '-' – a punctuation mark. It is used for a variety of purposes.

declarative (sentence/statement) – its order is:
subject ⇒ verb ⇒ verb complement (if any).

declarative structure – it means the structure of a declarative sentence or statement.

defining relative clause – see ⇒ identifying relative clause.

definite article – see ⇒ article.

degree (adverb of) – a word such as *very*, *rather*, *somewhat*, **quite**, *pretty*. It shows the extent of quality, e.g. ⇒ she is very clever. Here, very ⇒ adverb of degree.

demonstrative pronoun – it is used to refer to a particular person, or thing, e.g. ⇒ *this* is a car. Other demonstrative pronouns are *that*, *these* and *those*. These are also demonstrative determiners.

dependent clause – it cannot stand alone, e.g. ⇒ *when I gave him a cup of tea*, he drank it fast.

determiner – a simple word that is placed before a noun phrase,
e.g. ⇒ this.

direct object – I gave students passes. In this sentence: passes ⇒ direct ob- ject because the direct effect of the verb *gave* is on passes. In the same sen- tence: students ⇒ indirect object because the indirect effect/ secondary ef- fect is on students.

direct speech – the exact words of the speaker which are enclosed within the quotation marks, e.g. ⇒ ' We were aware of your financial problems,' said the chairman. It is quoted in someone's words.

dummy subject – when the word *it* or *there* is used in the subject position and does not relate to any specific thing, e.g. ⇒ **It** appears she is late again. It is also known as an empty subject. It is used because it is needed in the sub- ject position.

E

ellipsis – usually three dots are used to indicate that some words are left out, e.g. ⇒ get the---out of here!

embedded prepositional phrase – prepositional phrases are embedded in the noun phrase, e.g. ⇒ you spoke to Rachel about her journey. In this sentence: [Rachel about her journey] ⇒ noun phrase   and [about her journey] ⇒ prepositional phrase.

empty subject – see ⇒ dummy subject.

empty verb – *have* is the most commonly used empty verb but there are other empty verbs, e.g. ⇒ take, give, do. We use them as: *give* an example, *have* tea. In these examples, the action is indicated by the nouns *example*, and *tea*.

exclamation mark – it is a punctuation mark represented by **!** e.g. Cheers! It is a terminator.

F

finite clause – He walks to work. In this clause, the verb walk is marked for tense ⇒ present tense. When in a clause the verb is marked for tense it is called a finite clause. See ⇒ non-finite clause.

finite phrase and finite verb – a finite verb or finite phrase such as *talk, went, was going, will be* are finite verbs and finite phrases. These are marked for tenses, e.g. ⇒ he is singing a song. In this clause, the finite phrase is singing and is marked for tense ⇒ present continuous.

footnote – it is a punctuation mark. It is written below the text to give further information.

formal style – it is used in official and important situations. It often indicates a distant rather than a close relationship. It is very correct in both writing and speech.

fraction – a number which is not a whole number, e.g. ⇒ half, two-thirds, four fifths.

full stop – it is the most commonly used punctuation mark. In the USA it is called a period.

future (tense) – it is a state or action that will take place in the future, e.g.

⇒ I will come. It is formed as: auxiliary verb (will or shall) + bare infinitive verb.

future continuous(progressive)– it expresses a state or action that will continue in the future. It is constructed as ⇒ shall/will + participle –ing form, e.g.⇒ *I will be thinking of you*.

future perfect – it refers to our thinking in the future and then looking back when something will be completed at a specific point in the future, e.g. By next Friday, I will have met him in Paris. It is constructed as:
will/shall + have + past participle.

future perfect progressive – it is as future perfect, but the action. or state of something continues in the future, e.g. Next month, you will have been studying at the university one year. It is constructed as:
will/shall + have been + participle –ing form.

G

gender – in English the gender classification is: feminine ⇒ woman, masculine ⇒ man, and neuter ⇒ artefacts/things such as radio.

genitive case – it shows possession . It is a noun in its possessive form, e.g. John's car.

gerund – When a participle verb formed with *-ing* is used in a clause or a sentence as a noun, it is known as a gerund, e.g. *Dancing* is her favourite hobby. In this sentence, dancing is a gerund.

grammar – it has rules for combining words together for a meaningful communication in spoken and written language.

H

headword – it is a main noun or pronoun in a phrase, clause or sentence. For instance: a **bundle** of files. a paperback **book**. Headwords are highlighted.

hyphen '**–** ' – it is a punctuation mark. It is used either to join two words together or to split the word at the end of a line of print.

I

identifying relative clause – its purpose is to identify the earlier noun in the main clause, e.g. 'The young man **who is smartly dressed** is my son.'

idiom or idiomatic expression – it is a group of words. Its meaning is different from the meaning of individual words forming the idiomatic expression.

imperative mood – it is a command and an order. It can also be a polite order, e.g. *forgive me.* **go away. please take a seat.** There is no subject and the verb is in the base form.

indefinite article – see ⇒ article.

indefinite pronoun – a word which does not refer to any particular person or thing, e.g. ⇒all.

independent clause – see ⇒ main clause.

indicative mood – when we make a statement, ask a question or state a fact, e.g. ⇒ I'm here. See ⇒ moods.

indirect object – see ⇒ direct object.

indirect speech – it is not in the words of the speaker but its meaning is reported in our own words, e.g. I said she told me about her love affairs.

infinitive – it is the base form of the verb. e.g. ⇒ **go**. See ⇒ base form and bare infinitive (without the participle to-) as shown in a dictionary.

infinitive clause – it has an infinitive verb, e.g. We **walk** every
evening. I wanted **to go**.   bare infinitive ↵
       to-infinitive ↵

infinitive particle – see ⇒ particle.

inflection – it means changing the ending or spelling of a word in accordance with its grammatical function, e.g. ⇒ She studies French.
The verb **'study'** is inflected to match the present tense of its subject.

informal style – the use of the English language in social circumstances, e.g. both - spoken and written communication between relatives and friends.

ing- form – when *-ing* is added to a verb and used as a participle, or gerund e.g. write⇒writing.

interjections – a minor class of word. Used for expressing feelings,
e.g. ⇒ *Gosh!*

interrogative pronoun – what and which are used with nouns to ask questions, e.g. ⇒*Which* book was it?

intransitive verb – it does not take an object or complement, and it can stand alone, e.g. ⇒ I talk.

****

inversion – it occurs when the regular word order is changed to form a question, e.g. ⇒ Has she finished that job? In this sentence: the subject *she* has changed (inverted) place with the auxiliary verb *has*.

irregular verbs– they do not follow the pattern of adding '-ed' to form the past tense, e.g. ⇒ begin: its irregular past tense ⇒ began.

L

linking verb – see ⇒ copular verb. Linking and copular both mean the same.

M

mass noun – it is an uncountable noun. It refers to things such as grass, hair, sugar, medicines. Sometimes it can be used as a countable noun, e.g. ⇒ two sugars. one hair. It is used for quantities.

main clause – any clause which can stand alone is a main clause, e.g. ⇒ I walk. It stands alone as a meaningful clause or a short sentence.

main verb – it is the finite verb in the main clause, e.g. ⇒ When the doorbell rang, I *opened* the door.

manner – it is the adverb of manner. It tells us *how* something happened, e.g. ⇒ she cried *loudly*.

modal (auxiliary verb) – these are auxiliary verbs, e.g. ⇒ can, could, may, might, etc.

modify (modifier) – it means giving further information about a word or phrase, e.g. It is a *tall* tree. 'tall' modifier is an adjective, but functioning as a modifier. It gives further information about ⇒**tree**.

moods – see ⇒ indicative, imperative and subjunctive entries.

N

negative – a phrase, clause or sentence which has a word meaning 'no', 'not' is a negative phrase, clause or sentence.. You can have a negative question as well. For instance: Didn't you shout at her? ⇐ negative interrogative sentence. I never went to Paris. ⇐ negative declarative sentence.

negative word – a word like never, nothing and nowhere is a negative word, e.g. ⇒ I can see nothing wrong with her idea. ⇐ negative meaning intended by the word ⇒ **nothing**.

non-finite clause – it has a to-infinitive verb form, ⇒ We asked them. *to return* our camera.

noun – it is a name given to a person, place, object, etc., e.g. ⇒ John, London, book ….

noun (nominal) clause – it can act as the subject, object or the complement of the main clause, e.g. ⇒ He thought *that she was not at home*. Here, the noun clause is acting as an object.

noun phrase – it has a noun or pronoun as its headword, e.g. ⇒ I wanted John *as our leader*.

number – in grammar, the distinction between singular and plural is expressed as number, e.g. cap ⇒ singular noun and two caps(plural) number of the same object ⇒ cap.

O

object – it comes after the verb in a clause. For example: this is Andrew. object ⇒ Andrew.

object complement – it comes after the verb in a clause, e.g. ⇒ we all paid her **our** respects.

object predicate – see ⇒ object complement.

ordinal numeral – it refers to the position of something in a series, e.g. ⇒ he was in *third* place. Some other examples: fourth, fifth, , hundredth, etc.

ordinary verb – there are thousands of ordinary verbs, such as ⇒ go, run, jump, write, etc. Auxiliary verbs are not included in ordinary verbs. See auxiliary and modal verbs.

P

participle – it is a non-finite verb form. It ends either with *–ing* or *-ed*. See ⇒ present and past participle.

participle clause – it has a participle verb form in it, e.g.⇒ *Coming* to London, we were late.

particle – it is the word *to* with the base form of the verb, e.g. ⇒ to run.

particles class – it is a minor word class, e.g. ⇒ she *fell off* her bicycle on to the road.

passive – in a passive clause/sentence something is done to the subject (agent), e.g. ⇒ the report *is being typed*.

passive verb (or passive voice) – when the subject is affected by the action. The passive voice involves the use of the **auxiliary verb.** For instance, the house **is** occupied. Here is ⇒ auxiliary verb.

past continuous/progressive – it expresses what was happening at some point in time in the past, e.g. ⇒ I *was working* in London.

past participle form – Regular verbs: it ends in **–ed**. Irregular verbs: it ends in some other ways. e.g. ⇒eaten, drunk, etc. In the perfect it comes after 'have, e.g. I have *finished* it.

past perfect – it is formed with 'had' and a past participle e.g. ⇒ she *had received* my letter.

past perfect continuous/progressive – it is formed with 'had been' and an active participle, e.g. ⇒ We *had been dancing* all night. Here, *dancing* ⇒ active participle.

past simple – it is the past tense, e.g. ⇒ they *returned* home. It tells what happened or existed at a particular time (then) before the present time (now).

perfect – it expresses an action completed by the present, or a particular point in the past or future. It is constructed with 'have' with the past participle of the main verb, e.g. ⇒ *I have left* (present perfect), *I had left* (past perfect), and *I will have left* (perfect future).

perfect aspect –it is the underlined in: She *has been living* in Germany. See ⇒ aspect.

performative verb – it means the action it performs, e.g. ⇒ *I accept*. The action ⇒ accept.

person (singular and plural) – first person ⇒ **I, we.** Second person ⇒ **you.** Third person ⇒*he, she, it, they*.

personal pronoun – I, you, he, she, etc.

phrasal verb – it is a verb combined with an adverb or a preposition, e.g. ⇒ fall off, break down, etc.

phrase – a word or some words, e.g. ⇒ rubbish, a white elephant. There are five types of phrases: verb phrase, noun phrase, adjective phrase, adverb phrase, and prepositional phrase.

plural – it means more than one, e.g. ⇒ a song is the singular form but songs ⇒ the plural form of the noun.

possessive determiner – it is a possessive pronoun, when it replaces a noun, e.g. ⇒ this is *my* car.

possessive pronoun – mine, yours, ours, etc. This coat is mine. Possessive pronoun ⇒*mine*

post-modifier(post- modification) – it comes after the head noun in phrases, e.g. It is a nice **car** fitted with audio equipment.
          post-modification ↲⇒ head noun

predicate – in a clause, it is the verb element and any other elements that follow the verb, e.g. ⇒ England is the largest part of the UK. The underlined part is the predicate.

prefix – many words can be created by adding the beginning to a word, e.g. ⇒ *un*necessary. It is *un* + *necessary*. See ⇒ suffix.

pre-modifier(pre-modification) – an adjective (sometimes an adverb) that comes before a head noun is a pre-modifier. There can be several pre-modifiers, e.g. ⇒a **tiny shining** star. star ⇒ head noun/head word.

preposition – a class of word, e.g. ⇒ over, since, for. Also more than one word, e.g. ⇒ instead of.

prepositional idioms – it is the preposition used with an idiom, e.g. ⇒ *at heart*.

prepositional phrase – it is the preposition plus a noun or an adverb e.g. ⇒ in our school, over there.

prepositions of relationship – express a variety of relationships. Most common are time and place.

present continuous/progressive – it is the present tense that shows the action is continuous.

present participle form – it is the part of the verb which ends in –*ing*, e.g. ⇒ missing, crossing, etc.

present perfect – it indicates that the action or state was complete in the near past up to the present time, e.g. ⇒ The parcel has arrived.

present perfect progressive – an action or state in the past which continues up-to the present time, e.g. ⇒ it has been raining. It is formed as: have/has + been + active participle.

present simple – it is the present tense, e.g. ⇒ I work. It expresses a current action or state.

pronoun – a word used instead of a noun or noun phrase, e.g. ⇒ *You* are kind.

Q

Qualifier (s) – postmodifier and premodifier are qualifiers.A qualifier can come before or after a head word, e.g. ⇒ He has a corner shop near here. corner ⇒ premodifier and near here ⇒ postmodifier element.

qualify – see ⇒ modify.

question – it is a sentence for asking a question, e.g. ⇒ What's wrong with you?

Question tag – a short question at the end of a statement, e.g. ⇒ She loves him, doesn't she?

question word – these are:
       what, when, where, who, whom, which, how, whose, why.

R

reciprocal pronoun – it is used to express mutual relationships, e.g. ⇒ they love *each other*. There are only two reciprocal pronouns each other and one another.

reflexive pronoun – it refers to the subject, e.g. ⇒ They can do it *themselves*. I do it *myself*.

regular verbs – they change their forms in the past by following a set pattern of *–ed ending*, e.g. ⇒ verb 'help' its regular past tense form ⇒ 'helped'.

relative adverb – where, when and why are used in relative clauses as relative adverbs, e.g. ⇒ the house *where* I was born.

relative clause – it modifies a noun, e.g. ⇒ the salesman *who talked too much*.

relative pronoun – it links a subordinate clause to a main clause, e.g. ⇒ it is not me *who* hit first.

S

s-form of the verb – it is the inflected form of the bare infinitive. It is formed with either *s*, or *es* added, e.g. ⇒ he *runs.* Here *s* is added.
She *cries*. Here, cry is inflected by *es*.

sentence – a sentence is the largest syntactic unit which has at least one clause.

simple tense – it is without the auxiliary verb, e.g. ⇒ I go.

singular form – it means one thing only, e.g. ⇒ noun 'man' refers to only one person/man.

slang style – it is an informal way of speaking used between a specific group of people, e.g. ⇒ criminals.

split infinitive – the placing of a word or words between the *to* and the *verb* creates a split infinitive.

standard English – a form of the English language that is nationally used. Speakers of other languages learn standard English. For instance, broadcasting services use standard English.

statement – it is a declarative sentence which gives information. It is not a question.

structure - for our purpose, it means the way some words are arranged in accordance with the rules of grammar, e.g. ⇒ I went there.

style – it is a distinct way of doing something, e.g. writing or speaking in the language context. There are many styles. For instance, various styles are imposed on the use of idiomatic expressions.

subject –in a sentence, it comes before the verb, e.g. ⇒ he writes a letter. he ⇒subject/agent.

subject complement – in a clause/sentence it comes after a linking verb. e.g. ⇒she appears *calm*.

subject element – it precedes the verb in a clause. It is the agent of an active clause, e.g. ⇒ I'm writing this text. Here, I'm ⇒ **subject** or subject element. It is also the agent of this active clause.

subject position – it is the first element in a clause, e.g. ⇒ she loves you. subject ⇒ begins the clause.

subject predicate – see ⇒ subject complement

subjective pronoun – *I, you* (both singular and plural) , *he, she, it, they* and *we*. They occur in the subject position in a clause.

subjunctive mood – it indicates possibility, uncertainty, wish, etc., e.g. ⇒ she wanted a baby.

subordinate clause – it supports the main clause. See ⇒dependent clause

subordinator – in a complex sentence clauses are of unequal status. We use a subordinator (**when** ...) to join two clauses of unequal status.

suffix – words can be created by adding **an ending** to a word, e.g. ⇒ soft + *ly* = *softly*.

superlative – the form of an adjective for comparing three or more things, e.g. ⇒ highest, tallest (adjectives).

SV – it is an acronym for <u>s</u>ubject and <u>v</u>erb

SVO – it is an acronym for <u>s</u>ubject <u>v</u>erb and <u>o</u>bject

T

tense – it is a form of the verb which indicates when the action of the verb occurs, or the state affected by the verb, e.g.

- I talk ⇒ present tense
- she cried ⇒ past tense
- We will dance tonight. ⇒ future tense

It indicates a particular period of time or a point in time.

to-infinitive – it is a verb form which is preceded by 'to', e.g. to run, to sign, to smile.

transitive verb – it cannot stand alone and it is followed by an object, e.g. ⇒ she *rang* the <u>bell</u>.
           object ↵

U

uncountable noun – it has only one verb form. Some uncountable nouns are only plural such as jeans, e.g. ⇒ **a pair of jeans**. On the other hand, some uncountable nouns such as **space** are only singular, e.g. ⇒ There **wasn't much space** in the room. When an uncountable noun is the subject, the verb is singular, e.g. ⇒ Some *money is* in Euro currency.

V

verb – doing, action/state word. It is the most important part of speech, e.g. ⇒ she *loves* her children. Without the word *loves* which is a verb, the sentence will not make any sense.

verb aspect – see ⇒ aspect.

verb element – it is the focal point of a clause, e.g. ⇒ she has completed her assignment. In this sentence, the underlined element is the verb.

verb group – a main verb preceded by one or more auxiliary verbs, which combines with a subject, e.g.
          . He will do it.
       verb group↵

verb phrase – it is an ordinary verb, e.g. ⇒ run, have gone, etc. it may also have an auxiliary verb and other words, e.g. ⇒ will go, had gone away.

verbals – these are derived from verbs but are not used as verbs, e.g. ⇒ it was a *horrifying* scene.

voice – see ⇒ active verb (voice) and passive verb (voice).

vocabulary – it consists of words, e.g. all words in the English language.

W

wh-question – it is the question which begins with a question word or wh-word, e.g. ⇒what, where., etc. See⇒wh-word.

wh-word – there are nine such words: how, what, when, where, why, which, who, whom, whose.
word class – it is another name for parts of speech, e.g. ⇒ noun, adjective, etc.

word formation – it is a process of forming new words. For instance: 'mis' and 'apprehension' are two different words. By means of word formation, we can form another meaningful word, which is 'mis-apprehension'. Mis-apphension is another noun. Some people spell it without the hyphen.

XYZ

'yes/no' question – a question which can lead to a simple answer whether 'yes' or 'no', e.g. Were you present in the class at that time?

```
┌─────────────────────────────────────────────────────────────┐
│                                                             │
│                    __Addendum__                             │
│                  __Word Formation__                         │
│                                                             │
└─────────────────────────────────────────────────────────────┘
```

Word formation is an important learning activity. It enables us to spell words correctly. Thousands of words have a base form, e.g. chair, book, etc. These base forms are changed to make other words. For instance:

    . book ⇒singular noun – base form ⇒ **b<u>oo</u>ks** ⇒plural noun

a new word formed by adding *s* to the base form ↵

    . sad ⇒ adjective – base form ⇒ **<u>sadly</u>** ⇒ adverb

a new word formed by adding *ly* to the base form ↵

    . direct ⇒ verb – base form ⇒ **<u>misdirect</u>** ⇒ adverb

a new word formed by adding *mis* to the base form ↵

These examples illustrate that you can change the base form of a word by adding something to the beginning or the end of a word to convert it into a new word. You can also make multi-words, i.e. milk-man, mother-in-law, etc. **Multi-word verbs** are mainly **idiomatic** or **phrasal verbs** whose overall meaning is different from the meaning of the individual words they contain. For instance, **<u>drop off</u>** is a multi-word. It is used in idiomatic expressions such as:

    . Jane **dropped off** during the lecture.

This sentence has a **phrasal verb** (multi-word) which consists of two individual words (verb + preposition). It means fall into a light sleep. A phrasal verb may consist of a verb plus a preposition or a verb plus an adverb. It may also be a combination of: verb +adverb + preposition. On page 8, some examples of phrasal verbs are already given. Indeed, phrasal verbs form a special group of verbs. Here is an example of the use of a phrasal verb:

    . Please **<u>fill in</u>** an application form.

The underlined phrasal verb is a multi-word, which consists of a verb(fill) and an adverb(in).

<u>Some phrasal verbs</u>
⇓

```
┌─────────────────────────────────────────────────────────────┐
│ back down, balance out, bear up, boil down  to, bounce back,│
│ call out for, come down, come forward, come up, creep in,   │
│ cut in, die away, die down, do away with, drop by, drop out,│
│ ease up, end up, face up to, fade away, fall apart, fall    │
│ behind, fight back, fool around, get about, get along, go   │
│ along with, hang together, hold on, inflict yourself/       │
│ somebody on somebody, inform on somebody, insist on doing   │
│ something, keep under, live up to, match up to, mess about, │
│ push around, play around with, run away with, run off, show │
│ off, shy away from, wriggle out of.                         │
└─────────────────────────────────────────────────────────────┘
```

Since a particular phrase or a multi-word has a verb in it, it is called a phrasal verb. A phrasal verb gives a specific meaning, which may or may not be obvious. It may not be possible to work out the meaning from the words within the phrasal verb, because the meaning of the phrasal verb is almost idiomatic. There are very many phrasal verbs in English. You can even buy a dictionary of phrasal verbs in a reputable bookshop.

Word formation has been introduced when the idea of inflection, prefixes, suffixes, converting adjectives to adverbs, etc. is discussed in this book. The book contains many examples of word formation. In this limited space, suffice to say that the bulk of word formation is by the **process of affixation**. This process involves prefixes and suffixes, that is fixing something in front of a word or at the end of a word. There are many recognisable forms of both prefixes and suffixes in modern English. Here are a few examples of each type of affix.

Prefixes	word formed	Suffixes	word formed
after-	**after**noon	-able	advis**able**
ana-	**ana**logy	-age	marri**age**
anti-	**anti**pathy	-ant	pregn**ant**
auto-	**auto**bigrophy	-craft	handi**craft**
bi-	**bi**cycle	-ee	divor**cee**
counter-	**counter**attack	-en	gold**en**
ex-	**ex**-wife	-friendly	user-**friendly**
hand-	**hand**some	-ish	sheep**ish**
il-	**il**legal	-ly	year**ly**
off-	**off**spring	-ware	hard**ware**

There are certain rules of spelling which apply to the process of affixation. For instance, if the suffix begins with a vowel, the last consonant in the base word is doubled, e.g., regret ⇒ regrettable. The other methods of word formation include **acronyms**. It is not the oldest method of word formation. Nevertheless, it is used to form new words by using the first letters of the words that make up the name of something. For example:

NATO ⇒ North Atlantic Treaty Organisation.

If you are fascinated by word formation techniques: **go for** it.

a phrasal word – multi-word formation.⏎

Some people research into word formation and have developed specific strategies and terminology for this work. The term word formation to such experts is an umbrella term. They apply different methods of deriving, compound words, complex words and multi-word verbs. They study how words can be broken down into smaller meaningful units, the origin of words, import of words into the language and some other aspects such as the spelling of words. It is all part of linguistic study. See books on linguistic topic.

Suggested Answers

1. Your explanation should include:
 . distinct sound – can be a combination of sounds
 . intended meaning or definition of the word
 . word's structure so that it can be recognised when written
     . Use any English word to explain the above requirements
     for the recognition of a word – both spoken and written.

2.

Proper Nouns:
John Smith, Jane Clarke, Epping Forest (a particular place),
Forest Hotel, London (also a particular place), British, England,
Ireland.
John Smith and Jane Clarke are proper names, because they refer to distinct
individuals. Of course, John, Jane, Smith and Clarke are also proper nouns
when these are names of specific individuals.

Common Nouns:
secretary, delegates, countries, hotel, bedroom/s, bathroom,
restaurant, cafeteria, hall, recreation, facilities, amenities,
adult, children, delegates, ideas, information, book, trade,
trading, conditions, requirements, pressure, multimedia,
publishers, products, booksellers, aims, discount, structures,
representatives, distributors, wholesalers, goods, ordering
(the way in which something is arranged or ordered), facilities,
accounts, president, persons, members.

Collective Nouns:
UK Branch, International Association of Booksellers,
conference, seminar, forum, Multimedia Book Forum,
Booksellers Clearing House.

3. The following personal and possessive pronouns are inserted:

Personal Pronouns

a) .We sell most------------. **They** are also printed outside London.
   subjective personal pronoun ↵
   as it is in the subject position

b) . My friends wrote ------------------I wrote to **them**.
                objective personal pronoun ↵
                as it is in the object place

c) . We have just received---------- . **It** has 500 pages.
        subjective personal pronoun ↵

d) . He was here----- We were enjoying talking with **him.**
                objective personal pronoun ↵

e) . This job----- me. I have done **it** before.

   objective personal pronoun↵

Possessive Pronouns

f) .They telephoned us-----.I cannot guess **their** reason for doing so......
    possessive pronoun dependent form ↵
    because it is used with a noun ⇒ **reason**

g) . Certainly, this old car is not **mine**. I ....motorcycle.
        possessive pronoun.↵
            independent form because it is used in place of a noun

h) . At last, we bought-------. It is **ours**.
        possessive pronoun.↵
            independent form used in place of a noun

i) . My wife and------ guests. They were **our** old friends
        possessive pronoun ↵
dependent form as it is used with a noun phrase ⇒ old friends

j) . There is a big difference between our opinions and **theirs**.
        possessive pronoun.↵
    independent form used in place of a noun

4. Blank spaces are filled in with words shown in **bold style**:
a) Can you **fix** up a meeting?
b) We were looking **at** the photo.
c) Their car's noise woke us **up**.
d) Please do not **throw** away these papers.
e) Mary **looks** after her sick mother.
f) Fame has crept **up** on him after just one television appearance.
g) Don't just fool **around/about**.
h) I do not wish to hang **about** here.
i) I cannot put **up** with this sort of behaviour.
h) You ought to get **out** of the house more.
i) She gave **away** one million pounds to charity.
j) We must set **up** a new system for dealing **with** so many claims.
k) He is so humble that he always talks **down** his own achievements.

5.

Finite verb	Non-finite verb
a) leave	b) to remedy
b) took	d) to help
c) interrogated	e) to know
d) tried	g) to come
e) want	h) to be assured
f) denied	J) to telephone
g) wished	k) bleeding
h) wanted	l) to work
i) crowded	m) do deliver
j) trying	n) to do
k) found	o) having seen
l) reported	
m) prepared	

   n) wondered
   o) recalled

* Finite verb inflects for tense and agrees in number with the subject.
 * Non-finite verb does not change its form for tense.

6 . Highlighted words are inserted in blank spaces. Required tenses
   are indicated with the aid of arrows below:

a) I **am happy**. ⇐ simple present
b) They **are** going to the beach now.⇐ present progressive
c) Two years ago, she **was** in England for three years. ⇐simple past
d) Recently, Harry **has** written to us from Cambridge.
         present perfect⤶
e) On my arrival, I **will** write to you from Spain. ⇐simple future
f) Now we **are** watching a film. ⇐present progressive/continuous
g) Last week they **were** skiing in Switzerland.
         past progressive ⤶
h) Not long ago, they **have** travelled to France. ⇐ present perfect
i) Last year, we **had** the Indian summer in the UK. ⇐ past perfect
j) She **had** never ridden a horse before she joined our club.
         ⇑
   past perfect
k) You must believe me I did not think that I **would come** First
   in London Marathon Race this year. ⇐simple future in the past
l)   The Indian summer **has returned** today. ⇐ present perfect
m) We will **be** arriving at 14.000 hours at Victoria Coach
   Station. ⇐ future progressive
n) Most certainly, I **will be staying** at The Regents Hotel in Paris.
         future progressive ⤶
o) By that time, we will **have** retired. ⇐ future perfect
p) The weatherman told us that it **was** going to rain all that day.
               past progressive ⤶
q) He had **been** talking to me. ⇐ past perfect progressive
r) At that time our train will **have** been travelling through ⇐ future
   the tunnel.   perfect progressive
 s) By that time, We **would** have returned to France.
            ⇑
         future perfect in the past
t)   At the end of this year, we **would have** been living in this house
   for ten years. ⇐ future perfect progressive in the past
u) Indeed, she promised that she **would be writing** to me soon about
   our plans for the future.   ⇑
               future progressive in the past
v) During our visit to Paris last year, you indicated that you **would**

have been moving to another flat. ⇐ future perfect progressive
in the past

w) We all knew Jane <u>would **be** working</u> at the post office.

⇑

future progressive in the past

x) Your father told me that you **had** served your country in Bosnia.

past perfect.⌋

7.   **Modifiers**   **Adjectives**

a) so ⇒ adverb   tired

b) absolutely ⇒ adverb

c) not at all ⇒ adverbial phrase   informative, interesting

d) really ⇒ adverb   nicest (superlative form)

e) by far ⇒ adverbial phrase   best (superlative form)

f) no ⇒ it is adverb here   better (comparative form)

g) enough ⇒ adverb   warm

h) somewhat ⇒ adverb   crowded

i) pretty ⇒ adverb   sure

j) quite ⇒ adverb   enjoyed

8.

a) Often one can buy fruit cheaper in the market.
An adverb of frequency usually is in the mid position in the sentence. Thus **often** is in the wrong place in this sentence.
. cheaper is an adjective ⇒ comparative form
. It is suggested to re-write it as:
. One can buy fruit **often** cheap(or cheaply) in the market.

b) Here the use of an adverb should be in the **comparative form**.
It should be re-written with **more** as:
She told the grocer that she could buy this **more** cheaply at a supermarket.

c) **On the left** – this is an adverbial phrase which is modifying the noun gentleman. It is in the wrong position as usually an adverb or adverbial phrase comes after the noun which it modifies.
It should be : The gentleman **on the left** is my uncle.

d) Usually is in the wrong place. An adverb of frequency **usually** goes in the mid position in the sentence. **It should be:**
This car park usually is full.

e) In this sentence the position of the adverb **probably** is correct. An adverb can come after the subject and before the negative form of the verb phrase such as does not.

f) The position of the adverb such as **purposely, deliberately** and similar adverbs depend on what is the intended meaning. If the intended meaning is to say that he has chosen not to greet, then the position of the adverb purposely is **correct.**

On the other hand, if the intending meaning is to say that he did not greet because of a mistake or did not get a chance to greet, then it should be re-written as:

. He did not **purposely** greet avoiding his opponents.

g) **much** is an adverb of degree modified by the adverb of degree to intensified the meaning of the adverb **much**. As an adverb of degree it can be used at the end of a statement.

h) The use of adverbial phrase **even more rapidly** in the given order and position in the sentence is correct. The reason is that the adverb **even** can be used before another adverb, if we wish to focus on it. This is a comparative use of the adverbial phrase.

9.

a) . basic and applied ⇒ adjectives
   . some ⇒adverb . of ⇒preposition

b) . worldwide ⇒ adjective
   . still ⇒adverb . of ⇒preposition
   . for ⇒ preposition

c) . distinct ⇒ adjective   . spontaneous ⇒ adjective
   . quite, more, evenly, slowly, now, almost, just,
     certainly ⇒ adverbs
   . up ⇒adverb but it is used with
     conjure (verb) to form conjure up ⇒ phrasal verb
 . **just now** - in this phrase both words are adverbs and
                 forming an idiomatic phrase
                 . from, for, by, without ⇒ prepositions

d) . constantly ⇒adverb
   . hard-working, healthy ⇒ adjectives
   . with⇒ preposition

e) . encouraging ⇒ adjective
   . just ⇒ adverb   . for ⇒ preposition
   . Since **than** is used before a noun to express a comparison,
     it is functioning here as a preposition.

10.

a) We all know that **a** bicycle does not run on petrol.
   The indefinite article before the singular noun is needed
   Here we are referring to bicycles in general – not uniqueness

b) You should get **the** parcel on Friday as it is a special delivery.
   the definite article requires as you are referring to a particular parcel

c) There is a lot to show **a** visitor.
   a – the indefinite article is required – here visitor is not unique

d) She was **the** only woman I loved.
   the is used with **only** and superlative adjectives

e) He is **the** right person for this job.
   the is used with **right** and superlative adjectives

f) We invited some friends for lunch. Luckily **the** sun was brilliantly
bright in the afternoon. no determiner before ⇒ lunch
there is only one sun and thus **the** comes before ⇒ sun

g) In the dark, I was searching for **the** switch button of my radio.
radio has one switch button **the** switch button ⇒uniqueness

h) Suddenly, **a** car in front of us stopped and **the** driver of this
car ran fast to escape arrest by the police.
Here the indefinite article is required because **car** ⇒ not unique
When referring to its driver the definite article is needed
because now we are referring to a particular driver

i) **The** night Mary was taken ill.   night ⇒ a particular event ⇒the

j) Our new car is as big as **the** jeep we saw the other day.
The definite article before jeep as you are referring to a specific jeep.

11.

a) **Dear me!** - what else can you do now? indicating ⇒ surprise

b) **Oh blast!** We won't make it on time. showing ⇒ annoyance

c) **Good grief!** What a disaster! expressing ⇒ shock

d) **Good heavens!** What are you doing in my office without
my permission?   showing ⇒ surprise and annoyance

e) **Goodness me!** What a wonderful place! expressing ⇒ surprise

f) How **nice** to see you!

g) What a pleasant **surprise!**

h) **Ow!** It hurts! pointing to ⇒ sudden pain

i) **Whoops!** You almost dropped it on my new carpet. Be careful!
   - giving a warning about ⇒ accident , bad thing to happen

j) **Yuck!** Let's get out of here. expressing ⇒ feeling

g) What a pleasant **surprise!**

h) **Ow!** It hurts! pointing to ⇒ sudden pain

i) **Whoops!** You almost dropped it on my new carpet. Be careful!
   - giving a warning about ⇒ accident , bad thing to happen

j) **Yuck!** Let's get out of here. expressing ⇒ feeling

12.

a) The traffic lights changed to amber <u>**as**</u> I approached.
                    subordinator ↵

b) It is possible <u>**that**</u> Yvonne has not received our letter.
subordinator ↵

c) Our tutor said <u>**that**</u> we can leave <u>**as soon as**</u> we answered the
   subordinator 1↵   subordinator 2↵   question.

d) My wife went to the Chelsea Flower Show <u>**and**</u> she enjoyed
her visit.
The coordinator   '<u>**and**</u>' is joining two clauses of equal status/important.

e) Our tutor was unhappy <u>**because**</u> we came fifteen minutes late.
                    subordinator ↵

f) She was very kind to us, **and yet** she hurried us.

        two coordinators↵ - units of equal status

g) Milk **and** sugar.

      ⇑

coordinator – two words ⇒ still units of equal status.

h) Our roof leaked **whenever** it rained last year.

      subordinator↵

i) We can finish early **in order to** get ready for the dinner

      subordinator↵   and dance tonight.

j) He is working very hard **so that** the report can be submitted in time.

      subordinators↵

k) I liked her very much, **even though** I did not have much chance to

      subordinator↵   to meet her after work.

l) Hurry up , **or** you'll be late for work.

  coordinator↵ - used here with the imperative clause – hurry up

m) I have no car , **so** I'll hire one just for tomorrow.

      coordinator↵

n) She is not a racist **and** a feminist.

      coordinator↵ - these are clauses of equal status but

               referring to the same person without

repeating the same subject ⇒ she and the same verb ⇒ is

o) Some of the overseas students are very hard working **whereas**

  others aren't.   subordinator used to compare/contrast↵

13.

A prepositional phrase always has a prepositional complement which is a noun phrase. The reason is that a preposition cannot act alone as the head-word of a phrase. For instance:

  . Maria will buy a present **from us all**.

      prepositional phrase ↵ - us all ⇒ **complement**

            noun phrase↵

You can see that the preposition **from** is not functioning alone but in association with its complement. Thus a preposition can be the headword of a phrase but it must be followed by a prepositional complement.

14.

  a) I am looking for a young man **who used to live in this house**
  with his girlfriend.

relative clause ↵ identifying relative clause/ identifying a young man

No comma is needed between identifying and main clauses.

  b) I told you **that it happened on Christmas Day**.

        noun clause ↵ - it begins with **that**

c) This new car is not as smooth to drive <u>as the salesman told us</u>.
    comparative clause ↲ - no comma needed
-began with **as** the second subordinator in this sentence.
d) <u>When I rang this number</u>, no one answered my call.
adverbial clause ↲ - it is an adverbial of time

15.
a) <u>**Compound sentence**</u> - it has two clauses of equal status
    joined together by ⇒ **but** ⇒ coordinating conjunction
b) <u>**Complex sentence**</u> - it has two clauses of unequal status
    joined together by ⇒ **since** ⇒ subordinator
    since introduced the subordinate clause
c) <u>**Simple sentence**</u> - it has only subject, verb and complement
    complement is after the <u>**linking verb**</u>
                    be (is) ↲ - complement ⇒adjective phrase
d) <u>**Compound sentence**</u> - two independent clauses joined together
    by a coordinating conjunction ⇒ but
e) <u>**Complex sentence**</u> - it has three clauses:
    - subordinate clause 1 began with although ⇒ conjunction
        - it contrasts with the truth statement in the main clause
        - it is an adverbial clause of exception or concessive clause
    - subordinate 2 clause began with because ⇒ conjunction
        - it is an adverbial clause of reason
    - main clause ⇒ I enjoyed
        - it tells the truth which is contrasted by clause 1
f) <u>**Simple sentence**</u> – it consists of
                    subject + verb + object + **adverbial**
    - from a rented small premises ⇒ adverbial phrase
    - it refers to the object ⇒ my business
g) <u>**Simple sentence**</u> – it consists of
                    subject + verb + object + **object complement**
    - bankrupt ⇒ object complement and it refers to the <u>**object**</u>
                                        John ↲
h) <u>**Compound sentence**</u> - it is composed of three clauses, each of
    which is an independent clause – can stand alone.
    1 - We went to Scarborough
    2 - (we) came across Colin Smith
    3 - (Colin Smith) was with his family on a day trip to the seaside

    These short independent sentences/clauses are joined together by
    two suitable **conjunctions** to form a compound sentence.
i) <u>**Complex sentence**</u> – it has three clauses:
    - it begins with a subordinate and an adverbial clause of time:
        'As soon as, our stores' gates were open'

Test Your Knowledge   **Suggested Answers**   **335**

****

  - **'sales hunters(shoppers) rushed in'**
    independent clause ↵ - complete in itself
  - (they) '**grabbed high quality merchandise at the lowest prices**'
    independent clause ↵ - complete in itself
  These clauses are joined together to form this complex sentence.

j) **Compound sentence** – it has three independent clauses joined
  together with **or** ⇒coordinating conjunction
  <u>These are imperative sentences (equivalent to independent clauses)</u>

16.
Suggestions are within boxes.

a) The importance of language skills in a literate society can hardly
  be exaggerated. People are judged on how they speak, **and** nearly
  all academic teaching is done by means of language. so anyone who
  has not achieved an average standard in literacy is likely to be
  seen as deficient across a wide range of skills.

Use of capital letters in correct places. A comma is needed to join main
clauses. Place a comma before **and**. No comma before **who** as it is introducing identifying (restrictive) clause. It is identifying the noun **anyone** in the
main clause. Full stops inserted.

b) Humour is a diffuse, fuzzy sort of thing - a matter of taste and
  something you do not expect to find in even the most sophisticated
  computer, unless it has been programmed in by human beings.

Began with a capital letter ⇒ H. A dash is used to add additional
information. A comma is essential before **unless** ⇒ conjunction. It is introducing a relative clause - adding information that we can leave out and the
sentence will still make sense. A full stop inserted. A complex sentence.

c) Unlike space, time, **as we understand**, has a direction. There is
  an asymmetry between the past (**fixed**) and the future (**yet to exist**).
   Time's arrow is whatever gives time this direction.

Capital letters used in appropriate places. The highlighted subordinate clause
is separated from the main clause by two commas for the same reason as
given for b) above. A couple of parentheses are used to enclose additional information. An apostrophe is added to show possession. Full stops inserted.

d) 'It's my nature to be like I am,' she said, ' I was fated to be
  unhappy.'

  'I believe you can learn to be happy and healthy,'
  I replied.

Capital letters are used as needed. Direct speech is enclosed within the single
quotation marks. Here an apostrophe is used for contraction of **it is** to

become **it's**. Two paragraphs – to denote change of speaker.

e) The man, Mr Joe Bloggs, was reported present when the morning
   roll call was taken, though officials are not sure now whether it was
   he, in fact, who replied 'Present'.

Capital letters used as necessary. The phrase –Mr Joe Bloggs has
commas around it. It is giving an additional information. The main clause is
'The man was reported present'. The phrase in fact has commas around it to
isolate it as it only additional information.

f) Did people really speak this way?

   Of course they did, but as with many other aspects of the language,
   the words and phrases, which people use change and change again
   as the years go by.

Question is mark needed. For the sake of clarity, it is a good idea to
have a question sentence on a separate line. There is a comma before **which**.
It is introducing an adding clause.

g) This woman was still unemployed. She had neither money nor
   prospects. Even so, her world was relatively good for she was
   at peace with herself. She was not eating away at her health, her
   resolve and stamina with angry self-defeating thoughts. She was
   not filling her mind with negative ideas.

   Positive thinking helped her to take great strides. She could sleep
   at night. Her stomach was better and she didn't blow her top
   like she used to. In other words, she was learning how to make
   the world a great place to be with her positive attitude. Soon
   she found a new job. A well paid job, in fact. Well done!

Punctuated text is in two suitable paragraphs. capital letters, commas, full
stops and apostrophe are added as required. The last paragraph ended with an
exclamation mark instead of a full stop.

h) The following members have won prizes:
   . Sarah Dean First Prize - £1000 (one thousand pounds)
   . Robert McDonald Second Prize - £200 (two hundred pounds)
   . Natasha Robinson Third Prize - £50 (fifty pounds)

   Our annual membership fee, in accordance with the cost of living
   index, will rise to £55 (fifty-five pounds) from £50, from
   1st January, next year.

   Finally, Our revenue for the year just ended amount to £550, 0000.
This exercise is all about numbers. Capital letters, dashes, commas,
hyphen, etc. are placed in correct places.

Index

338 **Index**

****

Index   **339**

****

340   **Index**

****

342   **Index**

****

****

****